THE
EVERYTHING®
GUIDE TO
SPORTS BETTING

Dear Reader,

For as long as I can remember, sports have been my number one passion in life. But it wasn't until I moved to Boston after graduating from the University of Vermont in 2009 that I started betting on them. At the beginning, I was a naïve twenty-two-year-old making all the rookie mistakes. I bet on the Red Sox every night and the Patriots every Sunday. I took every favorite, every home team, and I used my winnings to bet on more games. In other words, I parlayed everything. I rarely won, but I instantly fell in love with betting. To me, there is no better feeling than having action on a game and seeing the team you bet on come through for you. The adrenaline rush is unparalleled.

In 2011, a stroke of luck landed me an entry-level job at Sports Insights, a leading sports betting analytics company on the North Shore of Boston. Over the years, I learned the betting industry inside and out, slowly transitioning from a rookie schmuck into a smart and (somewhat) successful bettor. It took a long time, but eventually a light went on in my head.

Here's what I learned: sports betting isn't easy, and anyone who tells you otherwise is lying. But if you stay contrarian, follow sharp action, and remain disciplined with your bankroll, you can succeed.

Josh Appelbaum

T0059375

Welcome to the EVERYTHING® Series!

These handy, accessible books give you all you need to tackle a difficult project, gain a new hobby, comprehend a fascinating topic, prepare for an exam, or even brush up on something you learned back in school but have since forgotten.

You can choose to read an Everything® book from cover to cover or just pick out the information you want from our four useful boxes: e-questions, e-facts, e-alerts, and e-ssentials.

We give you everything you need to know on the subject, but throw in a lot of fun stuff along the way too.

We now have more than 400 Everything® books in print, spanning such wide-ranging categories as weddings, pregnancy, cooking, music instruction, foreign language, crafts, pets, New Age, and so much more. When you're done reading them all, you can finally say you know Everything®!

QUESTION

Answers to common questions

FACT

Important snippets of information

ALERT

Urgent warnings

ESSENTIAL

Quick handy tips

PUBLISHER Karen Cooper

MANAGING EDITOR Lisa Laing

COPY CHIEF Casey Ebert

ASSOCIATE PRODUCTION EDITOR Jo-Anne Duhamel

ACQUISITIONS EDITOR Zander Hatch

DEVELOPMENT EDITOR Peter Archer

EVERYTHING® SERIES COVER DESIGNER Erin Alexander

Visit the entire Everything® series at www.everything.com

THE
EVERYTHING®
GUIDE TO

SPORTS
BETTING

From pro football to college basketball,
systems and strategies for winning money

Josh Appelbaum

Adams Media
New York London Toronto Sydney New Delhi

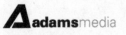

Adams Media
An Imprint of Simon & Schuster, Inc.
100 Technology Center Drive
Stoughton, MA 02072

An Everything® Series Book.
Everything® and everything.com® are registered trademarks of Simon & Schuster, Inc.

First Adams Media trade paperback edition February 2019

ADAMS MEDIA and colophon are trademarks of Simon & Schuster.

For information about special discounts for bulk purchases, please contact Simon & Schuster Special Sales at 1-866-506-1949 or business@simonandschuster.com.

The Simon & Schuster Speakers Bureau can bring authors to your live event. For more information or to book an event contact the Simon & Schuster Speakers Bureau at 1-866-248-3049 or visit our website at www.simonspeakers.com.

Manufactured in the United States of America

6 2023

Library of Congress Cataloging-in-Publication Data has been applied for.

ISBN 978-1-72140-021-8
ISBN 978-1-72140-022-5 (ebook)

Contents

Acknowledgments

First and foremost, I'd like to thank Dan Fabrizio. Dan took a shot on me when I knew nothing about betting (except how to lose). He welcomed me into the Sports Insights family and taught me how to be a contrarian bettor. I'd also like to thank my great friend and mentor P.J. Walsh. P.J. guided me from day one and turned me into a sharp bettor.

Thank you to The Action Network, specifically Chad Millman. Chad took me under his wing and showed me how to be a professional, for which I am forever grateful.

Thank you to my Sports Insights coworkers. Whether we're up, down, or treading water, they've always had my back. There's no one else I'd rather sweat games with: Mark Gallant, Travis Reed, Danny Donahue, John Ewing, Keith LeBlanc, Mike Marsh, Dan McGuire, Jason Awad, David Solar, Dan St. Pierre, Danner B and, of course, the Hangout Boys.

Thank you to Simon & Schuster for believing in a first-time author. A special thank you to Alexander Hatch and Peter Archer for being the best editors I could ever ask for.

Most of all, thank you to my family. To my agent, my idol, my dad: thank you for instilling in me a die-hard love of Boston sports and showing me how to be a stand-up guy. To my mom: thank you for teaching me how to write and always pushing me to meet my potential. To my sister: thank you for always being there for me and looking out for me. You guys are my rock. Without your love and support, none of this would be possible.

Introduction

GAMBLING IS AS OLD as civilization. Games of chance, luck, and skill are one of the first forms of entertainment ever recorded. From dice games in ancient Troy and Egypt to the invention of playing cards in China a thousand years ago, gambling is a universal human activity.

We can see that today: sports betting is spreading like wildfire. Many analysts have predicted the American betting industry will rake in $3 to $5 billion by 2023, putting the US on pace to overtake England and China as the gambling capital of the world.

As this betting gold rush heats up, millions and millions of you will be looking to join in on the fun and enter the market, many for the first time. If you're going to be successful at it, you need to know the basic principles of betting. The language gamblers and oddsmakers use can seem strange ("over," "moneyline," "the juice"), but this book will help you understand it. You'll learn how to take calculated risks and how to rate your success as a bettor. You'll learn about the range of bets available—you can bet on virtually every aspect of every sport—and you'll find detailed advice on how to bet on the big sports: baseball, football, and basketball. The goal of this book, in short, is to provide you with all the tips, strategies, and insights you need to get started (and more importantly, not lose all your money). You'll need that advice, because today we are witnessing a betting renaissance and the dawn of a new gambling golden age.

You can ride the crest of this wave of sports betting. All you need to do is master the skills and information this book will teach you.

CHAPTER 1

The Basics of Betting

No one becomes a sports betting expert overnight. It takes months, if not years, to turn from a rookie bettor into an experienced veteran. The first step is learning how sports betting works and some of the language bettors and oddsmakers use. This means mastering the fundamentals like:

- How are odds created?
- What is a favorite and what is an underdog?
- What is the difference between the spread, the moneyline, and the total?
- What is the juice?

Once you've grasped these guiding principles, then you can move on to bankroll management, betting strategies and, eventually, toward placing your first bet.

The Oddsmakers

The most common way of placing a bet is through a sportsbook. These are facilities that accept bets and give out money. A sportsbook can either be a physical place where you go to bet in person or an online account where you place bets from your computer or mobile phone. There are hundreds of different sportsbooks. Many of the biggest and most famous ones are located inside casinos in Las Vegas, such as The Venetian, Caesars Palace, Westgate, or The Mirage. Here, the walls are covered with massive TVs so bettors can watch all the games. Other sportsbooks are smaller and lesser known. They might be independent of casinos and tucked away on the outskirts of town. Online sportsbooks can be accessed anywhere, but there is no physical place to go bet and watch the games. Most online sportsbooks are located outside of the US, in places like Canada, Europe, or countries like Panama or Costa Rica.

A sportsbook requires a vast staff of employees to make the operation run smoothly, especially if they're located inside a large casino. The staff includes cashiers, ticket writers, surveillance officers, security guards, gaming supervisors, accountants, managers, and technicians, as well as servers, bartenders, cooks, and the entire hospitality staff. But when it comes to sports betting specifically, the most important person at a sportsbook is the head oddsmaker.

Betting Analysts

Every sportsbook has a team of betting analysts, led by a head oddsmaker. This is the person who creates the odds for all the different games, matchups, and events that people can bet on. Creating the odds is popularly referred to as "setting the line." The head oddsmaker is the smartest person at the sportsbooks. They are math experts with unparalleled betting knowledge and decades of experience in the industry. They know money and betting like the backs of their hands.

It's important to note that not all sportsbooks have the same exact odds. This is for two main reasons. First, not all sportsbooks are created equally. They all have different types of clientele. Some cater to professional bettors, also known as sharp bettors, while others cater to amateur players who bet for fun, also known as square or recreational bettors. Some sportsbooks allow bettors to bet large amounts on games, while others force bettors to bet lower amounts.

FACT

In the late 1920s, the state of Nevada was in serious decline. Its economy and mining industry were in shambles because of the Great Depression, and many of its citizens were fleeing the state. In an attempt to save their tanking economy, the Nevada State Legislature decided to legalize gambling in 1931. Over the years, Las Vegas became the gambling capital of the world.

Second, no two oddsmakers are exactly alike. One might have a different opinion on a particular game than another. By taking the odds from the most popular sportsbooks and finding the middle ground, bettors can get the market average odds, also called the consensus line. But how exactly do oddsmakers set the line?

Setting the Line

In order to determine what the odds on any game should be, the oddsmakers rely heavily on advanced mathematics, scientific formulas, and computer algorithms. This gives them a rough estimate on what the odds should be. Then the oddsmakers use what are called power ratings to refine the odds. A power rating is a statistical representation of how strong every team is compared to each other. It focuses on key statistical categories and considerations like margin of victory and strength of schedule. The strongest and best team is ranked number one.

Oddsmakers also factor in win totals and futures odds into their power ratings. Win totals are how many games the oddsmakers think each team will win during the upcoming regular season. They are historically known to be incredibly accurate. Before every new season, oddsmakers will take each team's win total from the previous season and then adjust the number based on the Pythagorean differential, also known as the Pythagorean expectation. This converts each team's point differential into an expected win percentage. Point differential is the number of points a team scored compared to the number of points they allowed to their opponent. It is one of the best ways to rank how good or bad a team is.

By comparing the number of actual wins to the projected Pythagorean record, oddsmakers can see which teams got unlucky the previous season and are bound to bounce back. At the same time, they can also find out which teams got lucky and are bound to regress and get worse.

Say the Dolphins won ten games last season, but their point differential was heavily in the negative (they gave up more points than they scored). That means the Dolphins exceeded their Pythagorean win total. Their overall record was better than how they actually performed. Thus, the Dolphins would be a good bet to take a step back the following year. On the flip side, maybe the Chiefs went 7–9, but they had a positive point differential. This means they outscored their opponents but got unlucky in the number of games they won. Basically, they performed better than their record dictated. As a result, the Chiefs would be a good candidate to have a bounce-back season.

After they've crunched all the numbers, the oddsmakers set a win total for every team. This is the best and easiest way to judge the strength of a team. For example, oddsmakers might project the Patriots to win 12.5 games this year, the highest of any team. The Patriots win total would then be pegged at 12.5. Meanwhile, the Browns win total might be set at 3.

Oddsmakers also set futures odds, which factor into the power ratings. These are the odds that a team will win their division, their conference and, most importantly, the championship. The Patriots might be the Super Bowl favorite at 5/1, which is the same as +500. This means that if you wanted to bet $100 on the Patriots to win the Super Bowl, you would win $500 if they hoist the Vince Lombardi Trophy (plus you'll get the $100 you risked back).

On the flip side, the Browns are a massive long shot, so their Super Bowl futures might be +7500. That means a $100 bet would pay out $7,500 if the Browns could shock the world and win it all.

The Popularity of Win Totals and Futures

The reason why win totals and futures odds are so important to power ratings is that they're available for bettors to bet on for months in advance of the season starting. They are incredibly popular bets with casual and professional bettors alike, which means the sportsbooks take in tons of bets and dollars on them, also known as taking in "action." Year in and year out, you'll see fans bet on their favorite team to exceed their win total or win the Super Bowl, just for the fun of it. Other professional bettors bet based on which teams they think provide the most value. Based on the action that the sportsbooks are taking in, the oddsmakers will adjust the win totals or futures odds, either raising them or dropping them depending on the liability they have on each team. Liability is the amount a sportsbook stands to lose if a particular outcome occurs.

If professional bettors are placing big bets on the Browns over win total and Super Bowl futures, that creates big liability for the sportsbooks and casinos. If the Browns win five or more games, or, god forbid, win the Super Bowl, the sportsbooks and casinos would lose huge amounts of money. As a result, the oddsmakers might adjust the Browns' win total up from 4.5 to 5 and their futures down from +7500 to +5000 so they can limit their risk. Because so much money is at stake with win totals and futures, the oddsmakers pay extra close attention in order to make sure they get them right. This makes win totals and futures one of the strongest overall betting markets and most representative of how good or bad a team is.

When two teams are set to play each other, the oddsmakers run their math models and compare each team's power ratings. If the two teams are closely rated the odds will be small, which is also referred to as short odds. If there is a large gap between the two teams, the odds will be much bigger, also known as long odds.

Adjusting the Line

Oddsmakers will tweak or adjust the line further based on a number of critical factors. These include home-field advantage, weather, injuries, unique schedule spots, and specific head-to-head matchups. If a team is coming off a blowout win or just lost their star player to injury, the odds-makers will factor that into the odds. If one team has a specific edge over another, like a bad offensive line going against a great defensive line, that will also be taken into account. If a team is playing their second game in two nights, that is factored into the odds as well.

ESSENTIAL

Oddsmakers lean on a team of consultants to help them set the line. This means getting feedback from their smartest and most trusted experts in the industry. Oddsmakers have go-to consultants for each sport. One might say the line should be 5 points, another says 3 points. Oddsmakers might settle somewhere in between at 4 points.

Once oddsmakers set the line, they release it to the public. The initial line is called the opening line. Bettors can then pick which side they want to bet on. Generally speaking, the goal of the oddsmakers is to release an opening line that will garner 50/50 action on both sides so they can limit their risk and mitigate their liability.

When a line is first released, the limits are low. This means that bettors can only bet up to a certain amount of money on the game. The sportsbooks use this initial period when the line is first released as a "feeling-out" stage to see how the early market reacts. They want to protect themselves from professional players betting big amounts early and taking advantage of an incorrect or off line, otherwise known as a "soft" line. The sportsbooks will allow professional bettors to bet on games at low limits in order to help them shape the line and get it as close to the most accurate number possible.

Once a universal number is established, the market takes over. The oddsmakers will sit back and see how the betting is coming in. They will adjust the line up or down depending on how much money or "action" a team is receiving. When it gets closer to game time, the sportsbooks and casinos will raise the limits to allow bigger bets on the game. This is only after they've gotten a chance to read the market and gotten a good grasp on which side is the smart bet and how much they stand to win or lose depending on which team wins, either the favorite or the underdog.

Favorites versus Underdogs

For every game, regardless of the sport, the first thing oddsmakers must decide when they set the line is which team is the favorite and which team is the underdog. Many different factors go into this process. It's not as simple as the team with the better record being the favorite. Things like home-field advantage, injuries to key players, and even the weather that day can help the oddsmakers decide that one team is more likely to beat the other.

Favorites and underdogs are not determined by the number of bets or the amount of money placed on a team. The underdog could have more bets and more money wagered on them than the favorite. Favorites and underdogs are selected by the oddsmakers based on their computer models and power ratings.

The favorite is considered to be the "better" team. Generally speaking, favorites have superior players, better coaching, a better track record of success, and, most of all, match up better against their opponent. As a result, they are expected to win the game. The underdog is the "worse" team and they're expected to lose the game. They do not match up well against their opponent. Their players might be less talented, they might have less experience, inferior coaching, and a track record of losing. However, because favorites are the better team and win the majority of games, oddsmakers must make betting fair by providing advantages to betting underdogs and creating risks for betting favorites.

FACT

In 2012, New Jersey Governor Chris Christie signed legislation to allow sports betting within state borders. The major professional leagues sued New Jersey to stop it. The case eventually made its way to the Supreme Court. On May 14, 2018, the Supreme Court ruled that the 1992 Professional and Amateur Sports Protection Action, known as PASPA, was unconstitutional. This allowed states to decide for themselves whether they wanted to legalize sports gambling or not.

The Pros and Cons of Favorites and Underdogs

Favorites either give points to the opponent, meaning they have to win the game by a certain number of additional points, or they come with heavy betting odds. This means bettors have to risk more money and pay a high price in order to bet on them. Conversely, an underdog will get additional points, meaning as long as the team loses by a certain amount or less, the underdog wins the bet. Underdogs will also come with juicy "plus-money" payouts, meaning you can risk a small amount but win a big amount if they pull off the upset. You can quickly identify if a team is a favorite or an underdog by whether they have minus sign (–) or plus sign (+) to the left of their odds. If a team has a minus sign before their odds, that means they're the favorite. If they have a plus sign before their odds, that means they're the underdog.

What If the Teams Are Even?

While almost all games have a favorite and an underdog, there are certain situations in which the teams are evenly matched. In other words, the oddsmakers' computer models and power ratings for each team are roughly equal, which means there is no clear favorite or underdog; the oddsmakers believe both teams have a 50 percent chance of winning the game. Think of this as a coin-flip game. In rare cases like this, the oddsmakers will set the line at a "pick," also known as a "pick'em." This means that the odds are zero. Bettors can then bet on which team wins the game "straight up." Winning straight up means the team just has to win the game by 1 point or more. The margin of victory does not matter. If a team is a pick or pick'em, bettors will see the odds listed as "0" or "PK." Is there more than one way you can bet on a favorite or an underdog?

The Spread

Once the oddsmakers set the line and distinguish the favorite and the underdog, bettors are given two basic options on how to bet one side or the other. The first is the spread (SPD). This is also referred to as the "point spread." The spread is a certain number of points taken away from the favorite and given to the underdog in order to level the playing field. Betting the point spread has nothing to do with which team wins the game. The only thing that matters is the margin of victory.

If you bet a favorite on the point spread, the favorite needs to win the game by a higher number of points than the spread. In other words, subtract the spread from the total amount of points the favorite scores. If that number is higher than the amount of points scored by the underdog, the favorite has won the spread bet. When a team wins a spread bet, it is popularly referred to as "covering." However, if the favorite wins by a fewer number of points than the spread, or loses the game straight up, the favorite has failed to cover and you lost your spread bet.

ALERT

When tracking how often a team covers or does not cover the spread, bettors use the term "against the spread," or ATS. It is a team's wins and losses based on the point spread. This record can be totally separate from a generic win-loss record. For instance, a team might have a win-loss record of 10–6, but they might be 6–10 against the spread. This means that they've won ten of their games, but only covered the spread in six of them.

If you bet an underdog on the point spread, the underdog needs to lose the game by less than the amount of points they're given by the spread. Think of it this way: when the game is over, add the spread to how many points the underdog scored in the game. If that number exceeds the total points scored by the favorite, you've won your spread bet and the underdog has covered. If the underdog wins the game straight up, without the benefit of additional points, this is also considered a cover and you've won your spread bet. However, if the underdog loses by any number of points that is higher than the point spread, the underdog has failed to cover and you lost your spread bet.

A Real-Life Example

Say the Eagles are playing the Giants. The oddsmakers crunch their numbers and the power ratings show that the Eagles are 7 points better than the Giants. This means that the oddsmakers think the Eagles will beat the Giants by roughly 7 points. The oddsmakers would then set the spread at Eagles –7 (meaning they are a 7-point favorite) and the Giants +7 (meaning they are a 7-point underdog). If you bet on the Eagles, you're saying that you think the Eagles will win the game by more than 7 points. If the Eagles win by 8 points or more, the Eagles have covered the spread and you win your bet. However, if the Eagles win by 6 points or less, or lose the game, you lose your bet. This means that the Eagles did not cover the spread.

On the flip side, if you wanted to bet the Giants, you are saying that you think the Giants will lose by 6 points or less, or maybe even win the game. If the Giants lose by 1 to 6 points, you cover your bet. If the Giants win the game, you also cover your bet. However, if the Giants lose by 8 points or more, that means they've failed to cover the point spread and you lose your bet.

If the Eagles win the game by exactly 7 points, with the Giants losing by exactly 7 points, that means the game lands on the spread. This is called a "push." It means neither team covered the spread. Anyone who bet Eagles –7 or Giants +7 would have their bets refunded to them by the sportsbook.

Not All Spreads Are Whole Numbers

It's important to note that not all point spreads are nice, easy round numbers. Depending upon where the computer models and power ratings line up, oddsmakers will also set spreads using half points. For example, maybe the power ratings show the Eagles as a slightly less than 7-point favorite over the Giants. The oddsmakers would set the spread at Eagles –6.5. This might seem confusing, because in a vacuum, the books are saying the Eagles are 6.5 points better than the Giants. However, no game can end with a half-point margin of victory. Still, the rules of spread betting are the same. If you bet on the Eagles –6.5, that just means they need to win by 7 points or more for you to cover. If they win by 6 points, you lose your spread bet. Conversely, if you bet on the Giants +6.5, they could lose the game by 6 points but you would still cover your spread bet. The extra half point is popularly referred to as the "hook." It is critically important and can be the difference between a win, a loss, and a push.

ALERT

There's no such thing as a guaranteed winner, no matter how high the spread. In 2007, the Patriots faced the Giants in Super Bowl XLII. New England was looking to complete the first-ever 19–0 perfect season in NFL history. They were 14-point favorites on the spread. Not only did they fail to cover, they lost the game 17–14.

Which Sports Use the Spread?

Spreads are available across almost all sports, but they are most commonly used in football and basketball. This is because the number of points scored in a football or basketball game is much higher than other sports, which means far fewer games are decided by exactly 1 point. As a result, it makes more sense to bet on the margin of victory instead of who wins the game. Spread betting is less common in baseball and hockey because the total number of runs or goals scored is much lower. Many games end with one team winning by 1 run or 1 goal. Because the margin of victory is much smaller, baseball and hockey bettors usually bet on which team will win the game, without having to worry about winning by a certain amount.

That being said, spreads do exist in baseball and hockey; they just aren't as popular to bet on. In baseball, the spread is popularly referred to as the "run-line." The favorite gives 1.5 runs to the underdog. This means the favorite spread is –1.5. The favorite has to win the game by at least 2 runs in order to cover the spread. If the favorite wins by exactly one run, they lose the bet and do not cover. The underdog is +1.5. They can either win the game or lose by exactly one run and they cover the spread. Because underdogs are getting an extra run and a half with the spread, bettors must pay a much higher price to bet on them. In turn, the price of betting a favorite on the spread is much lower because they have to win by more than one run.

The spread in hockey is called the "puck-line." The same logic in baseball spread betting applies to hockey spread betting. The favorite always gives 1.5 goals to the underdog. If the favorite wins the game by 2 goals or more, they cover the –1.5 spread and win the bet. If the underdog (+1.5) wins the game or loses by exactly 1 goal, the underdog covers the spread. Just like baseball, the price of betting the underdog on the spread is much higher because you're afforded an extra goal and a half. Conversely, the price of the favorite on the spread is much lower because they have to win by more than 1 goal.

What if you don't want to worry about covering the spread and only want to bet on which team wins the game? Is that a betting option?

The Moneyline

The second-most popular way to bet a favorite or an underdog is on the moneyline (ML). The moneyline is only based on which team will win the game. The margin of victory does not matter. The oddsmakers set prices on every team. The amount of money you must risk is determined by the price of the moneyline. If you win your bet, the price of the moneyline also determines your payout.

All moneyline prices begin at even money, also known as even odds. This is considered to be +100 or –100. It means that regardless of which team you bet on, you will win or lose the same amount of money that you risked on the game. Think of even money like a pick or a pick'em. Both teams are equally matched with no clear favorite or underdog, so the prices are even on both.

A moneyline favorite is given a minus price, which means bettors have to risk that amount in order to bet on them. A moneyline underdog is given a plus price, which means bettors stand to win that additional price if the underdog wins the game.

The Pros and Cons of Favorites and Underdogs

Because favorites win the majority of their games, the oddsmakers force bettors to pay higher prices on favorites and assume more risk. For example, in baseball a common moneyline price for an average favorite is –150. This means you have to risk $150 in order to win $100. If the favorite wins the game, you win $100 plus you get back the $150 you risked. However, if the favorite loses, you lose the entire $150 that you initially risked. So while favorites will win the majority of their games, they also come with big risk. When they win, you only win what you risked. But if they lose, you lose much bigger amounts.

On the flip side, because underdogs win less often, the oddsmakers need to make them more attractive to bettors so they can entice even betting on both sides. To make them more appealing, oddsmakers add a sweetener to underdogs in the form of plus money. This affords bigger payouts on underdogs when they win. Whatever price is listed after the plus sign next to the underdog, a bettor will win that additional amount if they pull off the victory. For example, let's say the moneyline price on a baseball underdog is +150. This means that if you risk $100 on the underdog, you win $150 if they win the game, plus you get back the $100 that you risked. If they lose the game, you just lose the $100 that you risked. With underdogs, bettors are assuming less risk and getting bigger rewards if they win.

FACT

Since 2005, there have only been three underdogs in the MLB with a moneyline price of +375 or higher. The Nationals +395 against the Twins in 2007, the Braves +425 against the Dodgers in 2016, and the Tigers +383 against the Indians in 2017. The Nationals won as +395 underdogs, while the other two teams lost. To this day, the Nationals hold the record for the biggest upset since 2005.

Which Sports Use the Moneyline?

Moneylines are available across almost all sports, but they are most popularly used when betting baseball, hockey, and soccer. This is because baseball, hockey, and soccer are low-scoring sports and the large majority of games are decided by 1 run or 1 goal. As a result, it makes more sense to just bet on who will win the game, not on their margin of victory. Football and basketball offer moneyline betting, but it's not nearly as popular as betting on the spread.

With football and basketball, the oddsmakers convert the spread into a moneyline price, which bettors can then pay. For example, if the New England Patriots are 10-point favorites on the spread, that would translate to roughly –700 on the moneyline. If you think the Patriots will win the game, but you aren't sure if they'll win by 11 points or more, you could bypass the spread and bet New England –700 on the moneyline. However, because of the high price, this means you would have to risk $700 just to win $100. If the Patriots win, you win your $100 and then get the $700 you risked back. But if they lose, you lose the full $700. This is why point spreads are much more common in football and basketball. They're much easier to understand and carry far fewer risks. Are spreads and moneylines the only ways to bet on a game? Can you bet on anything besides the favorite or the underdog?

The Total

In addition to designating the favorite and the underdog, oddsmakers will also set a total for every game. The total is the cumulative number of points scored in the game by both teams combined. Oddsmakers will set the total based on the same high-level algorithms they use to set spreads and moneylines. Once the total is set, bettors can wager on whether or not the game will go over or under the total. For this reason, the total is popularly referred to as the "over/under" (O/U).

In the NBA, you typically see each team score about 100 points per game. As a result, a common total is in the 190 to 220 range. Let's say the Warriors are playing the Cavaliers and the oddsmakers set the total at 215. This means bettors have the option of either betting over 215 or under 215. If you bet the over 215, both teams would need to score a combined 216 points or more in order for you to win your bet. It doesn't matter who wins the game. The margin of victory doesn't matter either. All that matters is the total number of points by both teams exceeds 215. If the Warriors win 109 to 107, you win your over bet. If the Cavs win 120–96, you win your over bet. However, if the total combined points scored in the game is 214 or less, you lose your total bet. If the game ends with exactly 215 points combined, your over bet would push and you would get your money back from the sportsbook.

ESSENTIAL

Betting on totals is a different way of betting. Instead of rooting for one team to win and the other team to lose, you are rooting for both teams. If you bet the over, you are rooting for both teams to score a lot of points. If you bet the under, you are rooting for both teams to score a low amount of points.

Not All Totals Are Whole Numbers

Just as spreads can involve half points, so can totals. Instead of setting the Warriors versus Cavs total at 215, maybe the oddsmakers set it at 214.5. This means that if you bet the over, you would need 215 or more total points to be scored in the game. If you bet the under, you would need 214 points or less to be scored in the game. In situations where totals involve half points, there is no way for a total to push. There has to be a clear winner and loser. Half points are also crucial depending on which side you're betting on. There is nothing worse than losing a total bet by a half point.

All total bets are based on the full game results, not the regulation time results. If a game goes into overtime or extra innings, it can have a massive impact on a total. All points or runs scored in overtime or extra innings count toward the total. If it's late in the game and a bettor is losing his under bet, he'll hope for overtime so there will be more scoring and a chance to win his over bet. However, if an under bettor is winning late and it's a close game, he'll pray the game ends in regulation time and doesn't go into overtime, since a longer game will lead to more scoring and could sink his under bet.

Which Sports Use Totals?

Totals can be bet on almost all sports, but they are most popular in basketball and football. This is due to the fact that basketball and football are higher-scoring sports, so betting on the total points scored is more meaningful (an average total in the NFL is about 45). Totals are also available in baseball and hockey, but they aren't as popular. An average total in baseball is roughly 8.5 runs, while an average total in hockey is typically 5 goals.

Win Totals and Prop Bets

It's important to note that totals aren't just set for individual games. Totals extend to season win totals and into the prop bet market as well. A prop bet, also known as a propositional bet, is any kind of bet on a game or player that isn't tied to the outcome or final score. The most common prop bet for an NFL game is the total amount of passing yards for a quarterback. The oddsmakers might set Aaron Rodgers's total passing yards in a game at 333.5. If you think Rodgers will throw for 334 yards or more, you can bet the over on the prop bet. If you think he will throw for 333 or fewer yards, you can bet the under. There are also season-long prop bets involving totals. A common one in baseball is the number of home runs a batter will hit in a season. The oddsmakers might set Mike Trout's home run total at 35.5. Before the season starts, you can bet either over or under 35.5 homers for Trout. Is there any fine print that comes with placing a bet on the spread, moneyline, or total? Are there any additional fees bettors should be aware of?

The Juice

Oddsmakers place a tax on every bet; this is popularly referred to as "the juice" or "the vig." *Vig* is short for *vigorish*, which originates from the Russian word for "winnings." This is a commission you must pay the sportsbook in order for them to accept your bet. The juice is added to all bet types, including spreads, totals, and moneylines. It will appear as a second number to the right of the spread or total, usually in parentheses. The juice won't appear in parentheses next to a moneyline price because it's already built into the line.

Standard juice is considered to be –110. This is also referred to as "ten-cent juice." This means that for every spread, total, or moneyline bet you make, you must pay a fee of 10 cents to the sportsbook. The oddsmakers constantly adjust the juice based on the action they're taking in, either raising or dropping the juice depending on which side is getting the most money. The juice is almost always a negative number that bettors have to pay an extra fee for, but on rare occasions the juice might be plus money, which means bettors can win a few extra cents.

FACT

The goal of any oddsmaker is to set a line that brings in equal action on both sides. If the betting is even, this limits their risk and liability, ensuring that regardless of which side wins, they won't take a major loss. But more importantly, if the action is equal, the books are guaranteed a profit based on the juice that bettors on both sides must pay.

Adjusting the Juice

To put the juice in perspective, say Florida State opens as a 7-point favorite on the spread against Auburn in a college football game. The oddsmakers would likely set the line at Florida State –7 (–110) and Auburn +7 (–110). The –110 number in parentheses is the juice. This means if you wanted to bet Florida State –7 you would need to risk $110 in order to win $100. If you wanted to bet Auburn +7, you would also need to risk $110 in order to win $100. In a way, the juice is kind of like a second moneyline.

If the sportsbook is taking in heavy betting on Florida State –7, they will adjust the juice higher from -110 to -115 or -125. This is how the juice moves when one side is getting the majority of the bets. The books compensate for the lopsided action by forcing bettors to pay a higher fee on the popular side.

Anytime juice moves toward one team, it simultaneously moves away from the opponent. At the same time that the oddsmakers raise the juice on Florida State from -110 to -115 or -125, they will drop the juice on Auburn from -110 to -105 or -100. Because Auburn is getting so few bets, Auburn bettors are afforded a smaller tax because they are backing the unpopular side.

Heavy Juice Moves the Line

By monitoring the movement of the juice, bettors can see which team is getting the majority of dollars and also predict which number the spread moves to. In the earlier example, if Florida State continues to get all the action, the juice will keep on rising until it hits a limit. Anything –125 or higher is considered heavy juice. The juice might rise further to –130 or –140, but that's about as far as it goes. If the action coming in on Florida State is overwhelming, raising the juice isn't enough to deter further Florida State betting or entice new Auburn betting. Instead of reaching –150 or –160 juice territory, the books will instead move the entire point spread a half point. Florida State might reach –7 (–145), but then the next move the oddsmakers make is moving the spread from –7 to –7.5. By moving a half point, the sportsbooks hope to entice action on Auburn at +7.5 so they can limit their liability on Florida State.

In the same scenario, while the juice increases on Florida State, the juice on Auburn (+7) would move from –100 to a plus-money payout of +105, +110, or +115. (This is referred to as a money plus juice.) In this case, the sportsbooks are taking in such heavy betting on Florida State that they're offering an underdog payout to anyone willing to bet on Auburn. Just as minus juice reaches a limit, so does plus money juice. Typically +115 or +125 is as high as plus money juice will go before the books move the number. So the next move after +7 (+125) would be for Auburn to go to +7.5.

Reading Juice Movement

Deciding when to pay the juice is a tricky game. Just remember: which-ever direction the juice is moving toward, that's the side getting the most money and the side the spread will move to next.

In the example with Florida State and Auburn, if you wanted to bet Florida State and you saw the line move from –7 (–115) to –7 (–125), you would want to bet Florida State immediately because the line will get worse. Even though you are paying a high juice, you can still lock your bet in at Florida State –7. If you wait too long, chances are that based on the juice movement, Florida State will move to –7.5 next. As a result, if you jumped on Florida State before they moved from –7 to –7.5, you just saved yourself a half point and increased your chances of winning. Now, if Florida State wins by seven, you push your bet instead of losing.

On the flip side, if you wanted to bet Auburn and saw the juice on Florida State move up, you would wait it out. If Auburn moves from +7 (+115) to +7 (+125), chances are the next move will be to Auburn +7.5. By reading the juice movement and waiting for the line to move, you just got an extra half point. Now if Auburn loses by seven, you still cover and win your bet because you got +7.5 instead of +7.

Now that we've discussed how lines are set, the difference between favorites versus underdogs, the spread, the moneyline, the total, and the juice, it's time to answer the next pressing question: how much should I bet on a game?

CHAPTER 2

Bankroll Management

Bankroll management is arguably the most important discipline needed to be a profitable long-term bettor. If you bet too much on a game, you can quickly go bankrupt. If you don't bet enough on a game, you won't see any profit when you win. You'll have to learn how to answer these questions:

- How can you distinguish between too much and too little?
- If you like one bet much more than another, should you bet more on that game and less on the other?
- How many games should you bet per day?
- Should you bet to risk or bet to win?
- Should you buy picks from handicappers?

Believe it or not, bankroll management can be just as important as picking winners. The goal is to map out a disciplined, consistent strategy that allows you to maximize your profits and minimize your losses, providing long-term sustainability. Think of it as investing, not betting.

Setting Up Your Bankroll

Before placing a single wager, ask yourself this fundamental question: how much can I afford to lose?

Everyone's answer is different. For some people, this might be $100. For others it might be $1,000, $10,000, or $100,000. Regardless of your income level, you first have to decide on a number that you're comfortable risking. Consider it disposable income. If you lost it all, would it drastically change your life? Would it negatively impact you to the point of missing car, rent, or mortgage payments? Would it bankrupt your life savings? Would it force you to default on your loans, cancel a vacation, or cut back on groceries? If the answer to any of those questions is yes, then that number is too high. Only bet what you can afford to lose. You never want to put yourself in a situation where you go broke and have to take out a loan because you've dug yourself a massive hole betting on sports.

Whatever number you decide upon, this is called your bankroll. It is the total amount of money that you have set aside for gambling.

Make Sure You Are Properly Funded

One of the most pivotal factors of bankroll management is making sure you're properly funded at the beginning. The more money you start with, the stronger position you put yourself in when it comes to turning a profit over the long haul. There's no way around it: when you first get started, you'll make mistakes. You'll lose more often than you win. If your starting bankroll is too small, you won't be able to weather the initial storm and survive the beginner's learning curve.

It's important to set a hard number for your starting bankroll. This will allow you to map out your bankroll management strategy much more easily. It also gives you a good benchmark to track your performance and chart your progress. A good minimum starting bankroll is $1,000. If you can start off with $2,000, $5,000, or $10,000, that's even better. The key is beginning with an even, round number that is large enough to keep you afloat through the rough early days when you're learning how to bet.

More importantly, you want to make sure that you are approaching sports betting with a clear mind and a level head. If you are worried about losing money and constantly stressed out, you will lose focus and be more prone to mistakes. Your judgment will be clouded and your decision-making won't be sound.

The Importance of Flat Betting

Once you've decided on your starting bankroll, the next step is determining how much to bet on each game.

The most common mistake a new bettor can make is being reckless with her bankroll. This means betting different amounts on different games based on how confident you are in the bet. Typically, if a new bettor loves a game, he will bet a large amount on it. If he likes a game but isn't as confident, he'll bet less. In betting circles, if you like a game but aren't completely sold on it, that is considered a "lean."

When a new bettor is doing well and riding a hot streak, he feels invincible, so he'll double down and start to risk more because he's overconfident. Conversely, if a new bettor is mired in a cold stretch, he'll start to chase and risk more on each game with the hopes of winning it all back in one fell swoop. All new bettors should resist these urges. This strategy, or lack thereof, is unsustainable, dangerous, and can quickly lead to bankruptcy.

Instead, bettors should adhere to a consistent, disciplined approach. This allows bettors to maximize their winning streaks but also weather the inevitable cold stretches that come with betting. Betting can be very volatile and unpredictable, with massive ups and downs in a short period. This is also referred to as "variance."

We all want to get rich quick, but that just isn't realistic. The ultimate goal is to steadily build your bankroll over time, not become a millionaire overnight.

Consistent Unit Size

In order to determine how much to bet on each game, take your starting bankroll amount and divide it into equal units. Once you decide this number, it becomes your unit size. This is the amount you are betting on every game. A good medium is 3 percent per play. To calculate what this means for you, multiply your starting bankroll by .03. If your starting bankroll is $1,000, this means you are betting $30 per game. In other words, your unit size is $30.

Not all bettors are exactly alike. Some are more conservative, while others are bolder and prefer to take more risks. As a result, your unit size can be tweaked slightly based on your comfort level. However, you never want to stray far from the 3 percent medium. If you'd like to be more conservative, consider risking 1 percent or 2 percent per play. If you prefer to be more aggressive, you might settle on 4 percent or 5 percent per play. But no matter what, never exceed 5 percent. Anything beyond that point is dangerous. You assume massive risk and set yourself up for volatile swings in your bankroll. Betting more than 5 percent per game puts you at the mercy of how well (or how poorly) you're doing at that particular moment. One losing streak could wipe out your entire bankroll and lead to ruin.

ALERT

Many professional bettors tend to only bet 1 percent per play. Because they've been in the game so long, they know the massive ups and downs that come with betting. As a result, they are more cautious and focus on the long game. Also, professional bettors are typically operating with much larger bankrolls than average bettors. Betting 1 percent might not seem like a lot, but if your bankroll is $100,000, this means every bet is $1,000.

Hope for the Best, but Plan for the Worst

Say your starting bankroll is $1,000 and you decide to bet $200 each on five games. This means your percentage play is 20 percent and your unit size is $200. If you win all five, that would be fantastic, but it just isn't realistic, especially if you're a new bettor. Everyone is excited when they first start betting, but you have to be prepared for the worst case scenario. You could very easily lose all five bets, and then you're bankrupt and have no more money to bet with. Just like that, you're out of the game before it even started.

If you drop the unit size to 10 percent and you're betting $100 on each game, you diminish your possible losses but you are still assuming far too much risk. If you lose all five bets (0–5) at $100 per bet, you just cut your bankroll in half, from $1,000 down to $500.

On the flip side, if you bet 5 percent per play, which means every bet is $50, going 0–5 would drop your $1,000 bankroll down to $750. Betting 3 percent per play ($30) would drop your bankroll down to $850. Betting 1 percent per play ($10) would drop your bankroll down to $950. By staying at or below the 5 percent threshold, you limit your losses substantially and keep yourself in the game.

However, what if you have a profitable night and go 3–2 (three wins, two losses) with your bets? The 5-percent-per-play bettor would increase his bankroll from $1,000 to $1,050. The 3-percent-per-play bettor would increase her bankroll from $1,000 to $1,030. The 1-percent-per-play bettor would increase their bankroll from $1,000 to $1,010.

ESSENTIAL

In 1956, J.L. Kelly Jr. created the Kelly criterion system. This is a famous mathematical formula used to determine how much to bet or invest in order to maximize the amount of profit. This is the opposite of flat betting. Instead of risking the same amount on every bet, you are weighting your bets based on confidence level. This system is used by experts and can be highly profitable, but also highly dangerous because it is very complex and hard to calculate.

Flat betting also allows you to eliminate damaging bias that could hold you back and cut into your potential profits. For example, say the $1,000 bankroll player only makes two bets. One of the games he really loves, but the other is more of a lean. As a result, he bets 10 percent on the game he loves (betting $100) and only bets 5 percent on the game he leans (betting $50). If he wins the game he leans but loses the game he loves, the bettor loses $50 overall. However, if he adhered to flat betting and risked the same $50 on both bets, he would break even instead of losing.

Once you've established your unit size, stay with it. Don't change day-to-day based on your performance or confidence level in a particular play. Always bet the same amount on every game: one unit per play and 3 percent of your bankroll per play. Flat betting will allow you to maximize your return on investment (ROI) and build your bankroll when you're doing well, but also guard against losing it all when you're struggling. It is the smartest and best way to keep you in the game long term.

What if I start winning consistently; do I ever increase my unit size?
A good rule of thumb is to re-evaluate your performance and analyze your bankroll once per year. The best time to do this is in mid-to-late August, right before the return of the football season. If you've turned your bankroll from $1,000 into $1,500 over the course of the past year, this means you can reset your unit size based on your updated bankroll. You would stay at 3 percent per play, but now with the $1,500 bankroll each unit is $45, not $30.

Bet to Risk versus Bet to Win

Bettors have two options when placing a wager: you can either bet to risk or bet to win. They might sound similar, but knowing the distinction is critical.

Betting to risk means you are betting a specific amount of your choice, regardless of the odds. If you lose the bet, you lose whatever amount you risked on the game. If you win the bet, your payout is determined by the price of the odds. Betting to win means you have to risk a different amount based on the odds in order to win your desired amount. Betting to win oftentimes means having to risk more, especially when it comes to betting on favorites.

Betting to risk and betting to win can be very confusing for new bettors. So let's take a look at a real-world example to illustrate the difference.

Let's say the Cubs are a –150 favorite on the moneyline and you wanted to bet on them. If you bet to risk $100 on the Cubs and they win the game, you win $66.67 based on the –150 favorite price, plus you get the $100 that you risked back. If the Cubs lose the game, you lose the $100 that you risked.

However, if you bet to win $100 on the Cubs, you have to risk $150 based on the -150 favorite price. If the Cubs win the game, you win $100, plus you get the $150 you risked back. But if the Cubs lose the game, you lose the entire $150 that you risked.

By betting to risk, you have far more control over your bet. You decide how much you want to risk, instead of letting the price of the odds dictate the amount.

FACT

According to a 2013 University of Nevada, Las Vegas (UNLV) Center for Gaming Research study, the fastest growing gambling hub in the world is Macau, an autonomous region on the southeastern coast of China. In 2012, Macau took in more than three times the total revenue of Nevada. The most popular table game in Macau is baccarat, while in Nevada it is the slot machine. American gambling mogul and billionaire Sheldon Adelson has invested heavily in Macau, opening the Sands Macao Hotel in 2004.

The Dangers of Betting to Win

The dangers of betting to win become more amplified as you make more and more wagers. For example, say you wanted to bet the Cubs, Red Sox, and Yankees, and all three teams are –150 favorites. If you bet to win $100 on each, this means having to risk $450 combined ($150 on each). If all three lose, you lose $450. However, if you bet to risk $100 on all three and all three lose, you only lose the $300 that you risked. By betting to risk instead of betting to win, you save yourself $150 in losses.

Does betting to risk and betting to win change if you bet on underdogs instead of favorites? The short answer is yes. Let's flip the moneyline prices and say the Cubs are a +150 underdog. If you bet to risk $100 on the Cubs and they win the game, you win $150 based on the underdog price, plus you get the $100 you risked back. If you bet to win $100 on the Cubs, you would only have to risk $66.67 based on the +150 underdog price. If the Cubs win the game, you win $100 plus you get back the $66.67 you risked. If the Cubs lose the game, you only lose the $66.67 that you risked.

On the surface, it might seem as though betting to win is the smarter bet when it comes to underdogs. After all, it allows you to risk far less up front. However, you must remember that betting to win on underdogs cuts into your potential profits and forfeits the advantages of plus-money payouts. Say the Cubs, Red Sox, and Yankees are all +150 underdogs. You bet to win $100 on all three, which means you risk $66.67 on each, totaling roughly $200 overall. If all three win, you win $300, plus you get the $200 you risked back.

However, if you bet to risk $100 on all three and all three win, you win $450 based on each team's +150 price, plus you get the $300 you risked back.

By betting to risk instead of betting to win, you increase your underdog pay-outs substantially. In this case, you win $450 instead of winning $300, earning $150 more in profit.

For these reasons, always bet to risk, never to win. Sure, there are pros and cons when it comes to favorites and underdogs, but overall the name of the game is limiting your risk and maximizing your reward. Betting to risk affords bettors this opportunity. Betting to win does not.

Limit Your Plays

Wayne Gretzky famously said, "You miss 100 percent of the shots you don't take." But the same logic can't be applied to betting. If a hockey player misses a shot, there is no penalty or consequence. But if a bettor misses her shot, she loses money. While it may be extremely frustrating to not bet on a team and see it win, always remember: you can never lose a play you don't make.

Being disciplined with your bets is something almost all new bettors struggle with. There's no denying it: having action on a game is exhilarating. The adrenaline rush that comes with betting on a team, watching the game, and rooting for them to win (or cover) is unmatched. There is absolutely nothing like it. When you win a bet, it makes you want to bet more. You can find yourself betting on more and more games in the hopes of recapturing that adrenaline rush.

However, this can become a slippery slope. The more bets you make, the more risk you assume. As a result, you should do everything you can to limit your plays. If you are betting ten games per night, you are opening yourself up to massive fluctuations in your bankroll. While one great night could result in huge profits, one bad night could give back all your hard-earned gains and clean out your bankroll. Having too many plays cuts into your win percentage and allows the juice to chip away at your winnings. It is the quickest way to go bankrupt. There's nothing wrong with having one glass of wine per night. But if you're having ten per night, you have a problem. Everything is better in moderation, especially your number of bets.

You should never bet on a game just for the sake of having action. Just because the Steelers are playing the Ravens on *Monday Night Football* doesn't mean you have to bet on it. Sure, having action on the game makes it more exciting and entertaining, but that should never be the only reason to bet on a game. Instead, only bet on your most confident games, where you've done all your research and believe you have a clear advantage—also known as an "edge."

FACT

The Action Network conducted a research study in 2018 that found fifty million to seventy million Americans place at least one sports bet per year, while eight million to ten million place at least one sports bet per week. With New Jersey, Delaware, and Mississippi having legalized betting after the Supreme Court ruling, and dozens more states to follow, this number is expected to grow by up to ten million over the next five to ten years.

While the number of bets made can vary based on the season, the schedule, the sport, and how many games you believe present value, a good rule of thumb is to cap yourself at five bets maximum per day. If you find yourself betting more than that, you are approaching dangerous territory. Always err on the side of caution. If you aren't totally confident in a play, lay off. If you run through all the games and don't find any presenting value, move on and live to fight another day. Many professional bettors only make one or two bets per night. Pick your spots. Remember, just like in life, patience is a virtue when it comes to gambling. There will always be more opportunities. Never lose sight of the fact that you're playing the long game.

Beware of Gambling Addiction

In many ways, gambling is a drug just like coffee, alcohol, cigarettes, or any other activity that you become reliant upon and can't stop doing. When you bet on sports, your brain releases a chemical called dopamine. This is a neurotransmitter that sends signals to your brain and makes you feel pleasure. It mediates your behavior in terms of desire and seeking rewards. In the case of gambling, you can become addicted to the thrill of betting. Once you're hooked, your body craves more and more of it. This causes your tolerance to rise, which means you need to bet compulsively in order to generate enough dopamine to achieve the same level of pleasure.

Signs of a gambling addiction include losing vast amounts of money but continuing to bet; betting more and more money in order to achieve the same level of pleasure; being restless, irritable, or going through withdrawal when you're not betting; lying about your gambling habits; jeopardizing your job or career; and destroying your relationships with friends, family, or a loved one.

FACT

The first Gamblers Anonymous (GA) meeting was held on September 13, 1957, in Los Angeles, California. Today, there are over 1,000 GA groups in America and hundreds of others across the globe. For more information, go to www.gamblersanonymous.org. You can also call the National Council on Problem Gambling (NCPG) helpline at 1-800-522-4700. It is available 24/7 and totally confidential.

A 2013 National Council on Problem Gambling survey showed that less than 2 percent of Americans have a gambling addiction. This translates to roughly six million people.

If you ever find yourself spiraling out of control and on the verge of addiction, seek out Gamblers Anonymous. Just like Alcoholics Anonymous, it's a free service where addicted bettors can meet with each other, discuss their problems, receive counseling, and begin a twelve-step program to recovery.

Avoid Handicappers and Touts

Although the Supreme Court legalized sports betting on the state level, the sports betting industry remains largely unregulated. It's tightening up, but a gray area still exists. This means that almost anyone can start a company or website and begin selling their picks. In betting circles, people who sell picks are popularly referred to as handicappers. This means that they study the games and make an educated guess on which team is the smarter bet.

While legitimate and transparent handicappers do exist, the overwhelming majority cannot be trusted. You have to remember that the number one goal of a handicapper who sells picks isn't to win their bets. It's to get people to buy their picks. Once you've purchase the picks, the handicapper has won. It doesn't matter if the pick wins or loses, the handicapper keeps the payment.

FACT

The most famous and successful handicapper in modern times is Billy Walters. In the 1980s, Walters created the Computer Group, which is considered the first-ever computer-based analytics program to analyze games and predict outcomes. Walters is credited with a thirty-year winning streak and claimed to have made up to $50 million per year betting on sports. In 2017, he was found guilty of insider trading. He was fined $10 million and sentenced to five years in prison.

Sure, if the picks win, that increases the likelihood that someone will continue to buy them, which benefits the handicapper long term. However, many handicappers concentrate solely on the here and now. If the picks lose and someone stops buying them, there will always be someone new willing to take their place. As the famous showman, businessman, and god-father of the circus P.T. Barnum is credited with saying: "There's a sucker born every minute."

The Used-Car Salesmen of Betting

Handicappers will go to absurd lengths to get people to buy their picks. They often seem like used-car salesmen, using fake names, fancy cars, and scantily clad women to get new bettors' attention. Additionally, many lie about their records. They pretend to be industry experts, promising and promoting unrealistic win percentages without any documentation of past performance. Many will claim an absurd win percentage: 75 percent to 90 percent, having won ten games in a row, or fifteen of their last sixteen. They hope you take them at face value and accept their claims as truth. Right off the bat, if a handicapper does not show a complete record of all of his picks, be suspicious. Many will call their picks "guaranteed winners" in order to sway a new bettor to purchase them. They may also call them "five-star locks" or "plays of the year" in an attempt to drive sales. Handicappers who use over-the-top tactics like this are popularly referred to as "touts" or "scam-dicappers." Consider them the con men of sports betting.

One of the most notorious games touts play is sending out one side of a game to half of their member list and the opposing side of that same game to the other half. This is called "double-siding" and is considered the oldest trick in the tout playbook. For example, say the Red Sox are playing the Yankees. The tout has 100 members paying for his picks. He sends the Red Sox as a pick to the first fifty members and then sends out the Yankees as a pick to the second fifty members. No matter what happens, half of the member base is guaranteed to win, which means at least half of them will continue to buy picks.

Don't Buy Picks

What if you find a diamond-in-the-rough handicapper who documents all of his plays, is honest with his records, doesn't oversell his performance, and turns a consistent profit? That means you should buy his picks, right? Not exactly. Even if the handicapper is legitimate, the deck is already stacked against you.

For instance, a common price point that handicappers set for a season picks package is $500. Let's say you've set aside $1,000 for betting and you spend half of it on the handicapper's picks. You are automatically starting $500 in the hole. You then risk $30 per game. Even if the handicapper has a profitable season, you may not even be able to offset the initial cost of the subscription. If you bet $30 per game and the picks profit $400 over the course of the season, you are still down $100. If the handicapper has a losing year, you are down even further.

The safest and best course of action is to avoid handicappers entirely. A great rule of thumb to live by in betting and in life: if it looks too good to be true, chances are it is.

Now that we've mapped out our bankroll management strategy, the next step is to set our sports betting goals and expectations.

CHAPTER 3

Realistic Expectations

Thanks to movies, TV shows, and popular culture, gamblers are often thought of as millionaire rock stars living a lavish lifestyle. They're usually depicted as bold and attractive celebrities, frequenting the most glamorous bars, restaurants, and nightclubs. They walk around casinos as if they own the place. They drive fancy cars, have beautiful women on their arm, and wear expensive suits and gold watches. They have deep pockets filled with $100 bills. They're always winning and they make betting look easy. While some bettors like this do exist, they are in the minority. If you think you're going to strike it rich overnight and become a millionaire, you are setting yourself up for disappointment.

Luck and Randomness

New bettors need to know what they're getting into before making their first wager. There's no way to sugarcoat it: betting is hard. The main reason why is because, at its very core, gambling involves a great deal of luck and randomness. If you're playing poker at a casino, your chances of winning are determined greatly by the cards the dealer hands out. You might get a great hand, you might get a lousy hand. You are at the mercy of luck. If you're playing roulette, you can pick red, black, or a specific number, but the outcome is determined not by skill, but by how the ball rolls along the wheel. Sometimes luck breaks your way, sometimes it doesn't.

FACT

One of the oldest and most famous gambling resorts in history is Monte Carlo. Located in the small country of Monaco along the French Riviera, Monte Carlo features the world famous Casino de Monte-Carlo, built in 1863. The casino is featured in the James Bond film *GoldenEye* and Alfred Hitchcock's *To Catch a Thief*. A famous computer algorithm betting system was named after Monte Carlo, which uses randomness to generate probability distributions.

Luck is amplified even further when it comes to betting on sports. This is because, unlike a deck of cards or roulette table, betting involves a human element. We all know that humans make mistakes. If you're betting on an individual sport such as tennis, you are counting on one person to play better than the other. But when you're betting on team sports, you're relying on multiple players—five, ten, twenty, or more—to work together efficiently toward victory. You're crossing your fingers that they play well that day, and that their opponent does not. But what if a player is distracted by something in his personal life? What if he stayed up late the night before and didn't sleep well? What if he's playing with an injury? Even if he's 100 percent healthy and his mind is laser-focused, he can still make errors.

There are countless other variables at play that make or break a bet. A baseball can stray foul by a quarter of an inch. The wind can push a field goal wide left. A basketball can bounce off a rim. A hockey puck can ricochet off multiple players and find its way into the net. An umpire or official can make an incorrect call that blows the game for one team and wins it for the other.

For these reasons and many more, there is no such thing as a guarantee when betting on sports. Anything can happen. This can be a gift and a curse. It is one of the main reasons why betting is so exciting, but also why it can be so frustrating. You can do zero research on a game, flip a coin, and blindly bet one side, and you might win. You can spend all day analyzing a matchup, studying every possible angle, dissecting every stat, and make the perfect pick, and it still might lose. No one has a crystal ball. This is why it's called gambling.

Superstitions

Luck is the elephant in the room when it comes to gambling. Before and during every bet, bettors pray that luck is on their side. This is why bettors are some of the most superstitious people in the world. If they think something can bring them luck and increase their chances of winning, they'll continue to do it. If they think something will jinx their bet, they avoid it like the plague. Every bettor has his own set of unique rituals and good luck charms. Maybe it's a lucky hat or a lucky T-shirt. If the team you bet on just scored a huge touchdown while you were sitting on the left side of the couch, you won't move from the left side of the couch the rest of the game. If you won a big bet after eating a turkey sandwich, you'll continue to eat turkey sandwiches before every game until you start losing. On the flip side, if you lost a bet wearing a specific T-shirt, you'll never wear that T-shirt again. There's no evidence that any of these superstitions work, but nonetheless, almost all bettors have them.

FACT

In betting circles, the worst thing you can be called is a *mush*. It's a term for someone who creates bad luck for others. This person will be known to "jinx" bets and it seems like anytime they're around, your bet loses. They feel like your personal kryptonite. The term comes from the 1993 movie *A Bronx Tale*, where Robert De Niro famously said, "Eddie Mush was a degenerate gambler. He was also the biggest loser in the whole world. They called him Mush because everything he touched turned to mush."

The House Always Wins

If betting were easy, casinos would go bankrupt. Average Joes would all quit their day jobs and live like modern-day kings. There's a reason why Vegas makes millions and millions every single year. It's cliché but true: the house always wins.

According to the UNLV Center for Gaming Research, more than $81 billion has been bet on sports in Nevada since 1984. Of that $81 billion, Nevada won $3.9 billion. Why does Nevada win so much money? Not only do they capitalize on the luck and randomness of betting, but they also hold a built-in advantage over bettors. This is popularly referred to as "the house edge," or the expected value. It is a mathematical formula that shows the average profit that the house stands to make on every bet for every game. Simply put, the rules of the game make it such that the odds are stacked against bettors before they even start.

FACT

In 1990, Mike Tyson and Buster Douglas squared off for the heavyweight championship of boxing. Tyson entered the fight with an undefeated 37–0 record, including 33 knockouts. Douglas was a 42/1 longshot to win the fight. In the tenth round, Douglas knocked out Tyson to become the new heavyweight champion of the world. To this day, it is widely considered the greatest upset in boxing history.

Calculating House Edge

Let's take a look at the dimensions and set up of the roulette table. In America, the roulette wheel has thirty-eight different numbers: eighteen red, eighteen black, and two green (zero and double zero). If you select red or black, the payout is small and only 1/1 if the number hits. That means if you bet $1 on red and it lands on red, you win $1 and get the dollar you risked back. Because there are eighteen red or black numbers and thirty-eight numbers overall, it means you have an 18/38 chance of hitting, which translates to 47.37 percent. In other words, you have a less than 50 percent chance of winning. You might win your first roll and maybe even your second roll. Heck, you may even win five in a row. But the longer you keep playing, eventually you will lose. It's mathematically guaranteed that house will come out on top 52.63 percent of the time.

FACT

Roulette comes from the French word meaning "little wheel." It was invented in the mid-seventeenth century by French mathematician Blaise Pascal. Originally, Pascal was trying to create a perpetual motion machine. It wasn't until the late 1700s and early 1800s that roulette became a popular gambling game. In America, roulette wheels feature double zeros, while in Europe, roulette wheels only feature a single zero.

Now let's look at the chances of hitting not red or black, but an exact number, which wins a payout of 35/1. This means if you bet $1 on a certain number and the ball lands on that number, you win $35. As a result, this means bettors have a 1/38 chance in winning and a 37/38 chance of losing. To calculate the expected value, you use the following formula: $-1 \times 37/38 + 35 \times 1/38$. This comes out to 0.526. In other words, the house holds a 5.26 percent edge in roulette. This means that for every dollar bet at the roulette table, the house wins about 5 cents. As a result, the house always comes out on top. The house edge varies based on the game, with some games providing a much larger edge than others, but all games provide a positive edge for the house. The biggest edge is with slot machines, where the edge can be up to 15 percent or more. What about the edge for sports betting? Is it more or less than casino games?

Sportsbooks Win Mostly Because of the Juice

In sports betting circles, the house always wins, although for slightly different reasons. If you've watched enough games as a bettor, it's hard not to think Vegas is some kind of mind-reading soothsayer who knows the outcome of every game beforehand. Oftentimes you'll turn on a game late in the fourth quarter and see that the score is 24–21. You check what the spread was and, sure enough, it was –3. A common response among recreational bettors is, "Vegas knew!"

However, the main reason why sportsbooks have an edge isn't because they're smarter than the average bettor and set hard-to-beat lines. Sure, that plays to their benefit, but it's not the only reason they always come out on top. After all, when it comes to betting, you always have a 50 percent chance of winning if you're betting on the moneyline. One side has to win and one side has to lose. If you're betting on the spread, you could always push, but in that rare instance you get your money back; you don't lose your bet.

The main reason why sportsbooks make so much money is because they are able to charge a 10 percent tax on all their bets. It's the juice that provides such a massive edge and makes them so profitable, not the fact that they set perfect lines or seem to predict the outcome beforehand.

Whether it's roulette, craps, poker, or betting on sports, the goal of the house is to keep bettors betting. They might win their first bet. They might go on an epic hot streak. But the longer they keep playing, the greater likelihood that they start to lose. This is why casinos give out free drinks and comp rooms. They want you to stick around and keep betting because they know that the law of averages is in their favor.

FACT

In 1987, Illinois sports bettor Robert P. Groetzinger sued the IRS over whether or not gambling qualifies as being either a trade or business, and thus is eligible to deduct business expenses. In *Commissioner v. Groetzinger*, the Supreme Court decided in favor of Groetzinger, stating that "if one's gambling activity is pursued full time, in good faith, and with regularity, to the production of income for livelihood, and it is not a mere hobby, it is a trade or business." In other words, if this is the case, then it is a trade or business under IRS tax code. This is the first time that professional sports bettors were given an official legal designation.

The Break-Even Point

The odds are stacked against bettors and the house always wins. But that doesn't mean it's impossible to win money betting on sports. It just means we need to adjust our expectations and set realistic goals. What is the break-even point for bettors? Do they need to win 50.1 percent of their bets in order to turn a profit? What is the magic number they should strive for?

Let's start with a simple example. Say you place two NFL bets, the first on the Cowboys (+7) and the second on the Chargers (+7). If you win one and lose the other, that means you break even, right? Wrong. You have to remember that all bets include the juice. So assuming standard –110 juice, if you went 1–1 with your two picks, you would actually lose money because of the tax on both bets. In other words, you had to risk $110 in order to win $100 on both teams. One team wins, so you win $100, plus you get your initial $100 back. But the other loses, so you lose $110. As a result, despite going 1–1, you lost $10 overall.

That means we just need to win 50.1 percent of the time in order to compensate for the juice, right? Wrong again. In order to calculate the break-even point, we can use the following formula: the price of the bet / (1 + Price of the bet). Since standard juice is –110, this translates to 1.10 / (1 + 1.10), or 1.10/2.10. This comes out to .5238. This means that in order to break even, assuming standard –110 juice, bettors need to win 52.38 percent of their bets.

ALERT

The break-even point changes depending on the price of the juice. If a bettor pays –115 juice instead of –110 juice, they would need to win 53.48 percent of their bets in order to break even. On the flip side, if a bettor pays –105 juice instead of –110 juice, they would only need to win 51.2 percent of the time in order to break even. As a result, bettors should always search out the books offering the lowest possible juice.

This is the magic number that bettors should always keep in the back of their head: 52.38 percent. This is the number you're trying to beat. Anything 52.39 percent or higher means you're turning a profit. To make it easy on yourself, set a nice round number of 53 percent. That is your goal and what you should always strive for. Anything above that is gravy.

70 Percent Win Rate Is Unattainable

For brand-new bettors, it's hard to understand why a 70 percent win rate isn't realistic. After all, if you get a 70 on a school paper or a test, that's a C–. So surely we can strive to be at least a C– bettor, right?

This kind of logic is why many inexperienced bettors fall for the traps set by handicappers and touts online. They often boast about winning 70 percent, 80 percent, or even 90 percent of their plays; a new bettor naïvely accepts it as doable. While bettors can win seven out of ten plays, it's all about the long term. Anyone can get hot for a short period of time, but almost no one can sustain that level of excellence. Simply put, it's almost impossible to win at such a high rate over a long period.

QUESTION

How often to do you have to win in order to be considered a professional or sharp bettor?
Generally speaking, sharp bettors win at a rate of 55 percent on average. If someone wins at a 55 percent rate over the course of one year, they aren't automatically considered sharp. You must maintain a 55 percent win percentage year in and year out, over the course of many years. Some of the sharpest bettors in the world hit at a 58 percent clip, but it is very rare. The best handicappers in the world hit 60 percent of their plays. Only 0.5 percent of bettors approach the 60 percent win rate.

Let's use some hard math to dispel the myth that a 70 percent win rate is easily attainable. In statistics, there is a formula called a z-score. It measures the relationship between one data point compared to the average, also known as the mean. For example, say a group of 30 students take a test and the average score is 75. If one student got exactly 75, that means their z-score is zero. If the student got above a 75, their z-score would be a positive number. If the student got below a 75, their z-score would be a negative number. The greater the number, positive or negative, the further you are from the mean. The size of the difference between the data point and the mean is called a standard deviation.

Applying this to betting, let's say the average bettor makes 1,000 picks at the standard −110 juice and he hits 50 percent of his plays. This would mean his z-score is zero.

Using the z-score, this 50 percent bettor would only have a 1/44 chance (or a 2.3 percent chance) of winning 53.2 percent of his plays, thus breaking even. This same bettor would only have a 1/700 chance (0.1 percent chance) of winning 54.8 percent of his bets, which would be considered an impressive win percentage.

What are the chances that a 50 percent bettor with no edge hits 70 percent of her plays? According to z-score, less than one in a trillion. Basically, a bettor with no edge is better off playing the lottery.

No Overnight Millionaires

There will be instances when you bet a game and there is zero sweat. This means that from the very beginning, the team you bet on jumps out to a big lead and cruises easily to victory. There are other times when you bet on a team and they battle back and forth and come up huge for you in the end. There are times when your team is down big early in the game and you write them off, but they mount a furious late comeback and cash for you in the end. Maybe you bet on the Jets +14 and they're down by 23 points late in the fourth quarter, but then they score a touchdown, recover an onside kick, and kick a field goal, losing by 13 and giving you an improbable late win, also known as a backdoor cover.

FACT

In Super Bowl LI, the Patriots closed as 3-point favorites against the Atlanta Falcons. Nearly two-thirds of bettors took New England minus the points. The Patriots trailed 28–3 in the third quarter but then roared back to score 31 unanswered points, winning in overtime 34–28. Miraculously, New England ended up covering the 3-point spread.

But then there are times when the opposite happens. From the very beginning, the team you bet on gets blown out of the water. Or your team battles and battles but comes up short. Or, worst of all, your team is leading the entire game but blows it at the very end in heartbreaking fashion. You bet on the Mets +150 and they take a 4–0 lead into the ninth inning, but then give up 5 runs and lose 5–4. Or you bet on UCLA –15 and they're up by 17 points with less than ten seconds left, but then the opponent hits a meaningless last-second 3-pointer and you lose. These are called bad beats, or mooses. They happen to all of us. They are the most difficult part of betting.

The truth is that no bet is ever safe. There are no guarantees. Sometimes the luck breaks your way, sometimes it doesn't. What you think might be impossible often ends up happening. All bettors must prepare themselves for the Jekyll-and-Hyde emotional aspect of betting.

The most important thing to remember is that you're always playing the long game. Everyone wishes they could become a millionaire overnight, but it just doesn't work that way. Betting is a grind. You'll have good days and bad days. The key is never letting the ups and downs throw you off course. Always stay even-keeled. When you're hot, you're never as good as you think. When you're cold, you're never as bad as you think. You're always somewhere in between. Stay focused on the 52.38 percent magic number. Stay true to your bankroll management plan. Never lose sight of the forest amongst the trees. It isn't about today or tomorrow, it's about next week, next month, and next year. Stay the course and think long term. Always be disciplined and patient.

FACT

The phrase "patience is a virtue" comes from the Latin epic poem *Psychomachia*, which translates to *The Battle of Spirits* or *Soul War*. It was written by Prudentius in the fifth century C.E. and is considered the first medieval allegory about good versus evil. It describes a battle between seven vices and seven virtues. Chastity defeats lust, temperance defeats gluttony, charity defeats greed, diligence defeats sloth, kindness defeats envy, humility defeats pride, and patience defeats anger.

This mindset will keep you in the game and set you on the road to success. But before you can step inside the gambling arena, there is more work to be done. You must forget everything you know about sports. It is only after you've rid yourself of all subjectivity that you start analyzing games correctly. This means approaching bets with a completely objective perspective and an open mind.

CHAPTER 4

Remove All Bias

Once you've gotten a handle on key betting terms, mapped out your bankroll management plan, and set realistic expectations, the next step is to begin mentally preparing yourself to enter the betting market. This means getting rid of preconceived notions and personal bias and not buying into conventional wisdom or media hype. All it does is wear you down, cloud your judgment, and talk you into poor betting decisions. If you enter a bet already thinking one team will win, for no other reason than your own bias, you are already putting yourself behind the eight ball. You should enter every bet with a clear head and let the data tell you where the value is. New England Patriots head coach Bill Belichick always tells his players to "ignore the noise." Sports bettors should do the exact same.

Don't Bet Like a Fan

In order to succeed at betting, the first thing you need to do is stop being a fan and let go of all your long-held allegiances. It's natural to want to bet on your favorite teams, but it's just not smart. If your only reason to bet on the Lakers is because you're from Los Angeles and grew up rooting for them, you're already jeopardizing your bet by injecting personal bias into the equation. Just because you're a die-hard Yankees fan doesn't mean you should bet on the Yankees and against the Red Sox every night simply because they're your archrival and you want to see them lose. Never bet a team just because they have more star players, or a famous coach, or because they're a historically successful franchise. Never bet against a team simply because they lack those things. None of that matters. Always bet with your head, never with your heart.

QUESTION

What separates a professional bettor from a novice bettor?
Professional bettors bet games based on hard data. They analyze the matchups and let the numbers and prices tell them where the value is and which side is the smarter bet. Novice bettors largely ignore data. They bet based on gut instinct. They bet on teams and players, not numbers and prices.

Allegiances Hold You Back

Here's the problem with betting on your favorites: if the only reason you're betting on a team is because you like them, you're assuming unnecessary risk and forfeiting possible value. Let's say you're an avid Packers fan. Green Bay is hosting the Bears at Lambeau Field. You're going to the game and you want to make it more fun, so you bet on the Packers as 7-point favorites. Because you love the Packers, you overlook the data that shows the Bears are the smart pick. Maybe the Packers are getting 80 percent of bets and the line opened at –6 and moved up to –7 because of heavy public betting on Green Bay. Maybe the Packers are coming off a win and are being overvalued. Maybe they suffered an injury to one of their offensive linemen. Maybe the over/under is low, which benefits the underdog. Maybe you overlook the fact that historically, underdogs inside the division play better than underdogs outside the division, especially when they're on the road. All the signs are pointing to the Bears +7 as the smart play, but because you love the Packers, you bet Packers –7.

In 1969, investor George Soros formed the Quantum Group of Funds. It became one of the most successful hedge funds in history. Today, Soros is worth over $8 billion. Soros credits much of his success to "the theory of reflexivity." This is the idea that people's biases can move the market in directions that don't align with reality, creating valuable opportunities for savvy investors.

These are just a few of the many reasons why betting on your favorite team is dangerous. You ignore meaningful data and often bet bad numbers without even being aware of it.

Now let's imagine that the Packers win the game, but only by 6 points. Everyone in the stadium is celebrating and going wild, but you're upset and mad that the Packers failed to cover. You are angry at your favorite team for not winning by enough. If you'd done some research, you would have either decided to lay off the game and enjoy the victory, or bet on the Bears and enjoy the best of both worlds: you win your bet and your team wins the game.

Ignore Media Hype

In the same vein, new bettors should block out media bias. It's just noise that manipulates public perception, which the sportsbooks capitalize upon. For example, maybe the Saints (–7) are playing the Lions on *Sunday Night Football*. The game is several days away. You turn on ESPN and see commentators hype up the Saints every day leading up to the game. They show highlights of how the Saints crushed their last opponent by two touchdowns. They feature a one-on-one interview with Drew Brees, cutting away to clips of him throwing touchdown pass after touchdown pass. The anchor talks about how the Saints are red-hot and have won eight of their last ten home games by 14 points or more, whereas the Lions have never won on the road in the Superdome. Then *SportsCenter* cuts to *NFL Live*. They go around the ten-person panel, and all ten analysts pick the Saints to beat the Lions in a blowout.

If you did all your research and decided that the Saints were the smart play before the week-long hype tour began, that's fine. But if you failed to do any homework and decided to bet on the Saints simply because the media talked you into it, that is a mistake.

FACT

One of the most successful businessmen in the world is Warren Buffett. As the CEO of Berkshire Hathaway, Buffett has amassed a fortune of over $84 billion, making him the third-wealthiest person in the world. One of Buffett's biggest investment tips is to not overreact to news stories and headlines. Always abide by the 99/1 Rule. This means only listening to 1 percent of the financial news you hear.

Beware of Shaded Numbers

You have to remember that if you're watching ESPN pump the tires of the Saints all week, it means hundreds of thousands, if not millions, of other bettors are watching it too. They're hearing the same exact things you are. They're going to want to bet the same exact way. This is a problem because the sportsbooks take notice of which direction public sentiment is trending and shade their lines accordingly.

Shading lines means that sportsbooks move the odds further in the direction of the popular public side, forcing recreational bettors to take bad numbers. Maybe the oddsmakers crunched the numbers and their power ratings and matchup adjustments landed on the Saints –6.5. But because they knew the public would load up on the Saints no matter what, they decided to open the line at –7. Then maybe throughout the week, the heavy Saints betting caused the oddsmakers to adjust the line even further to –7.5, causing late Saints bettors to lay a bad number a full point higher than the true opener. The line movement wasn't caused by professional bettors betting the Lions, which is also known as sharp action. Instead, the line movement was based solely on the public overreacting to media bias and overvaluing the Saints.

Cover Up the Team Names

Never make a bet based solely on fandom, media bias, or gut instinct. Instead, you should bet based on solid analysis. A good way to make sure you're avoiding even the slightest chance of bias is by covering up the names of the teams and betting on the smarter play. By doing this, you force yourself to dissect the game from an unbiased perspective. It allows you to cancel out the noise and block subjectivity from influencing your decision.

Using the same *Monday Night Football* example above, maybe you crunched all the numbers, examined the opening line, saw where the bets and dollars were, studied how the line had moved, dug deep into historical data, dissected all the head-to-head matchups, and came to the conclusion that Detroit +7.5 was the smart play. But then after watching days of ESPN and media hype on New Orleans, you are lured into thinking otherwise. Not only do you not bet Detroit +7.5, you then decide to bet Saints -7.5. After all, the Saints are unstoppable in the Superdome and average a 14-point margin of victory. In the end, maybe the Saints win the game by 6 or 7 points, just as the oddsmakers predicted. But because you listened to the media hype and took a bad shaded line, you lost your Saints –7.5 pick.

Always trust your own data you so carefully crafted and analyzed, not some ex-jock or talking head in a borrowed suit reading off a teleprompter.

FACT

In 1976, Steve Jobs cofounded Apple Computer, which later became Apple Inc. In a 2005 commencement address at Stanford University, Jobs said, "Your time is limited, so don't waste it living someone else's life. Don't be trapped in dogma—which is living with the results of other people's thinking. Don't let the noise of others' opinions drown out your own inner voice." In 2018, Apple became the world's first-ever trillion-dollar company.

Don't Overreact to Recent Trends

Inexperienced bettors who fall in love with trends are victims of recency bias. If a team is coming off a 20-point blowout victory, an ill-informed bettor will be inclined to bet them again because they looked great their last time out. Similarly, if a team has won five games in a row, a naïve bettor will automatically assume the hot streak must continue. On the flip side, if a team just suffered a humiliating loss or is riding a five-game losing streak, the natural instinct is to bet against them. After all, only bad teams lose five games in a row.

Bettors should reject this kind of thinking. Despite how a team looks recently, good or bad, it may be completely out of the historical norm. Instead, bettors should focus on sample sizes larger than a handful of games because they more accurately represent a team's overall strength and performance.

Long-Term Trends Are More Meaningful

Long-term history is a much better indicator of success than short runs. Over the course of a season, teams experience ups and downs. A great team can hit a rough patch and lose three or four games in a row. A bad team can get hot and enjoy a three- or four-game winning streak. However, the law of averages always wins out in the end. As a result, bettors should judge teams based on their overall body of work. This means looking at a larger sample size of games that take into account the entire season thus far, not just a small part of it.

Say the Tigers are playing the Blue Jays. Advanced trends might tell you that the Tigers are 0–5 in the last five games, 1–7 in their last eight road games, and 2–10 in their last twelve games against the Blue Jays. Meanwhile, the Jays are 8–1 in their last nine games and have won six in a row at home. The advanced trends may also state that the under has hit in seven of the last nine Tigers games and eight of the last ten Jays games. An inexperienced bettor reads these trends and says, "Stop right there. Bet the Jays and the under!"

You have to remember that all of these trends, and hundreds of others, are already baked into the cake. The oddsmakers set the line with all of this in mind. Don't think you've discovered a Holy Grail stat that the oddsmakers have overlooked. The oddsmakers know these types of trends are easily available and that many ill-informed bettors pick games solely based on them. In the example above, this means that the oddsmakers will shade the lines toward the Blue Jays and the under, forcing ill-informed bettors to take a bad number. Never fall into the recency bias trap. Select your games based on season-long performance, not recent history.

Buy on Bad News, Sell on Good

Just like stocks on Wall Street, sports bettors should look to buy on bad news and sell on good news. The reason is simple: by going against the grain, you can take advantage of public bias. By capitalizing on the overvaluing (or undervaluing) of teams and recent results you'll get artificially inflated lines, which is a direct result of sportsbooks shading the odds. This means getting better prices, which, in turn, increases your chances of winning.

The most common buy-low, sell-high situation is taking teams coming off a loss, especially a blowout, and fading (or going against) teams on a sustained winning streak. Another example is betting on teams with losing records and against teams with winning records, or betting on teams who missed the playoffs the previous season and against teams who made the playoffs the previous season. It also means betting on teams who just suffered injuries. In its simplest form, buying low and selling high means betting on bad teams and against good teams. It might sound crazy, but there's a method to the madness.

FACT

In the opening weekend of the NFL, ill-informed bettors don't have much data to go on, so they'll look back to the previous season. If a team made the playoffs, they will bet on them in Week 1. If they missed the playoffs, they will bet against them. However, this is a losing strategy. Since 2005, teams who missed the playoffs the previous year went 135–118 against the spread (ATS) (or 53.4 percent against the spread) in Week 1 of the following season. If they are playing a team who made the playoffs, they improve to 52–35 ATS (59.8 percent).

Let's say a football team is coming off a 24-point loss in which they committed multiple fumbles, threw several interceptions, and failed to reach the end zone. The bookmakers know that the public won't want to touch the team coming off the blowout loss. After all, they looked terrible in their last game. So instead of opening the team off the blowout at +10, the oddsmakers set the line at +11 instead. The public expects another easy blowout and proceeds to hammer the favorite, pushing the line from −11 to −12. Savvy bettors could then bet on the team coming off the blowout at a more valuable and inflated +12. By allowing public perception to undervalue the team off the blowout, overvalue the opponent, and then influence the odds, bettors just got free points and additional line value.

ALERT

Since 2005, NFL underdogs coming off a loss of 20 points or more have gone 266–218 (55 percent) against the spread in their next game. Underdogs coming off a loss of 30 points or more have gone 82–51 (61.7 percent) against the spread in their next game. A $100 bettor taking every underdog off a blowout loss of 20 points or more would have made $3,338 since 2005.

On the other hand, say the star quarterback of the best team in the league just threw for 500 yards and five touchdowns in a 35–7 victory, the team's fifth win in a row. Now that team travels on the road to face a divisional rival. The oddsmakers open the line at the best team in the league −3 and the public immediately hammers them, remembering how great they've looked in the last five games. This heavy betting pushes the league leader from −3 to −3.5. Experienced bettors could sell high on the team riding the winning streak and grab the divisional opponent at an inflated +3.5.

A good rule of thumb: a team is never as bad as they played in their last game or as good as they played in their last game. They are always somewhere in between.

The Gambler's Fallacy

One of the most common mistakes bettors make is falling victim to the gambler's fallacy. This is the widely held belief that if something happens at a high rate in a short time, it's bound to happen less often in the future. The problem is, that it isn't true.

Say you flip a coin ten times. Because the odds of a coin landing on heads or tails are 50/50, you would assume that five of the flips would be heads and five would be tails. However, you flip the coin ten times and notice that it lands on heads seven times and tails three times.

You automatically say to yourself, "Wow, that's weird. I should bet on the next coin flip being tails because tails has only hit three out of ten times. It's bound to hit on the eleventh flip."

At first glance, this seems like a logical conclusion. But if you dig a little deeper, you realize that the logic is flawed because every coin flip is independent of previous flips. It's incorrect to assume that probability changes based on past results. Just because you notice a pattern doesn't mean it's linked. It could just be coincidence. The coin doesn't abide by the law of averages over a small series of flips. In the short term, anything can happen. It's only when it's compounded over a massive sample size that the law of averages takes over.

If we flipped the coin a thousand times we would see a ratio much closer to 50/50 than if we only flipped it ten times. If we flipped it a million times, we would get even closer to exactly 50/50 heads and tails. However, if we dissect every single flip along the way to a million, we would almost certainly see small bunches in which heads landed more often than tails, or vice versa.

ALERT

The gambler's fallacy is also known as the Monte Carlo fallacy. It got its name in 1913, when bettors at the Monte Carlo Casino noticed that the roulette ball kept landing on black. As a result, nearly everyone at the casino jumped in and kept betting on red, thinking that black streak must end. Eventually it did, but not until the twenty-seventh spin. No one knows how much money the bettors lost betting on red every time, but legend states it was more than a million dollars.

The same logic can be applied to sports betting. For example, say the Cubs have the best record in baseball and travel to San Diego to take on the last-place Padres. The Padres win the first two games of the series. An ill-informed bettor might put a huge piece of his bankroll down on the Cubs to win the third game, saying to himself, "the Cubs are a great team, they can't possibly get swept by the lowly Padres." Sure enough, you check the box score the next morning and see that the Padres won 4–2. If the Cubs played the Padres one hundred times, they would probably win seventy times. Over the long haul, they are a much better team and the results would bear that out. However, in the short term anything can happen, just like the coin landing on heads seven out of ten times.

Just because a good team is on a losing streak doesn't mean they're destined to win their next game. Just because a bad team is on a winning streak doesn't mean they're destined to lose their next game. In the end the law of averages wins out, but in the interim a streak can continue.

ESSENTIAL

The Martingale betting system was named after John Henry Martindale, a famous London casino owner in the eighteenth century. (Martindale's name was incorrectly referred to as Martingale, but it stuck.) The system is to bet double after each lost bet so you can recoup your losses and turn a profit. It was successfully used by Charles Wells in 1891 to win 1.5 million francs playing roulette in Monte Carlo. He was known as "the man who broke the bank at Monte Carlo." However, the Martingale system rarely ever wins and is more often considered fool's gold or a scam. By doubling down, you are increasing your risk and are more likely to go broke, rather than winning big.

The gambler's fallacy can also be applied to bettors themselves. If a bettor is enjoying a hot streak, she might convince herself that the streak will continue. She bets on more and more games and places bigger and bigger wagers. What she fails to realize is that her chances of winning are the same as her historical win percentage. So if you are a 52 percent bettor over the past five years, you have roughly a 52 percent chance of winning your next bet if you continue to follow the same methods and do the same level of preparation that you did before. Hitting 75 percent or 25 percent of your wagers over the past week doesn't change this.

Confirmation Bias

Another pitfall that new bettors are susceptible to is confirmation bias. This means seeking out data or trends that fit their opinion. In other words, they are looking for information that tells them what they want to hear. Once they find it, they end the search for more data. This is dangerous because it causes bettors to talk themselves into or out of play based on cherry-picked information that may not be truly indicative of the overall edge.

Let's say the Bruins are playing the Blackhawks in Game 7 of the Stanley Cup Finals. A hockey bettor scours the Internet for Game 7 betting trends. Does the home team have an edge? Is the away team undervalued? Does the team coming off a loss perform better historically? Does the team coming off a win carry over momentum? Which team has more experience playing in Game 7s? What is the record of both head coaches in Game 7s? What happened the last time each team played in a Game 7?

FACT

In an article for the website *FiveThirtyEight* titled "The Real Story of 2016," leading statistician Nate Silver blames confirmation bias as the main reason why the media failed to predict Donald Trump's presidential victory. "Journalists just didn't believe that someone like Trump could become president...so they cherry-picked their way through the data to support their belief, ignoring evidence—such as Hillary Clinton's poor standing in the Midwest—that didn't fit the narrative."

An experienced bettor finds a vast list of trends that favor both teams equally, with no discernable edge for either team. As a result, he smartly decides to lay off the game and not place a bet. However, if that hockey bettor was a Bruins fan, he would choose to focus more heavily on trends and articles that favor Boston, while disregarding or completely ignoring trends that favor Chicago. This thought process is natural, but it should be avoided at all costs because it leads to poor decision-making. Always enter a bet with an open mind. Let the data decide which team is the smart bet, not your pre-existing beliefs and emotions.

Now that we've removed our biases, stopped thinking like a fan, ignored media hype, and learned how to approach sports betting from an objective perspective, are there any other types of bets we need to be aware of before diving into betting strategies?

CHAPTER 5

Alternative Bets

The most popular bet types are full-game bets on the spread, the moneyline, and the total. However, bettors have a variety of other bets at their disposal. This includes first-half bets, second-half bets, quarter bets, live betting, alternative bets, props, parlays, and teasers. Knowing what wagering opportunities are available to you is critically important when trying to capitalize on certain situations that present an edge. But this is only half the battle. The other key factor is knowing what bet types present heightened risk and should therefore be avoided.

Partial-Game Lines

When oddsmakers set a line on a game, they don't just decide the full-game odds. They also set a series of partial-game lines on the spread, the money-line, and total. For these bets, the full game outcome does not matter. All that matters is what happens for that specific part of the game. This could be the first half, the second half, or each of the four quarters. Partial-game lines are available across almost all sports, but they are most popular when betting on football and basketball.

First-Half Lines

Oddsmakers set a first-half line (1H) on every game. This is based only upon what happens in the first half of the game. The end result is irrelevant. First-half lines are set in comparison to the full-game lines, with the odds-makers altering them slightly based upon matchups and adjustments. Typically, the first-half line will be about half of the full game line. First-half bets are available to all bettors right up until the game begins. Once the first half ends, the bet is decided.

For example, the oddsmakers might open the Raiders as a 7-point favorite for the full-game spread and 4-point favorite for the first-half spread. If a bettor took the Raiders −4 for the first half and the Raiders lead by 5 points or more heading into halftime, that bettor wins her first-half bet. It doesn't matter what happens in the second half. The Raiders could blow the lead and lose the game by 7 points. The first-half bet would still win.

In terms of the moneyline, the Raiders might be −350 for the full game and −220 for the first half. If a bettor took the Raiders −220 on the first half moneyline, the Raiders would need to win the first half in order to win the bet. As long as they win by 1 point or more, the bet wins. The margin of victory does not matter. Neither does the final score.

When it comes to the total, the oddsmakers might set the full game over/under at 41 and the first half over/under at 20.5. If a bettor took the first-half over, the combined points scored by both teams would need to be 21 or higher in order for the first-half over to win. The full-game total could land on 40, which would mean the full-game under wins. However, as long as the first-half total was 21 or higher, the first-half over wins. The final score does not matter.

Capitalize On Unique Situations

First-half bets can provide unique value to bettors based on matchups, weather, the schedule, and other variables. By understanding specific situations, bettors can take advantage of partial-game lines.

Let's say the Broncos host the Eagles for a 4:00 p.m. game. The full-game total is 41 and the first-half total is 20.5. The forecast calls for heavy, fifteen-mile-per-hour winds from 4:00 p.m. to 5:30 p.m., but from 5:30 p.m. on, the wind is expected to die down. A bettor could take advantage of this by betting the under 20.5 for the first half instead of the under 41 for the full game.

Maybe a cold-weather team must travel to play a team based in a hot climate, or vice versa. For instance, the Patriots, based in New England, always seem to struggle when having to play the Dolphins in hot and humid Miami. A bettor could capitalize on this by betting the Dolphins as a first-half underdog. If the Dolphins lead or cover the spread at halftime, the bet wins. That way, if the Patriots roar back in the second half to win the game and cover the full-game spread, it's irrelevant. The first-half Dolphins bet still wins.

Similarly, say the Pistons are playing the second night of a back-to-back and the previous game went to double overtime. The Pistons suffered a devastating 1-point loss and the team didn't get to the hotel until 4:00 a.m. Expecting a "hangover" or "letdown" situation and sluggish, tired legs to start off the next game, a bettor could take the under 109 for the first half instead of the under 218 for the full game.

Although it's not nearly as popular as other sports, baseball has a first-half line as well. It's called first-five (F5). This means it's only based on the results of the first five innings. For instance, maybe a team has their ace starting pitcher on the mound but they also have one of the league's worst bullpens. Instead of taking the team on the full game moneyline, a bettor could instead bet them on the first-five. That way if the relief pitchers blow the game, the bet will still win as long as the team leads by at least one run entering the sixth inning.

Second-Half Lines

The second-half line (2H) is based solely on what happens in the second half of the game. What happens in the first half has no bearing on the second-half line result. Neither does the full game final score. Second-half lines are not available until after the first half ends and are only available for basketball and football. Oddsmakers will set the second-half line based mostly on the first-half score and how that lines up with the full-game odds. They will also take into account the overall action they have on a game. Oddsmakers will be extra cautious with second-half lines to ensure they don't hand out an incorrect or "soft" line that cuts into their full-game edge.

Typically, second-half lines will appear about one or two minutes after the first half ends. They are very time sensitive. Second-half lines are only available during the halftime intermission, which is typically fifteen to twenty minutes. In order to bet on second-half lines, bettors must quickly access their sportsbook and place the bet in that short window between when the first half ends and the second half begins.

Let's say Alabama is a 3-point favorite against Georgia for the full game. However, Alabama trails at halftime 17–10. The oddsmakers might set the second-half line at Alabama –7.5, knowing that they are playing poorly but are still the team favored to win by roughly 3 points. If a bettor believes that Alabama will come back and win the game, he could take Alabama at –7.5 for the second-half line. As long as Alabama outscores Georgia by 8 points in the second half (which means they win the game by at least 1 point), the second-half bettor wins his bet.

ALERT

One word of caution to all second-half bettors: never bet a second-half line solely because your full-game bet is losing. This is extremely dangerous and can compound your losses by turning one potential loss into two. In other words, never try to "chase" or bet yourself out of a losing situation. If you bet an underdog at +3 and they're down 14 points at halftime, don't double down on the underdog or bet the opposite side on the favorite to try to save yourself. Oftentimes it's best to take your one potential loss instead of assuming more risk and tacking on another loss.

The main variables that go into second-half bets are momentum (how each team played in the first half), injuries, foul trouble, and weather. For example, maybe the halftime score doesn't accurately reflect how a game is being played. Maybe one team was the beneficiary of a lucky break or a call that went in their favor. Another team played nearly flawlessly but one mistake cost them the lead. Betting for or against these teams would provide value to second-half bettors.

Additionally, if a star player got hurt in the first half or a team lost several players to injuries, bettors could look to bet against that team in the second half. Or maybe a team has several key players in foul trouble, which means their minutes will be restricted and they may foul out early, in which case you would look to bet against them in the second half.

Maybe the Rockets are playing the Hornets and the total for the full game is 220. However, both teams shoot ice cold from the field and the score is 40–38 at halftime. The oddsmakers might open the second-half total at 105. If a bettor thinks both teams will shoot better and find a rhythm, he could bet the second-half over 105. If both teams combined for 106 points or more in the second half, the bettor wins their bet.

ESSENTIAL

Professional bettors typically gravitate more toward first-half lines, while public or recreational bettors tend to bet more second-half lines. Professional bettors prefer first-half lines because they are available all day or all week long. This means the bettors have much more time to research and analyze the first-half line. Casual bettors gravitate to second-half lines because they feel more confident in predicting the outcome, having watched the first half and seen how both teams are playing.

Quarter Lines

In addition to first half and second half lines, oddsmakers also set lines on all four individual quarters of football and professional basketball games (college basketball plays two halves). As a result, bettors can seek out valuable opportunities where they have an edge on a specific quarter but perhaps not for the first half, second half, or full game. For quarter bets, all that matters is the result of the individual quarter. No other quarters matter. Neither does the first or second half or full game. Quarter lines are typically one quarter of the full game line. Unlike second-half lines, quarter lines are available before the game starts.

ALERT

For example, in the NBA playoffs, teams coming home after being down in the series 0–2 typically perform well in the first quarter. They are desperate and come out firing because they are fighting for their playoff lives, while the team that is up 2–0 is usually playing with less urgency and less hunger. The sportsbooks know this and will set the lines accordingly.

For instance, the Cavaliers might be a 5-point underdog for the full game against the Warriors, but only a 2-point underdog for the first quarter. Bettors might love the Cavs to come out hot and win the first quarter, but they are worried the Warriors will be too good in the end and come back to cover the full-game spread. Instead of taking the Cavs +5 for the game, a bettor could bet the Cavs +2 for the first quarter. If the Cavs outscore the Warriors in the first quarter or only trail by one, that first-quarter Cavs bet wins.

Live Lines

Another alternative bet type is the live line. Betting the live line is also referred to as live betting, in-play wagering, or in-game wagering. This is the line on the game at any given moment while the game is in progress. The live line opens as soon as the game starts and closes as soon as the game ends. It changes almost every second, depending on the score and how the game is being played. Not all books post live lines. However, for the ones that do, bettors are afforded a unique opportunity to take advantage of certain situations.

To set live lines, sportsbooks use a computer algorithm that constantly updates the odds based on how the game is being played. The computer takes the full-game odds for the favorite and the underdog and then inputs the current score of the game. The algorithm compares the score to hundreds of thousands of past games that had a similar score at the same point in the game. The algorithm then forms a win probability percentage for each team. More closely, if a 6-point favorite trails by 3 points midway through the first quarter, the algorithm can determine how often in the past teams in that situation came back to win.

Most commonly, the live line is used when a bettor believes a team that is currently losing (usually a favorite) can come back and win. For example, let's say the Astros are a –150 favorite against the White Sox. But right off the bat, Chicago scores 6 runs in the first two innings to take an early 6–0 lead. The Astros live line to come back and win the game might be somewhere in the neighborhood of +500. If you think the Astros can come back and win the game, you could bet $100 on the live line. If Houston pulls off the come-from-behind win, your $100 live-line bet would net you $500, plus you would get your $100 back.

In America, live betting is a relatively new phenomenon that has become increasingly popular in recent years. It has coincided with advancements in technology that have allowed oddsmakers to calculate and set incredibly accurate in-game odds. Live betting began in Asia and Europe and was most popularly used betting on soccer, specifically the English Premier League. In 2017, live betting accounted for more than 20 percent of the money wagered at several Nevada sportsbooks. With the rising popularity of mobile betting (that is, betting using your cell phone), live betting is expected to become even more widespread in the coming years.

The most famous example of a live line cashing in was the 2017 Super Bowl between the Patriots and the Falcons. When the Patriots trailed 28–3 midway through the third quarter, some Vegas and offshore sportsbooks were posting a Patriots live line +1000 to +1200. When the Pats cut the deficit to 28–20 late in the fourth, the Patriots live line fell to around +500 or +600. But then the Falcons moved the ball deep into Patriots territory with under five minutes to play. With an 8-point lead and Atlanta looking like they were about to score again and ice the game, the Patriots' live line shot up to +1500 or +1700, depending on the sportsbook. As we all know, the Patriots pulled off the impossible comeback for a score of 34–28 in overtime, cashing massive live-line bet tickets for those brave enough to bet them.

Live lines aren't only for cashing a massive payout when a team is losing big. They are also used to get better odds on a team that falls behind by a small margin early in the game. Oftentimes, bettors will wait for a favorite to trail by a few points or one run and then bet them on the live line at a much better number. For example, say the Nationals are a –121 favorite for the full-game line. But in the second inning they give up a run and trail 1–0. The oddsmakers might post the Nationals at +125 on the live line. By waiting for a favorite to trail in the game, bettors can take advantage of plus-money payouts.

Live lines are also used to gauge how likely a team is to win at any given point in the game. For example, say you bet the Red Sox +130 and they jump out to a 9–0 lead in the third inning. The oddsmakers will run their computer algorithm to determine how often underdogs of +130 who led by 9 runs in the third inning ended up winning the game. Maybe the calculator says 90 percent. The oddsmakers then convert that percentage into betting odds, setting the Red Sox as a massive live-line favorite of –1000 or so.

This doesn't mean you would want to go bet the Red Sox live line. Sure, they look like a lock to win, but anything can happen, and if they blow the lead and lose, you'll take a massive hit based on the odds. Instead, the smarter play would be to just ride out your Red Sox +130 game bet. Because live lines change every second, timing is everything. Many bettors monitor the live lines during the game in order to track the progress of their full-game bet. By comparing the full-game odds to the live-line price, bettors can gauge how likely or unlikely they are to win their bet.

Parlays (And Why You Should Avoid Them)

One of the most popular bet types for novice or recreational bettors is the parlay. This is when a bettor makes multiple wagers (at least two) and ties them into the same bet. If any of the bets in the parlay loses, the entire parlay loses. However, if all wagers win, the bettor enjoys a massive payout.

For example, say a bettor wants to wager $100 on a three-team parlay with the Pittsburgh Pirates +150, Texas Rangers +100, and Cincinnati Reds +203. If all three teams win, the $100 bet would pay out a whopping $1,515.

Sounds pretty awesome, right?

This is precisely why public bettors love parlays. They want to get rich quick and the parlay affords them this opportunity. The possibility of striking it rich with one parlay bet is too irresistible to ignore.

Oftentimes you'll even see casinos or sportsbooks post screenshots on social media promoting parlay winners:

- "Check out this bettor who turned $500 into $100,000 with his six-team parlay."
- "Tons of big winners today—but none bigger than this guy. He turned $60 into $80,000 with a twenty-team parlay."

For casual bettors, hitting this type of epic parlay is the ultimate fantasy. But ask yourself this: why would casinos and sportsbooks be so willing to share and promote this information after they've lost such huge amounts?

It's because parlays provide the house with a much larger edge than straight, individual bets.

To understand just how great the edge is, we first must define the term *hold*. The hold is the percentage of money the bookmaker or house holds onto after all bets have been settled and paid out. It is calculated by dividing the gross winnings by the gross amount of bets that the sportsbook accepts. Think of it as a win percentage for the sportsbooks.

A UNLV Center for Gaming Research study showed that from 1992 to 2017, Nevada sportsbooks boasted a hold of just over 30 percent on parlays. In comparison, every other major sport averaged holds of roughly 5 percent. In other words, the house wins 30 cents on every $1 bet on parlays. They only win 5 cents on every $1 bet on regular, individual bets.

FACT

From 1992 to 2017, just under $81.9 billion has been bet on sports in Nevada sportsbooks. Of that $81.9 billion, the sportsbooks have won just over $3.9 billion. This translates to an overall hold of 5.52 percent. Here are the holds for each individual sport: football 4.91 percent, basketball 5.08 percent, baseball 3.32 percent, "other" 6.35 percent. Others include sports like hockey, soccer, tennis, golf, boxing, and mixed martial arts. Meanwhile, the hold for parlays is 31.17 percent.

Simply put, books made a killing off of parlays. They are the number one cash cow for the house, which is why sportsbooks and casinos are so happy to promote them on social media. Parlays are the sports betting equivalent of the penny slot. Bettors keep going back to the well in hopes of hitting a big payout. However, whether it's the penny slot or the parlay, the big winners are almost always the books, not the bettors.

Any seasoned wiseguy knows that sports betting isn't easy. It's hard enough to win one bet. So when you layer more and more bets onto the same wager, you're playing right into the sportsbooks' hands by assuming more risk and limiting your chances of winning. Sure, you might cash a juicy parlay once in a blue moon, but it will likely take you dozens and dozens of lost parlays until you finally cash big.

It's also important to note that if you have a five-team parlay and you win four out of five bets, you lose the entire bet. However, if you bet those five teams individually, you would have profited close to three units or more depending on the price.

There's nothing wrong with placing a parlay bet for fun every once in a while. But bettors should never make it a routine, daily occurrence. You greatly enhance your chances of winning by sticking to individual game bets.

Teasers

Another popular bet among recreational or novice bettors is the teaser. Teasers are similar to parlays. The big difference with teasers is that bettors can also adjust the point spread or the total in their favor, moving a line up ("tease up") or down ("tease down") a certain number of points. The more the bettor changes the line from the original spread or total, the lower the payout becomes. Just like parlays, all bets involved in the teaser must win in order for the teaser to win. If one bet in the teaser loses, the entire teaser loses. Because teasers are adjustments to the point spread, they are only available for football and basketball.

The most common teasers for football are 6, 6.5, or 7 points, but can be more or less at the bettor's discretion. You can tease spreads, totals, or a combination of both. Sportsbooks have their own payouts and rules for teasers. Depending on the sportsbook, you can combine up to ten bets or more in one teaser. The more teams you include in the teaser, the higher the payout. But of course, all must hit in order for you to win.

For example, say the Bills are a +2.5 underdog against the Dolphins and the total is 45.5. Maybe you are leaning Bills and the over but you aren't totally confident in both numbers. You could bet a 6-point teaser on both the spread and the total, teasing the Bills up from +2.5 to +8.5 and teasing the total up from 45.5 to 51.5. On the flip side, if you liked the Dolphins in a high-scoring game, you could tease Miami from –2.5 to +3.5 and the total from 45.4 to 39.5.

The price of a 6-point, two-team football teaser is typically –110. If you increase the 6-point teaser from two teams to six teams, the price improves to +610. A ten-team 6-point teaser would pay +2600. The price gets better as you add more teams to the teaser. However, the reward doesn't come without risk. By layering on more teams, you increase the likelihood that at least one of them will lose.

ESSENTIAL

One of the most popular teaser bets is the "sweetheart teaser," also known as the "monster teaser." In a sweetheart teaser, bettors pick three teams and get to tease each of them 10 points, with the price being typically –110 to –130. One big drawback with sweetheart teasers is that at most sportsbooks, if any of the bets tie or push, the whole sweetheart teaser loses. This is the fine print that sinks a huge number of bettors.

Just like parlays, teasers provide a massive hold for the books. This is why they are called "sucker bets." They are attractive to recreational bettors, but the real winner is almost always the house. Teasers get their name because, you guessed it, they're a tease. On the surface, the teaser sounds like a layup. You get much better numbers that look as if they can't possibly lose. But almost always, at least one of the bets will lose. As a result, bettors should tread lightly. If you'd like to place a teaser every now and again, go for it. But making it a daily habit is assuming risk and playing right into the sportsbooks' hands.

Some sportsbooks offer pleaser bets, also known as "pleasers." They are the opposite of teasers. Instead of getting better odds and additional points, you are getting worse odds but at a much better price. For instance, say the regular full-game odds were Panthers −3, Seahawks −6, and 49ers +3. If you wanted to bet those three teams in a 6-point pleaser, the odds would change to Panthers −9, Seahawks −12, and 49ers −3. If all three teams cover the pleaser spreads, the bettor would enjoy a massive payout of roughly +1500.

Teasers and parlays are also referred to as "exotics," which is short for exotic bets. Exotics are considered any kind of bet outside of the regular spread, moneyline, and total bets. Another popular exotic is propositional bets.

Propositional Bets

Propositional bets, popularly referred to as "prop bets" or "props," are bets on anything involved in the game that isn't tied to the final score. Props are often viewed as "fun bets" or scratch tickets. Recreational bettors love props because it makes the game more fun and exciting to watch. The limits are low, meaning you can't place big wagers on them. Some limits are as low as $25 or $50, depending on the sportsbook. Props are typically broken up into three categories: game props, player props, and entertainment props.

Game Props

Sportsbooks offer a variety of game props for bettors to bet on. These bets isolate specific parts of a game and are not dependent on the outcome. For instance, in baseball a game prop bet could be any of the following: will either team score a run in the first inning? Which team scores first? Which team is winning after the first inning? Will the game go to extra innings? How many combined hits, runs, and errors will both teams have?

In football, a game prop could be betting on which team will score first, which half will be the higher-scoring half, the over/under on the longest touchdown, whether the game will go to overtime, whether there will be a safety, whether a kicker will miss a field goal, how long the longest field goal will be, and many more.

Player Props

In recent years, player props have been widely popular among recreational bettors. Instead of betting on the entire team, or one team against another, bettors bet on how individual players perform. In baseball, this means betting on how many total hits, runs, or stolen bases an individual player will have, or the number of strikeouts a starting pitcher will have: will it be over 4.5 or under 4.5? Bettors can also bet on whether or not a player will hit a home run. Typically, these props are one-sided. This means a player might be +500 to hit a home run. So if you bet $100 and the player hits a home run, you win $500, plus you get your $100 back. If the player does not hit a home run, you just lose your $100. There is no option for a player not to hit a home run.

Player props are incredibly popular for the NFL and NBA. On any given Sunday, NFL bettors can bet on the over/under passing yards for a quarterback, the over/under receiving yards for a wide receiver, and the over/under rushing yards for a running back. Bettors can also bet on whether or not a player will score a touchdown; how many catches, tackles, or sacks a player will make; or if a player will throw or make an interception. In the NBA, the most popular player prop is the total number of points scored. Will it be over or under 21 points? Also popular are the number of rebounds, assists, blocked shots, turnovers, 3-pointers, or free throws.

ALERT

While prop bets can be highly entertaining and extremely fun, books usually make a killing off them. This is because sportsbooks typically charge a much higher juice on prop bets, anywhere from –130 to –150 instead of the standard –110. As a result, you should make a point to limit your prop bets to only situations that provide value. Do your homework. Make sure you've built a strong case as to why you're betting a prop.

Player props aren't just for individual games. They can also be season-long props. This means betting on who will win the MVP Award, Rookie of the Year, Offensive and Defensive Player of the Year, Cy Young Award, Coach of the Year, and many more. You could also bet on who will lead the league in specific stat categories and individual players' over/unders. For instance, will a player hit over or under twenty-five home runs this season? Will a quarterback throw for over or under thirty touchdowns?

Other Props

Aside from game props and player props, there is also a litany of other props available to bettors. This could be anything from which head coach will be fired first, which team a star free agent will sign with, or the draft position for individual players in the draft. Prop bets can range even further into things like politics, music, movies, and entertainment. For instance, bettors could bet on who will win the presidential election, or seats in the House of Representatives and Senate. Sportsbooks will also provide props on who will win specific categories at the Oscars, Emmys, and Grammys. You can even bet on who will become the next James Bond, how much money a movie will make in an opening weekend, or how many records an album will sell. Sportsbooks capitalize on current events or anything in the news cycle by offering these prop bets. Their goal is to take advantage of public interest and perception.

Super Bowl Props

Prop bets are available year-round for almost all sports, but the most popular prop-bet time of year is the Super Bowl. In recent years, Super Bowl prop bets have become a growing phenomenon in the gambling community, especially among casual bettors.

For example, here is a list of some of the prop bets offered for Super Bowl LII between the Eagles and the Patriots:

- Will the National Anthem be over or under two minutes long? Over –130, under +110
- Will the coin flip be heads or tails? Heads –120, tails –120
- What color hoodie will Bill Belichick wear? Blue +120, red +200, gray +500

- Which team will score first? Patriots –110, Eagles +120
- Which team will commit the first turnover? Patriots +115, Eagles –120
- Will the game go to overtime? Yes +700, no –1000
- Will there be a safety? Yes +600, no –900
- Will Al Michaels make a gambling reference? Yes +1500, no –2000
- Will there be a missed extra point? Yes +300, no –500
- Will there be over or under four and a half Budweiser commercials? Over +150, under –175
- Will Justin Timberlake cover a Prince song? Yes –150, no +200
- Will Britney Spears make an appearance on the halftime show? Yes +300, no –450
- Will Donald Trump tweet over or under two and a half times during the game? Over –115, under –115

Typically, recreational bettors focus on the prop bets that provide the biggest payouts because they want to turn a small wager into a big profit. In the examples above, a bettor might take a shot on yes to overtime at +700, hoping to turn their $10 wager into a $70 payout.

The books will also post cross-sport props, such as: who will have more: an NBA player's points or an NFL player's rushing yards? Or who will have more: Tiger Woods birdies or Tom Brady touchdowns?

FACT

Nevada's 198 sportsbooks took in $158.6 million in bets on Super Bowl LII between the Patriots and Eagles. It marked the third straight year setting a new record handle. "Handle" refers to the amount of total money bet on a game or event. However, the sportsbooks only made $1.17 million in winnings (0.7 percent hold), their lowest Super Bowl win percentage since 2011. This was due to the fact the majority of bets, including the biggest bets, were on the Eagles, who covered and won the game as 4- to 5-point underdogs. Also, sportsbooks took a big loss on props. The game set a Super Bowl record for scoring and yards. The vast majority of prop bets were all the over, with almost all of them cashing.

Team Totals

In addition to betting on the total number of points scored by individual players or both teams combined, bettors can also bet on specific team totals. This means betting the over/under points scored by just one of the teams involved in the game, not both.

For example, let's say the Dodgers are facing the Padres. Los Angeles is in first place with their ace pitcher on the mound, while the Padres are in last place with their worst pitcher on the mound. The game total is set at 9.5. You like the Dodgers to score a lot of runs against a sub-par, journeyman pitcher, but you're afraid to bet the over 9.5 because you think the Dodger's ace might pitch a shutout or only give up 1 or 2 runs. So even if the Dodgers score 9 runs and win 9–0, you would lose the over 9.5 bet.

Instead of betting the game total, you could bet the Dodgers team total, which might be 5 or 5.5, while the Padres team total might be 3.5 or 4. If you bet the Dodgers team total over 5.5 and Los Angeles wins 6-0, you win your bet. The game total of 9.5 has no effect on your team total bet.

Alternative Spread Bets

Some sportsbooks offer alternative spread bets, also known as alternate bets. In baseball, these are referred to as alternate run-lines. In hockey they are referred to as alternate puck-lines. Instead of a normal baseball or hockey spread bet, in which the favorite is –1.5 and the underdog is +1.5, alternative bets offer the favorite +1.5 and the underdog –1.5.

On the surface, it seems like a layup for favorites. You might already think the favorite will win the game, but now you can bet on the favorite to win or lose by just one run? Sounds too good to be true!

The catch is that the prices are exorbitant, which is great if you're betting on an underdog but extremely dangerous if you're betting on a favorite. For example, say the Angels are playing the Athletics and the Angels are a –140 favorite. You want to bet on the Angels; you aren't supremely confident that they'll win the game, but you think it will at least be close. Instead of betting Angels –140 on the moneyline, you could bet the Angels +1.5 on the alternate run-line. If they win or lose by one, you still win. However, the price on the Angels +1.5 is –270. It's a gift and a curse. You get an extra run and a half, but you are forced to lay a massive number. It's a very risky proposition with little reward.

The real value to alternate run-line is betting on underdogs. In the example above, the Athletics might be +122 on the moneyline to win the game straight up, but the Athletics alternate run-line would be –1.5 at +225. Sure, the Athletics would need to win by 2 or more runs instead of just one, but you'd enjoy a much bigger payout based on the alternate run-line. Not all games result in a team winning by exactly one run. Many times a team will win by two or more. By picking their spots with alternate run-lines, bettors take more risk but also enjoy a much bigger reward.

Many books also post 2.5 (or 2X) run-lines. That would mean the underdog is +2.5 runs and the favorites is –2.5 runs. For example, the Arizona Diamondbacks might be –200 favorites on the straight moneyline (with the San Diego Padres as +179 underdogs). The regular run-line would be Diamondbacks –1.5 +105. The 2.5 run-line would be Diamondbacks –2.5 +142. So if you think Arizona can win by 3 runs or more, you could get a juicy +142 payout, as opposed to a modest +105 payout to win by 2 runs, or a risky –200 price to win straight up. The double run-line creates value on favorites, but not as much on underdogs. In the example above, the Padres would be +179 moneyline underdogs to win straight up. On the regular run-line they would be +1.5 –125, while on the 2X run-line they would be +2.5 –167. Sure, the Padres would only need to win or lose by 2 runs or less, but laying the –167 isn't great value.

In football and basketball, alternate spreads are offered at varying prices based on how far the line has moved from the original spread. For example, the Colts might be a 3-point favorite on the full-game spread at –110 juice. However, alternate spreads could be offered with Colts –7 (+250) or Colts –10 (+350). On the flip side, the Colts could also be offered at +3 (–200) and +7 (–400). Just like alternate bets in other sports, these lines come with obvious pros and cons. By getting better odds you are forced to take on much higher risk and pay a high price. Conversely, by getting worse odds you are afforded much more of a reward.

Now that we've broken down all the different bet types, the next step is to discuss and map out the overarching betting strategies that we will use to make our bets.

CHAPTER 6

Contrarian Betting

In order to make sports betting a successful and sustainable endeavor, you must pick a strategy and stick with it. If you just chase what's hot, bet against whatever is cold, and don't have a solid and consistent philosophy or plan, you might as well be flipping a coin. The best way to win over the long haul is to embrace contrarian betting. This means betting against the average Joes who pick games based on gut instinct and lose much more often than they win. By going contrarian, bettors can capitalize on public bias and take advantage of artificially inflated or shaded lines. Best of all, contrarian bettors can place themselves on the side of the house—and in the end, the house always wins.

Betting Against the Public

Contrarian betting, also referred to as betting against the public or fading the public, is a sound betting strategy for one simple reason: more often than not, the public loses. As a result, the team getting the minority of bets provides much more value than the team getting the majority of bets.

It's a misconception that the public never wins. Make no mistake about it, they do win from time to time. Betting goes in cycles, with a series of ups and downs. There will be days, weeks, or even months where public bettors do well and turn a profit. However, over the course of the long haul, average Joe bettors end up losing in the end. This is why you want to bet against them, not with them.

Before going deeper into why betting against the public is a smart strategy, we must first define who the public is.

FACT

In the world of Wall Street, contrarian investors are known to buy stock when everyone else is selling and sell stock when everyone else is buying. They believe that anytime the herd instinct takes hold and public opinion sways heavily in one direction or the other, it leads to the overvaluing or undervaluing of a stock. This creates market inefficiencies that contrarian investors are then able to exploit.

Public bettors are hobbyists and fans. They bet as a form of entertainment. By and large, public bettors ignore betting analytics data. They might spend less than five minutes deciding who to bet on. Instead of analyzing betting percentages, dissecting line movement, and studying historical trends and head-to-head matchups, they bet almost solely based on gut instinct and emotion. They also love betting on their favorite teams. In the betting community, public bettors are referred to in many different ways: average Joes, novice bettors, casual bettors, recreational bettors, or "square" bettors. Although they bet small amounts on games, public bettors make up the overwhelming majority of the sports betting market.

Who Does the Public Bet On?

Because public bettors bet based on bias, emotion, and gut instinct, this means they gravitate toward certain teams and specific bet types: most notably favorites, home teams, and overs.

Public bettors love betting on favorites because it's human nature to want to root for winners. Think about it: if an average Joe is going to put his hard-earned money down on a game (also known as "getting down"), he wants to bet on the "better" team. Why would he want to risk his money betting on a team that is expected to lose? On its face, that seems counterintuitive. Public players also love betting on home teams because they overvalue home-field advantage. They will almost always take a team playing in front of their supportive home crowd over a team who has to travel on the road into a hostile environment.

Just as the public loves betting favorites and home teams, they also have a psychological bias toward betting overs. If a public player is betting a total, he wants to see a high-scoring, back-and-forth, entertaining game with lots of action and lots of points, cashing his over ticket in the end. It's not fun to root for low-scoring games and hope for missed shots, blocked shots, shot clock violations, strikeouts, double plays, and shutouts.

Overvaluing Non-Key Factors

Public bettors will also select games based on criteria that don't have nearly as big an effect as they think. This means almost always picking the team with the better record (or in college sports, the team with the higher ranking). Public bettors put too much weight into recent performance. If a team looked great in their last game and is on a winning streak, public bettors will automatically want to bet on them the next game. Conversely, if a team looked terrible their last game and has lost several games in a row, the bettors will want to bet against them. This is called recency bias.

Public bettors love basing their bets on players. If one team has more star players than the other, they will bet that team, no questions asked. They are also biased toward teams with rich histories, which come from successful, championship-winning franchises. Public bettors also bet on whichever team has the more famous head coach. Additionally, public bettors are incredibly susceptible to media bias. They fall in love with teams that get a lot of media attention and hype. If a team is on sports shows all day, on the cover of every magazine, and talked about constantly on the radio, a public bettor will be swayed to bet on them.

Public bettors also have great memories. If they bet on a team and the team wins for them, they will continue to bet on that team regardless of the betting data or head-to-head circumstances. Conversely, if they bet on a team and the team loses, they will never want to bet on them again. In fact, they will look to bet against them, or "fade" them, simply out of spite.

In the end, all of these biases meld together to form a herd betting mentality, also known as public betting. By going against the prevailing public beliefs and opinions, contrarian bettors can exploit these biases and increase their chances of winning by capitalizing on market inefficiencies.

FACT

In his 1893 dissertation *The Division of Labor in Society*, French sociologist Émile Durkheim coined the phrase "collective consciousness" to describe how a group of shared ideas, principles, and attitudes come together to form and govern societies. This creates a "group mind" or "herd mentality" that people are programmed to abide by. Durkheim described it this way: "The totality of beliefs and sentiments common to the average members of a society forms a determinate system with a life of its own. It can be termed the collective or creative consciousness."

Shaded Lines

One of the main reasons why contrarian betting is a sound strategy is because you almost always get better odds by taking the contrarian side. You have to remember that the oddsmakers aren't setting a line in a vacuum. Their number one goal is to maximize their profits. Because the overwhelming majority of bettors are public bettors and not professional bettors, oddsmakers always set lines with public opinion in mind. In other words, the oddsmakers know that the public loves betting favorites, home teams, popular teams, and overs. As a result, they will capitalize on public bias by shading their lines accordingly. Shading means setting a line that is further toward the popular side. This forces public bettors to assume added risk by betting artificially inflated or worse lines.

In baseball, the sportsbooks know that big-market teams like the Red Sox, Yankees, Dodgers, and Cubs will almost always get an overwhelming majority of bets. So instead of opening them as a –150 favorite, they might shade them to –160 or –170. The public could care less if the line is –150 or –170. They will bet on the big popular teams regardless. This means that public bettors are almost always getting a bad number on the popular, big-name teams.

Take the 2016 curse-breaking, World Series–winning Cubs. They had an impressive win-loss record of 103–58, winning almost two-thirds of their games. However, because they were a public darling and almost always a big favorite at a shaded price, a $100 bettor taking the Cubs in all 162 games only finished the year up $155.

FACT

Warren Buffett is arguably the most successful contrarian investor of all time. He defined contrarian investing in these terms: "Two super-contagious diseases, fear and greed, will forever occur in the investment community. The timing of these epidemics will be unpredictable....We simply attempt to be fearful when others are greedy and to be greedy only when others are fearful."

While shaded lines hurt public bettors who want to bet the popular side, they help contrarian bettors who are brave enough to bet the unpopular side. In the examples I just mentioned, just as the oddsmakers will shade the Red Sox or Yankees line negatively from –150 to –160, they will also shade the opponents' line positively. In this case, the opponent might open at +145 instead of +135. A contrarian bettor willing to back the unpopular opponent just got an artificially inflated line of 10 cents. A $100 bet now pays out $145 instead of $135, simply because public bias drove up the line.

Shaded lines are valuable in spread sports like football and basketball, where a single half point can make a world of difference. Say the undefeated Packers are playing at home against the winless Browns. The oddsmakers know that the betting public will want to pound Green Bay as a home favorite against an inferior team. After running their computer models and consulting their power ratings, they come to the conclusion that the spread should be set at 14 points in favor of Green Bay. However, knowing that the public will be inclined to bet Green Bay no matter what, the oddsmakers shade Green Bay from −14 to −14.5 or −15. As a result, contrarian Browns bettors are awarded better odds of a free half point or full point. Instead of betting Cleveland +14, contrarians can bet Cleveland +14.5 or +15. Now if Green Bay wins by exactly 14 points, Browns contrarian bettors win thanks to the +14.5 or +15 shaded line.

At its core, contrarian betting is all about value. When the public is heavily lopsided in one direction, it causes that particular side to be overvalued and overpriced. This is why contrarian bettors love to zig when the public zags. Instead of betting on popular teams, favorites, home teams, and overs, contrarian bettors largely focus on unpopular teams, underdogs, road teams, and unders, knowing that they are consistently undervalued and underpriced.

The Contrarian Magic Number

In order to bet against the public, we first need to know where the public is. It isn't enough to just blindly assume that they will bet every single favorite, home team, and over. There are always extenuating factors at play. Maybe they fall in love with a trendy underdog or bet an under because two teams have great defenses. Or maybe they bet a road team because they have their ace starting pitcher on the mound.

Contrarian bettors never place bets based on assumptions. To determine where the public is, they rely on hard data in the form of public betting trends. By knowing what percentage of bets each team is receiving, contrarian bettors not only determine which side the public is on but also gauge the level of public bias.

Technically speaking, anything below 50 percent is considered to be contrarian. However, in sports betting, the contrarian threshold is much lower. This is because not all contrarian value is weighted equally.

If the bets are split 51/49 or 55/45, there isn't much contrarian value on the team getting 49 percent or 45 percent because it means the public is relatively undecided. The key with contrarian betting is to look for the most lopsided games of the day, where the public is heavily biased in favor of one side. The more lopsided the betting percentages are, the heavier the public bias, and thus the more value there is in betting against the public. In other words, a team getting 30 percent of bets would have much more contrarian value than a team getting 40 percent of bets. And a team getting 15 percent of bets would have much more contrarian value than a team getting 25 percent of bets.

While betting against the public sweet spots can vary based on the sport, a good universal benchmark is betting on teams that are getting less than 35 percent of bets. Contrarian bettors should consider 35 percent the magic number at which to bet against the public. If a team is getting less than 35 percent of bets, that's a strong indication that the public is dismissing them. Therefore, they would be a smart bet because they are being undervalued and might be benefiting from a positively shaded line.

ALERT

When seeking out betting information, be sure to check the source. Many different sites claim to have betting percentages. But they might only come from one sportsbook and are not truly reflective of the betting market. Additionally, the information could be delayed or stale. Bettors should seek out live odds software that displays up-to-the-second data and pools betting percentages from multiple sportsbooks, giving bettors a much better sense of the overall market.

Sportsbooks Worry about Lopsided Action

Another important key to remember is that heavily lopsided betting attracts the most attention from the oddsmakers and the sportsbooks. If the betting percentages are relatively even, with close to 50 percent on both sides, the sportsbooks can sit back without fear of losing big. Based on the juice, it doesn't matter much to them which team wins. They will make money by taxing each side.

However, if a game is heavily lopsided, with the public betting one side in overwhelming fashion, this raises red flags for the sportsbooks because, depending on the outcome, they stand to lose a lot of money. For instance, if the Steelers are 10-point favorites against the Buccaneers and 80 percent of spread bets are taking the Steelers, the sportsbooks have huge liability on Pittsburgh. If the Steelers win by 11 points or more, the sportsbook will take a massive hit because they will have to pay out huge sums of money to public bettors who took Pittsburgh.

Could the Steelers reward public bettors and win by 11 points? Of course they could. But never forget: the sportsbooks are smart and not in the business of losing. They rarely put themselves in a position to take massive losses. They can predict which side will be the popular side and already set the spread with public perception in mind. By betting on the Buccaneers +10, contrarian bettors can take advantage of public bias and place themselves on the side of the house. Being on the side of the house is always a smart decision because, in the end, the house always wins.

Focus On the Most Popular Bet Type

To bet against the public, we want to focus on teams getting less than 35 percent of bets. But what type of bets are we talking about, exactly? Moneyline bets or spread bets? Can you bet against the public with totals? Does betting against the public work equally well for all sports?

Every sport is different and bettors need to be mindful of this. Contrarian betting only works by targeting the most popular bet types for each sport. Contrarian bettors need to go where the largest number of public bets are in order to truly capitalize on bias and shaded lines.

For football and basketball (both professional and college), the overwhelming majority of public bets are placed on the spread and to a lesser extent, the total. While the public does bet on moneylines in football and basketball, it accounts for a much lower share of bets compared to the spread and total. As a result, there is no contrarian value betting on the moneyline because there aren't enough public moneyline bets to bet against. In fact, you might even be betting against professional bettors who are risking large sums on the moneyline.

For example, say a football game is receiving 25,000 bets. Of those 25,000 bets, 15,000 are on the spread, 9,000 are on the total, and 1,000 are on the moneyline. In all three cases, the percentages could be exactly the same, with 70 percent on one side and 30 percent on the other. In all three cases, the side getting 30 percent of bets would be the contrarian side. However, the 30 percent side on the spread would be much more valuable than the 30 percent side on the total. That's because it's taking into account a higher number of public wagers, and therefore more accurately represents public bias. Meanwhile, the 30 percent of bets on the moneyline are so low that there is no value to taking the contrarian side. For these reasons, when betting against the public in football and basketball, bettors should be focusing on teams getting less than 35 percent of spread bets, because the spread is the where the highest number of public bets are.

FACT

Since 2005, NFL teams getting 20 percent or less spread bets have gone 113–91 ATS (55.4 percent), winning +16.53 units with a +7.8 percent ROI. This means a $100 bettor would have made $1,653. Teams getting less than 20 percent of moneyline bets have gone 83–124 (40.1 percent), losing –7.85 units with a –3.8 percent ROI. Because the spread is much more popular than the moneyline, it takes in a much higher number of public bets, which leads to much more contrarian value.

In baseball, the most popular bet type for public bettors is the moneyline. Sure, baseball bettors also bet the spread and total, but it pales in comparison to the number of bets that the moneyline receives. If a baseball game is receiving 10,000 bets, it's a good bet than at least 7,000 (or 70 percent) will be on the moneyline, while the total and spread account for the other 3,000. So naturally, contrarian baseball bettors should focus on teams getting less than 35 percent of moneyline bets, because the moneyline is where the highest number of public bets are.

FACT

Since 2005, MLB teams getting less than 20 percent of moneyline bets have gone 1,262–1,872 (40 percent). However, because these teams are almost all big underdogs at undervalued prices, they have produced +72.47 units won with a +2.3 percent ROI. A $100 bettor taking every team getting less than 20 percent of moneyline would have won $7,247 over the past thirteen years.

Betting Against the Public Doesn't Work with Every Sport

When betting against the public in hockey, bettors focus on the team getting less than 35 percent of moneyline bets. This is because the vast majority of hockey bets are placed on the moneyline, not the spread or total. However, contrarian bettors should tread lightly in hockey. Because hockey isn't nearly as popular as the other professional sports, there isn't as much public betting to go against. The average number of bets on an NHL game is much, much lower than an NFL, NBA, or MLB game, which leads to less contrarian value.

Always remember: betting against the public only works in the most popular sports that garner the highest amount of public attention and the largest number of public wagers. This is why it's best suited for betting on football, basketball, and baseball. Betting against the public does not work in supplementary or lesser-known sports like golf, tennis, WNBA, or the Canadian Football League (CFL). If the public isn't betting heavily on a sport, there isn't any contrarian value to be had. As a result, contrarian bettors should target only the big-name sports and ignore the lesser-known sports.

Target Heavily Bet Games

Isolating the correct bet type and focusing on the most lopsided games aren't the only requirements for betting against the public. You can't just blindly take every team getting less than 35 percent of bets. The last step is to analyze the number of bets a game is getting. The goal is to target the most popular games of the day that are getting the highest degree of public attention and highest number of total bets, or action.

Why is the number of bets so important? Because contrarian value isn't based solely on percentages, but also the size of the sample. If you were to poll ten people and seven of them are betting on Team A, that tells you 70 percent of the bets are on Team A. This means Team B is getting 30 percent and would therefore be the contrarian side. However, if the sample size is small, you don't know where the 70 percent of bets are coming from. The 70 percent on Team A might be professional bettors who win at a high rate. They crunched all the numbers, analyzed every matchup, and came to the conclusion that Team A was the smart bet. As a result, betting on Team B, while technically contrarian, would not be a smart idea because you are betting against professionals, not public players.

However, if you polled one hundred people instead of ten people and found that seventy of them were betting on Team A, that leads to much more contrarian value on Team B. Remember, the vast majority of the betting market is made up of public bettors, not professional bettors. So the larger the sample size, the increased likelihood that the majority of bets are coming from public players. As a result, the 30 percent on Team B in the game with one hundred bets is much stronger than the 30 percent on Team B in the game with ten bets.

FACT

Since 2005, NBA teams getting less than 35 percent of spread bets have gone 3,090–2,947 ATS (51.2 percent) in the regular season, losing –12.42 units with a –0.2 percent ROI. However, if the game is getting at least double the amount of bets compared to the average game that day, the team getting less than 35 percent of spread bets improves to 61–42 ATS (59.2 percent), winning +15.69 units won with a +14.85 ROI. If the average game is getting 5,000 bets that day, these games would be getting 10,000 bets or more. The higher amount of bets represents increased public action, leading to an elevated contrarian value.

Practically speaking, say there are two games in the NBA with the same exact lopsided betting percentages. The Hawks are +6 and only getting 25 percent of spread bets and the Knicks are +6 and only getting 25 percent of spread bets. However, the Hawks game is getting 8,000 bets while the Knicks game is getting 20,000 bets. Even though the lines are exactly the same and both games are equally lopsided with the same percentage of bets, the Knicks +6 would be much more valuable than the Hawks +6 because it's getting more than three times the number of tickets. As a result, it has three times the number of public bettors to go against, leading to three times the contrarian value.

Look for Televised Games, Rivalry Games, and Playoff Games

In order to identify the most heavily bet games of the day with the most public action, bettors need access to live odds betting software that displays the number of bets from not only one sportsbook, but a group of sportsbooks. However, a good rule of thumb for targeting a heavily bet game is to ask yourself this initial question: is the game on TV?

If the answer is yes, the game is likely to have contrarian value if the public is heavy on one side. This is because public bettors are much more inclined to bet on a game if it's on TV. After all, the most fun part of betting is watching the game and rooting for your team to win. If the game isn't on TV, public bettors will be less inclined to bet on it.

As a result, contrarian bettors should pay close attention to televised games, particularly nationally televised games between popular teams. These are the games that will garner the most public action and have the most contrarian value. If the Grizzlies are playing the Suns at 10:30 p.m. ET and the game can only be seen in local markets, it's probably not a game offering much contrarian value, even if the percentages are lopsided. However, if the Celtics are hosting the Lakers at 7 p.m. ET and the game is on ESPN, TNT, or TBS, it will likely be the most heavily bet and most watched game of the night and therefore, a good situation to go contrarian if the public is loading up one side over the other.

Another great spot to bet against the public is in rivalry games and playoff games. Rivalry games generate much more buzz and intrigue among public bettors than regular games, which provides added motivation to bet on them. This rivalry leads to higher ticket counts and more contrarian value. In baseball, a game between the Red Sox and the Yankees will garner much more public action than a game between the Rays and the Brewers. In football, a game between Ohio State and Michigan will garner much more public action than a game between Western Kentucky and Maine. Contrarian bettors should target these rivalry games if the percentages are lopsided, especially if they're on TV.

Playoff games are arguably the best situations to bet against the public because they receive the highest amount of public interest and media hype, and are all nationally televised. Even better, average bettors who may not have placed a bet all season long will come out of the woodwork and bet on playoff games just because they're the topic of conversation and generating all the headlines. Playoff games are the most heavily bet games of the season, which creates a perfect storm for contrarian bettors to bet against the public.

Since 2005, NFL regular season underdogs have gone 1,860–1,859 ATS (50 percent), losing –84.66 units with a –2.2 percent ROI. However, in the postseason, underdogs have gone 88–72 ATS (55 percent), winning +12.27 units with a +7.5 percent ROI. This is because playoff games attract a much higher amount of public bettors than regular-season games. The influx of public action, with the vast majority betting on play-off favorites, leads to increased contrarian value on playoff underdogs.

Be Aware of the Sports Betting Landscape

When betting against the public, contrarian bettors should always take a step back and look at the sports betting schedule, specifically what sports are in season and how many games are being played on a given day. The sports betting schedule is also called the board. Each day, the board will show the total number of games bettors can bet on.

One of the best days to bet against the public in baseball is on Fridays. This is because public bettors are wrapping up their work week and just got their latest paychecks. As a result, they are more apt to bet on games, specifically favorites and home teams. This leads to increased contrarian value on road underdogs. Since 2005, road under-dogs getting less than 35 percent of moneyline bets on Fridays have gone 627-925 (40.4 percent), winning +54.05 units with a +3.5 percent ROI. On all other days combined, they've gone 3,028–4,795 (38.75), losing –61.01 units with a –0.8 percent ROI. In betting circles, this is called "Fade the Public" Friday.

If the board is loaded with dozens of games and several different sports are being played all at once, this can hurt contrarian bettors. This is because public bettors are easily distracted. If there are dozens of different games to bet on, public bettors will spread their action across the board based on personal preference. If it's a busy night in the fall or winter and the NFL, college football, NBA, college basketball, and NHL are all playing games on the same night, public bettors might bet on a combination of games across each sport. As a result, the number of bets on each game will be lower on average because public bettors have so many games to choose from. This leads to decreased contrarian value.

On the flip side, if the board is light, which means there are only a few games to bet on, this is a great advantage for contrarian bettors. Public bettors will be thirsty for action, but they have far fewer games to choose from. This means they will load up on all of the same games, leading to higher ticket counts and increased contrarian value. Furthermore, they will likely know less about the games, which makes them more profitable to bet against. If it's a Thursday in the summer and there are only six MLB games on the board, all six games will be heavily bet because the public has nowhere else to turn. If it's a quiet Tuesday night in the fall and there is only one college football game on TV between Coastal Carolina and Georgia Southern, the public will bet on the game just for the sake of having action. They will likely take the favorite, home team, or over based on their gut instinct and bias, without having spent any time analyzing the game.

Bet Against the Popular Underdog

Because the public loves betting favorites, the vast majority of contrarian bets will be on underdogs. However, this isn't always the case. It doesn't happen often, but from time to time the public will fall in love with an underdog. The public almost never wants to bet on an underdog because underdogs are perceived to be the inferior team, and the public is programmed to want to bet on the superior team. As a result, in the rare instances that the public bets heavily on an underdog, or "loads up" on an underdog, it signals pure and heavy bias. This creates rare contrarian value on favorites.

For example, say North Carolina is traveling to Cameron Indoor Stadium to face archrival Duke in the most popular college basketball game of the week. The Tar Heels are coming off an impressive blowout win while the Blue Devils just lost their last game. The oddsmakers open the game at Duke −7. The public says that's way too many points and 70 percent of bets hammer the Tar Heels +7. This heavy public North Carolina betting might cause Duke to fall from −7 to −6.5. Contrarian bettors would then be afforded a rare opportunity to bet Duke at better odds. Instead of having to bet Duke −7, now they get a free extra half point and get to bet Duke −6.5. Not only is

Duke contrarian in a heavily bet game (only getting 30 percent of bets), but the public overvalued North Carolina so much that they moved the line and handed out an extra half point to contrarian Duke bettors.

Anytime the public bets heavily on an underdog, contrarian bettors are afforded the unique opportunity to bet an undervalued favorite. This is popularly referred to as "Fading the Trendy Dog." In the example above, the smart bet would be for savvy contrarian bettors to take Duke −6.5 and fade the trendy UNC dog.

QUESTION

Does this mean I should bet every favorite if they're getting less than 50 percent of bets?
Not exactly. Fading the Trendy Dog means focusing on favorites getting less than 35 percent of bets, but only in the most heavily bet games of the day. Since 2005, all college basketball favorites getting less than 35 percent of bets have gone 979–969 ATS (50.3 percent), losing −42.27 units with a −2.1 percent ROI. However, if the game is heavily bet, receiving at least double the average number of bets that day, the favorite getting less than 35 percent of bets has gone 145–124 ATS (53.9 percent), winning +12.95 units with a +4.7 percent ROI.

Playing the Long Game

Being a contrarian bettor isn't easy. It means you're almost always betting on the worst teams. You're relying on underdogs who look like they can't possibly win or cover. You're betting on cellar dwellers and teams coming off blowout losses. You're betting road teams in hostile environments. And when it comes to totals, you're almost always taking unders.

It seems crazy, but there's a method to the madness. If betting every favorite, every home team, and every over was the path to success, the public would be filthy rich and the sportsbooks would go bankrupt. But remember, the house always wins. It's the oldest phrase in betting. This is why underdogs, road teams, unders, and unpopular teams have so much value. There will be ups and downs along the way; that's betting. But if you always bet the side that offers the most value and you align yourself with the house, you'll set yourself up for long-term success.

Contrarian betting isn't the only key to being a successful bettor. It provides a solid foundation to build upon, but it's only a starting point. It gets you halfway to where you want to be. The second pivotal factor is making sure you are always on the same side as the professional bettors.

CHAPTER 7

Follow Sharp Action

It isn't enough to just blindly bet against the public in every single game. Contrarian bettors must also be selective and look for the most valuable contrarian spots. This means making sure you are always on the same side as the professional bettors who win at a high rate, also referred to as sharp bettors or sharps. There are several different ways to locate sharp action, including bet signals, steam moves, reverse line moves, line freezes, and bet versus dollar discrepancies. The ultimate goal is to search for games where you can simultaneously bet against the public, place yourself on the side of the house, and align yourself with the sharp professional bettors. When you find a team that checks off all three boxes, that is the smartest bet you can ever make.

Who Are the Professional Bettors?

A professional bettor is considered someone who wins at a high rate and has a long track record of success. Professional bettors aren't betting based on gut instinct or bias. They don't have favorite teams or favorite players. They never bet based on emotion. They're completely objective and analytical. They block out the media noise. They're betting solely based on data and value. Professional bettors are extremely calculating, patient, and disciplined. They only bet a game if they believe they have a clear advantage, called an "edge."

Unlike public bettors, who have day jobs and bet during their free time as a form of entertainment, professional bettors have no other jobs. As a result, while the average public bettor might spend five minutes deciding who to bet on, professional bettors spend hours every day dissecting data, statistics, and head-to-head matchups. They watch countless hours of game film, studying and scouting each team, looking for tendencies, strengths, weaknesses, and any pieces of information that could provide an edge against a particular opponent. They know every player, from the star to the last man on the bench.

FACT

Professional bettors who team up and combine their knowledge and resources are called betting syndicates. They work together to form sports betting enterprises, which they run like businesses. They are constantly running computer models and staring at the odds to capitalize on soft or mispriced lines. They have teams of specialists in different areas and bet large amounts at different sportsbooks to maximize their profits.

Professional bettors have their own power rating systems and handicap each game. Before the oddsmakers release a line, professional bettors will crunch their own numbers and come up with a number that they think the line should be. If the oddsmakers release a line that is far off from the line that professional bettors think it should be, professional bettors will bet the game immediately once the lines are available. For example, a professional bettor might analyze an upcoming game between the Bears and the Panthers and conclude the Panthers should be 4-point favorites. If the oddsmakers open the Panthers at –3.5, the professional bettor will bet Panthers –3.5 as soon as line is released, because his numbers say the line should really be –4.

Professional bettors are mathematicians at heart. Their number one goal isn't just to pick the right side, but to also get the best possible odds on a game. While a public bettor will only bet through one sportsbook, professional bettors bet through multiple sportsbooks so they have access to a wide range of different lines. Professional bettors almost never bet parlays and teasers. They are also well funded and disciplined with their bankroll management.

Bet with the Pros

Professional bettors are the experts of the betting industry. As a result, you always want to be on the same side of a game that they are. Think of it in investment terms. If a stock is rising, or a team is getting a huge majority of bets, who is buying the stock or betting on that team? If it's the public, or novice investors who don't have a track record of success, you want to be on the opposite side. However, if it's Warren Buffett buying the stock, that changes everything. You want to buy the stock and be on the same side as Buffett because he's proven to be a smart, sharp, and profitable investor. In the same vein, bettors always want to be on the same side of the sharps. They are the Warren Buffetts of sports betting.

QUESTION

Should you bet with the money or against the money?
It depends what kind of money it is. If the money is coming from professional bettors, you want to be with the money because it's considered "sharp money." If the money is coming from average Joes who are betting for fun, you want to be against the money because it's considered "public money."

It's a misconception that sharps never lose. They do, and they lose quite a bit. If a sharp bettor is hitting 55 percent to 60 percent of his plays, which is an impressive win rate, that means he's losing 40 percent to 45 percent of the time. Sharps are not infallible, but they've earned their name for a reason. This is why they're popularly referred to as "wiseguys." Going against sharp money, no matter how confident you might be in a play, is a mistake that all bettors should avoid.

Sharps Move Lines

Typically, professional bettors bet large amounts on games, but not always. Being sharp depends more on your win rate. Only those who have a high win percentage and have proven it over the course of the long haul are considered sharp.

When professional bettors bet on a game, it's called sharp action or smart money. Oddsmakers both fear and respect sharp bettors. As a result, sharps can force the oddsmakers to adjust the line, which is also known as "moving the line." Whichever side the sharps bet on, the oddsmakers will move the line further toward that side. Public bettors rarely cause sportsbooks to move a line. It's only when they are betting one side in overwhelming fashion that oddsmakers will adjust the odds.

For example, say a celebrity like Floyd Mayweather bets $1 million on the Super Bowl. Despite the massive bet, Mayweather may not move the line an inch because he is considered a public bettor. He doesn't have a high win rate or a long track record of success. He is betting for fun based on gut instinct, not because he crunched the numbers and has an edge on the game.

However, if a sharp bettor with a high win rate bets $100,000 on the Super Bowl, he could move the line because the oddsmakers know he is a placing a smart bet with strong and sound reasoning behind it.

This might sound strange and somewhat scary, but anytime you place a bet, the house knows who you are (unless it's your very first time betting at sportsbook). The house has a complete record of every member's betting history. By looking up your account number, they know how many bets you've placed, along with your win rate. They know immediately whether you're an average Joe betting for fun or a seasoned professional betting based on hard data and analysis.

FACT

Professional bettors rarely place bets in person. They do not want the sportsbooks to know who they are. If they did, the sportsbooks might reject their bets or shade the odds against them. As a result, many professional bettors hire runners, also known as number runners. These are individuals who will place the bet in person on behalf of the professional bettors. This allows the professional bettors to stay anonymous and keep their edge.

However, it's not always easy to tell who the sharps are betting on. It's not as if they release their picks to the public. There are a few tools you can use to get a feel for which teams and lines the sharps seem to prefer.

Bet Signals

The best and easiest way to identify sharp action is through the use of bet signals. Bet signals are automated alerts coming directly from the sportsbooks. They are triggered as soon as professional bettors get down hard on a specific game, a specific team, and at a specific number. Bet signals highlight market inefficiencies and come in three major forms: steam moves, reverse line moves, and line freezes.

Steam moves and reverse line moves are triggered on the spread and the total in basketball and football and on the moneyline and the total in baseball. One important thing to keep in mind with bet signals is that they can be triggered multiple times a day on different sides of the same game. The goal is to isolate games where sharps are all united on one side. If all the bet signals are coming in on the same team or same side of a total, that's an indication that sharps are in agreement all across the market. Despite the fact that they are betting at different books, they all agree on which side is the smart play, with no sharps voicing differing opinions. This gives you increased confidence in playing that particular side.

Late bet signals are more meaningful than early bet signals. This is due to the fact that early on, when the lines are fresh and just released, the limits are low at most sportsbooks, meaning sharps can still bet the game but they cannot bet massive amounts. Later in the day, once they've gotten a better read on the market, books will raise the limits. As a result, a bet signal coming in at 10 p.m. ET the night before a game would be much less meaningful than a bet signal coming in at 6 p.m. ET an hour before the game starts.

Steam Moves

A steam move occurs when professional bettors place large wagers at once across multiple sportsbooks. This causes sudden, drastic, and uniform line movement across the entire sports betting market. If a large wager is placed at one individual sportsbook but no other sportsbooks move their lines, that's not considered steam. A steam move must hit multiple sportsbooks and cause universal line movement across the entire marketplace.

Steam moves have a domino effect. First one sportsbook gets hit with a large wager from respected players, then a second, then a third, and so on. This is because sportsbooks have different limits on how much they are willing to accept in terms of maximum bets. If a professional bettor has a great edge on a game, he will bet the game at several different books in order to maximize his potential profits.

FACT

One of the best sportsbooks to keep an eye on when looking out for steam moves is *Pinnacle*. An online gaming site based in Curaçao, *Pinnacle* was established in 1998 and is considered one of the sharpest offshore sportsbooks in the world. They have some of the highest limits of any sportsbook, which means they attract lots of professional gamblers. When *Pinnacle* gets hit with a steam move, they will cause the entire market to move.

For example, let's say a handful of sportsbooks are posting $10,000 limits. This means they will not accept bets bigger than $10,000 each. If professional bettor bets $10,000 at one sportsbook on Packers –3 against the Vikings, he might cause the oddsmakers to move the line to –3.5. So if he wanted to bet it again, his second bet on the Packers would be at –3.5, a worse number. However, if he spreads his action across multiple books, he could place several $10,000 wagers at the exact same time on Packers –3. This means he's maximized his potential profit and gotten the best number available. When a sharp bettor bets big amounts at multiple books, it's called "getting down hard" or "getting down heavily."

Once the professionals start doing this, it forces the whole market to react, causing the oddsmakers to move their lines in the direction of whichever team the sharps just bet on. In this case, the oddsmakers would move the Packers from −3 to −3.5. We call this reaction steam, or a team getting "steamed." This is basically sharp bettors and big players spreading their money across multiple sportsbooks, getting down hard at the same time and causing the entire market to move.

If a bettor has access to live odds software, they can monitor the sportsbooks in real time. If they see all the sportsbooks move their odds in the same direction at the same time (or within thirty to sixty seconds of each other), they know a steam move took place. Whichever team the line is moving toward is the team the professional bettors just bet on.

Don't Chase and Beware of Buy Back

One big mistake that many bettors make is following every single steam move they see, which is also called "chasing steam." This is a bad idea and a losing strategy because, although knowing which side the professional bettors like is a massive advantage, you have to remember that the professional bettors might only like that team at the specific number.

For example, if the professional bettors steamed the Packers at −3 and now the market has moved to Packers −3.5, you would be chasing steam by betting Packers −3.5. The key with steam moves is to get the same number that the professionals steamed, also referred to as the triggering number. If the professional bettors steamed Packers −3, it means they only like the Packers at −3. If you were able to take advantage of a slow-moving sportsbook and quickly bet the Packers −3 before the market moves, that would be a smart bet. However, if you are too late and the line has already moved to Packers −3.5, you missed out on the key number and should probably lay off the bet.

Another thing to keep in mind is that steam moves can occur on both sides of a game. Sharp bettors aren't always going to bet on the same exact teams at the same exact odds. They might have differences of opinion based on what their number crunching is telling them and how the line has moved. As a result, you might see a steam move on Packers −3, which causes the market to move to −3.5. At that point, professional bettors might steam the Vikings +3.5 because their model says the Vikings have value with the extra half point. So you need to be prepared to bet both sides in those instances, or better yet, just lay off the game entirely.

Bettors should also be aware of the possibility that professional bettors are intentionally betting one side in order to move the number in their favor. Then once the odds move to their desired number, they bet the other side for an even larger amount than the original steam move. This is called "buying back." For example, maybe the professional bettors loved Vikings +3.5 all along. But in order to move the number to Vikings +3.5, they had to bet heavily on the Packers at −3. For example, they might bet $5,000 each on the Packers −3 at five different sportsbooks. Once the line moves to Packers −3.5, they bet $10,000 each on Vikings +3.5 at ten other sportsbooks. These situations are rare but do happen. In order to pull off these "buy back" moves, bettors need a massive bankroll at their disposal.

Reverse Line Movement

Aside from steam moves, the easiest and best way to locate sharp action is to search for reverse line movement (RLM). This is when the betting line moves in the opposite direction of the betting percentages.

Normally, when the majority of bets are heavily weighted in favor of one team, the oddsmakers will adjust the odds and move the line further toward that team. The reasoning is simple: they want to balance their action and limit their risk. By moving the line toward the popular side, not only do they make the odds worse for the popular side but, more importantly, they are hoping to entice action on the less popular side by offering better odds. The vast majority of the time, this is how the line moves. It is considered normal or standard line movement. However, sometimes you will see the opposite happen. Despite the heavy betting on one side, the line will move in the other direction, toward the team getting the minority of bets. This is called reverse line movement.

Anytime bettors see line movement that doesn't make sense, it's most likely reverse line movement. Stop for a second and think about: if the majority of bets are all on one side, why would the oddsmakers move the line the other way, toward the less popular side? Why would the sportsbooks make the odds better for public bettors who are already betting the popular side? No, they aren't being nice or handing out better numbers for free out of the kindness of their hearts. They are moving the line in the opposite direction because professional bettors just placed big wagers on the less popular side.

FACT

Since 2005, NBA teams getting less than 35 percent of spread bets with at least a full point of reverse line movement have gone 482–435 ATS (52.6 percent), winning +21.28 units with a +2.3 percent ROI. However, if the reverse line movement is 1.5 points or more, teams getting less than 35 percent of spread bets are twice as profitable: 253–192 ATS (56.9 percent), winning +47.64 units with a +10.5 percent ROI. The size of the reverse line movement directly correlates with how much money sharp bettors bet on a game. The bigger the movement, the more money they put down.

For example, let's say the Seahawks are 7-point favorites (–7) against the Dolphins and 80 percent of spread bets are taking the Seahawks. Normally in situations like this, the oddsmakers would move the Seahawks from –7 to –7.5. This way they can mitigate their liability on Seattle by offering the Dolphins at a better number, hoping to entice action on Miami at +7.5.

However, instead of seeing the line move further toward the Seahawks, you see the line move the other direction, toward Miami. So despite 80 percent of bets taking the Seahawks, you see the Seahawks fall from –7 to –6.5. This would be a reverse line move on the Dolphins. Despite the public hammering the Seahawks, the line moved toward the Dolphins even though they're only getting 20 percent of spread bets. Why would the sportsbooks do this? Because they just took in a big wave of bets from professional bettors on Miami +7.

FACT

Since 2005, when an NBA under is getting 40 percent or less bets but the total falls at least 1 point, the under has gone 1,419–1,227 (53.6 percent), winning +129.64 units with a +4.8 percent ROI. This means that 60 percent or more bets are taking the over, but the sportsbooks drop the total a full point, maybe from –210 to –209. In these cases, a $100 bettor would have made $12,964 betting the under every time from 2005 to 2018.

In the example above, an inexperienced bettor would see this unusual movement and double down on the Seahawks. If they already bet the 49ers once at –7, surely they will love the 49ers even more at –6.5. However, experienced bettors know better. One of the oldest and best sports betting mantras is this: if it looks too good to be true, it is. The line fell toward Miami because sharp professional players bet on Miami, forcing the line to fall. If bettors could react quickly and find a book that is still posting Miami +7, that would be a smart bet.

Just as in life, timing is everything when it comes to steam moves and reverse line moves. If you are able to pounce quickly and get the triggering number, you are in excellent shape. However, if you wait too long or miss the triggering number, you most likely missed the boat. If the line moves too much, that means a lot of the value is gone and you are now chasing a bad number.

In the example above, the professionals are telling you that the Dolphins are the sharp play, but only if you can get the triggering number of +7. If you're too late and can only get Dolphins +6, you should probably lay off and see if it rises back closer to the triggering number.

You should never blindly follow reverse line movement. Instead, it should be one of many tools in the toolbox when selecting a play.

FACT

Since 2005, MLB divisional underdogs getting less than 35 percent of moneyline bets with at least 5 cents of reverse line movement have gone 1,109–1,384 (44.5 percent), winning +128.39 units with a +5.1 percent ROI. This means that two teams in the same division are playing each other, and the underdog might be getting 32 percent of bets but has moved from +135 to +130 to +125. If you bet $100 on every team in that situation you would have made $12,839 from 2005 to 2018.

Line Freeze

The third and final bet signal used to locate sharp action is to search for line freezes. This takes place when there is heavily lopsided betting on one side but the line refuses to budge toward the team getting vast majority of bets. It's similar to reverse line movement, but instead of the line moving toward the less popular side, it doesn't move at all.

For example, say the Ravens are playing the Bengals and the oddsmakers set the total at 42. You see 78 percent of bets taking the over. In this case, you would expect the sportsbooks to adjust the odds and move the total from 42 to 42.5 in order to compensate for the heavy over betting so they can entice under betting and limit their risk. However, despite the heavy over betting, you notice that the total remains unchanged at 42.

This is a line freeze. Even though the public is hammering the over, the books are reluctant to move the line up because they have under liability. Either they've already taken in smart under money from respected players, or they're afraid that if they raise the total to 42.5 they'll open themselves up to a big wave of professional under bets. Sportsbooks may be taking in 78 percent of bets on the over 42, but if they're all $5 bets from public bettors, they aren't too concerned. Even if the over hits, they won't take a huge loss because they're all small bets. What they're really worried about is moving the line in favor of professional bettors betting $10,000, $25,000, or more on the under 42.5. They don't want to raise the total to give out an extra half point to sharp under bettors because then their liability would be seriously jeopardized.

Line freezes are most common in spread and total sports like basketball and football because a single half point could be the difference between a win and a loss. However, you will also see this happen in moneyline sports like baseball or hockey. For example, maybe the Cleveland Indians (–140) are a road favorite facing the Seattle Mariners (+130). Nearly 80 percent of bets are on the Indians –140. However, you see the line remains frozen and hasn't moved despite the heavy Cleveland betting. This signals reluctance by the books to raise the Indians line because they're worried about handing out better odds and an increased payout to sharp Mariners bettors.

Anytime you see heavy betting on one side, yet the line doesn't move, that should automatically trigger alarm bells. If the lack of line movement seems fishy, there's a reason behind it. The sportsbooks aren't asleep at the wheel or forgetting to adjust the number. They're staying right where they are because they've either taken in smart money on the other side, or they're afraid to move the line because they'll open themselves up for sharp bettors to bet big amounts on the unpopular side. The public can be hammering one side, but the books aren't worried. It's the other side that's more important. The sportsbooks are worried about getting hit with big sharp money, not public money.

Bets versus Dollars Discrepancies

Another way to locate sharp action is by comparing the percentage of bets to the percentage of dollars a particular team or side is receiving.

It's rare that bets and dollars will be exactly equal. This is because different types of bettors are betting on the game and they're risking varying amounts. By comparing the percentage of bets to the percentage of dollars, bettors can better understand which side the professional bettors are on. The ultimate goal is to decipher what kind of money a team is getting: is it sharp money from professional bettors (in which case you would want to be on the same side), or is it public money coming from average Joe bettors (in which case you would want to be on the opposite side)?

It's pretty simple: if a team or side is receiving a much larger share of money compared to bets, that's a good indication that it's sharp money. If a side is getting a much lower share of dollars compared to bets, that's a good sign that it's public money.

To illustrate the point, let's imagine one game is receiving ten total bets. Eight of the bets are on Team A, which means Team A is receiving 80 percent of bets. However, all eight bets are coming from public bettors risking $5 each, totaling $40 on Team A. Meanwhile, Team B is only getting two out of ten bets (or 20 percent), but the two bets are coming from professional bettors risking $20 each, totaling $40 on Team B. This means that Team A is receiving 80 percent of the bets wagered on the game but it only accounts for 50 percent of dollars wagered on the game. On the other hand, Team B is only receiving 20 percent of bets wagered on the game but it accounts for 50 percent of dollars wagered on the game. One could reasonably deduce that the majority of sharp bettors were on Team B based on the bets versus dollars discrepancy, because even though they're only receiving 20 percent of the bets on the game, it accounts for a much larger share of dollars. This means that betting on Team B would be the smart play because Team B is receiving the smart money.

In practical terms, say the Phillies are playing the Pirates. The Phillies are getting 58 percent of bets but it only accounts for 35 percent of the dollars wagered on the game. That's a difference of 23 percent. That negative discrepancy is telling you that the majority of bets on the Phillies are coming from public bettors risking small amounts. Meanwhile, the Pirates are getting 42 percent of bets wagered on the game but it accounts for 65 percent of dollars wagered on the game. That's a difference of 23 percent. That positive bets versus dollars discrepancy is telling you that the sharp money is on the Pirates.

ESSENTIAL

It's a misconception that public bettors and professional bettors are always on different sides of a game. Although somewhat rare, it does happen that they'll bet on the same side. However, if public bettors and professional bettors are on the same side of a game, it's likely for different reasons. Public bettors might like a team because they're popular favorite at home. But professional bettors might like the team because of matchups, power ratings, and value. Also, it's likely that professional bettors bet the team early at the best odds, while public bettors bet the team late after the odds got worse.

Bets versus dollars discrepancies aren't all created equal. They are more meaningful if the team getting the positive discrepancy is contrarian. For example, if the Cubs are getting 80 percent of moneyline bets wagered on the game but 90 percent of moneyline dollars wagered on the game, they would enjoy a 10 percent difference between bets and dollars. However, despite the positive discrepancy, they are still getting 80 percent of bets. This means they are still the public side, and we want to bet against the public, not with the public. So although the Cubs are getting more money, it's still mostly public money, not sharp money.

A good rule of thumb is to search for situations where a team is getting less than 50 percent of the bets (which means you are on the contrarian side and can bet against the public) and is also getting a higher share of dollars. In a nutshell, a team getting 20 percent bets but 30 percent dollars is much more valuable than a team getting 70 percent bets and 80 percent dollars. The discrepancy is the same, but the first example is more valuable because it's against the public, while the second is less valuable because it's with the public.

Make Sure Line Movement Agrees

The bigger the discrepancy between bets and dollars, the stronger the sharp money is. However, you can't just bet every team getting more money than bets. You also have to monitor how the line is moving. You want the line movement to be on the same page as the bets versus dollars discrepancy, meaning you want the line to be moving toward the team getting the lower percentage of bets but higher percentage of dollars.

For example, say the Angels are playing the Dodgers. You see 65 percent of moneyline bets on the game are taking the Dodgers, yet it only accounts for 51 percent of dollars wagered on the game. Meanwhile, the Angels are only getting 35 percent of bets wagered on the game, but it accounts for 49 percent of dollars wagered on the game. This bets versus dollars discrepancy is telling you that the majority of bets on the Dodgers are smaller wagers from public players, while the bigger, sharper wagers are on the Angels. In this instance, the Angels are the side getting the smart money.

However, in addition to the positive 14 percent discrepancy for the Angels, the line movement is also in the Angels' favor. The Angels opened at +110 and moved to +104. So even though the Angels are only receiving 35 percent of bets on the game, the line moved in their favor and their payout got smaller. This signals sharp reverse line movement on the Angels. In this case, the Angels are in the ultimate sweet spot: they're contrarian, have reverse line movement, and a positive bets versus dollars discrepancy. This is the sort of situation bettors should focus on.

Check the Source

When looking for bets versus dollars discrepancy plays, you must also be careful about where the numbers are coming from. Dozens of sites claim to provide this information. However, often you have no idea whether they're legitimate or not. The numbers might be fabricated. They might be real but only coming from one sportsbook. In this case, although the numbers are accurate, they don't accurately represent the entire market. Lastly, even if they're legitimate and come from more than one book, they might be delayed and not in real time, so you could be looking at stale information that doesn't account for the latest action.

Wait Until Close to Game Time

Another note of caution: when looking for bets versus dollars discrepancy plays, you should wait until as close to game time as possible. The betting market is fluid and constantly changing as more action comes in. What looks great early in the day might look completely different later in the day. If you wake up and see a massive 40 percent bets versus 80 percent dollars discrepancy at 9:00 a.m., take it with a grain of salt. While that information is accurate as of that moment, it wouldn't be wise to act on that so quickly because those percentages are coming from a small number of early wagers.

When the number of bets is low, the discrepancies can be massive. Throughout the day they tend to level out. Wait until within an hour of game time to lock in a bets versus dollars discrepancy play. That's when the number of bets are highest and the data is strongest.

Now that we've learned how to bet against the public and locate sharp action, we are almost ready to start making picks and placing bets. However, there is still one last thing we need to discuss. In order to put ourselves in the strongest position possible to succeed as sports bettors, we need to learn from the past so we can better predict the future.

CHAPTER 8

Learn from the Past

It's often said that those who don't know history are doomed to repeat it. The same can be said of betting on sports. While past performance in no way guarantees future results, being aware of specific historically profitable situations can provide bettors with an increased edge and account for overlooked or undervalued factors that current data may not reflect. If you finish your research on a game and find out that teams in a similar situation tend to win at an above-average rate, that strengthens your pick and makes you more confident in your play. However, if you crunch the numbers and find out that your play has been a consistent loser in years past, it may help you to lay off and avoid a loss. The key is to find a game that provides value not only in the present, but in the past as well. In doing so, you can be even more confident in the future outcome.

Betting Systems

Casual bettors approach a game solely through the lens of the two teams playing each other. They will look at both teams and compare and contrast them. Who is the favorite and who is the underdog? Who has the better record? Who is playing at home? How has each team played recently? Depending on how a casual bettor answers these questions, that's who they will end up betting on.

More advanced bettors will pore over higher-level statistics, head-to-head matchups, and power ratings. They will break down the betting data, looking at where a line opened and how it moved. They will analyze which side is getting the majority of bets and dollars in an attempt to locate sharp action. In the end, they make a pick based on which side they believe has more value.

However, very few bettors dig into the past and study historical data. This means dissecting information based on years and years of previous games to see if they can locate a profitable situational bet. Most likely this doesn't occur for one of two reasons: either they don't have the time to do the research, or they don't have access to accurate and reliable historical information. Either way, they are forfeiting an incredible edge that could help them greatly improve their chances of winning.

Professional bettors rely heavily on historical data and use past results to create betting systems. A betting system is a model that hones in on a profitable situation in the past and then looks for present-day games that fit the same criteria. This is a different way of betting on games. Instead of focusing exclusively on the present-day matchup and dissecting the two teams going head-to-head, you are instead betting on situations, not specific teams.

The ultimate goal of any betting system is to isolate a trend that provides a statistically significant edge. This means that no matter which two teams are playing, it still remains profitable.

Take Advantage of Historical Trends

An example of a betting system is the "Windy Under" system for totals in the NFL. Anytime the wind is blowing heavily, it can have a big impact on the game. Wind makes it harder for quarterbacks to throw the ball. A pass that would otherwise be caught can sail left, right, or come up short. This leads to more incompletions and fewer first downs. It also leads to more running of the ball and less passing, which chews up the clock and makes the game go faster. Wind also makes it harder for kickers to make kicks. If you add this all up, wind makes it harder for the offense to score points, which benefits the under.

The historical data proves it to be true. Since 2005, when the wind blows at least ten miles per hour, NFL unders have gone 418–335 (55.9 percent), winning +58.7 units. This is now your "Windy Under" system. Anytime you see an upcoming game with wind speeds of ten miles per hour or more, you will bet the under, regardless of which teams are playing, because you know it's a profitable edge and a smart play.

Another betting system can be based on a matchup that disproportionately benefits one side. For instance, in the NFL, underdogs playing divisional opponents perform much better against the spread than underdogs playing non-divisional opponents, especially when they're on the road. This is due to the fact that teams in the same division play each other twice a year, which means they're very familiar with each other. This levels the playing field and benefits the underdog. If they're on the road, that's even better because you can take advantage of public bias, which overvalues home teams.

Since 2005, teams fitting this criteria have gone 474–420 (53 percent) against the spread, winning +31.62 units. You can title your system "NFL Road Divisional Underdogs." Now the next time a team matches your system, you will bet the game with this trend in mind.

Depending on the strength of the system, bettors will either play every match no matter what, or use the system as an additional factor when deciding whether or not to bet a game. You know a game that fits your system has added value because teams in that same situation have turned a profit in the past. You then use this information to help you strengthen a potential bet or save you from betting against a profitable trend.

Say the Chiefs are 7-point underdogs on the road against the Broncos. You are thinking about betting the Chiefs because they're only getting 25 percent of spreads bets, providing excellent contrarian value in a heavily bet game. Even better, you see that Kansas City is getting more money than bets and also received a sharp reverse line move. Based on the present-day data, you are feeling confident in the Chiefs and want to bet on them.

Then you check the historical data and notice that the Chiefs also happen to fit your "Road Divisional Underdog" system. You liked them anyway based on the current data, but now you can tack on the profitable historical trend. This makes you even more confident in your Chiefs play because you know you're on the right side not only today, but historically as well.

On the flip side, maybe you are looking at a second NFL game between the Jets and the Bills. You are thinking about betting on the Bills as 3-point home favorite because you like the matchup. Buffalo has beaten the Jets in three straight games at home. The Bills are getting two starting players back from injuries and their defensive line is going against a porous Jets offensive line that just gave up seven sacks the previous week. Buffalo is also getting only 40 percent of bets, giving them decent contrarian value. However, you realize that the Jets match your "Road Divisional Underdog" system. Because the past and present data are in conflict, the smartest play is to lay off the game entirely.

The goal is to look for games where the historical data and the present-day data match. If a team looks great based on the present-day information but also matches a historically profitable situation, that is the best of both worlds because it places you in the strongest position possible. It adds a whole new layer of confidence to a play.

It's a constant trial and error. The key is to look for patterns and then backtest them to see if they're profitable. Sometimes you have ideas you think are great that end up not being a total loser, and other times you uncover a massive edge out of the blue. The goal is to constantly evolve, search for possible edges, and strive to improve. Always try to get .01 percent sharper each day.

ESSENTIAL

Many bettors believe that when it's freezing cold out, less points are scored in an NFL game. That's because the players are uncomfortable, their hands are stiff, and it's harder to throw and catch the ball. This theoretically benefits the under. However, historical data has proven the exact opposite is true. When it's 32 degrees or lower, the over has gone 117–95 (55.2 percent), winning +16.09 units since 2005. This is an example of a popular belief that isn't true. Cold temperatures don't have nearly the effect people think. The oddsmakers are setting lines to capitalize on this public bias.

Key Characteristics of a Winning Betting System

But what exactly makes a winning betting system? Is it solely based on the record of the system? Or is there more that goes into it than just wins and losses? In order to create a winning betting system, bettors must ensure that their system meets three key characteristics.

The first characteristic is a sound hypothesis. Every system starts with an idea. Does cold weather lead to fewer points being scored? If a team lost the first game of a doubleheader, are they more likely to win the second game? Do teams playing in the second game of a back-to-back lose more often? Do home teams perform better on Mondays? In order to uncover a profitable trend, you must first be able to explain the underlying reason why you think it's profitable. Having a great record isn't enough. If it doesn't make sense, you might just be targeting a random trend that doesn't have a clear real-world justification behind it.

The second characteristic is a big sample size. The bigger the sample size, the more confidence we have in the data because it's being pulled from a large group of results. The more results there are, the more likely the trend is because there really is an actual advantage for one team and it's not just pure luck.

FACT

Thomas Bayes was a famous English statistician in the eighteenth century. He was credited with creating the Bayes' theorem or Bayesian probability, which is the idea that in order to predict the probability of an event, you need to have massive amounts of empirical data and constantly update your predictions based on new evidence. In other words, predictions are never set in stone; they change as more information becomes available.

If the sample size is small, it might have a great record but that record might just be based on luck and isn't historically significant. For example, say you create a system that has gone 9–1 over the past five seasons. It would translate to an impressive 90 percent win rate, but the sample size is so small that there is no way to know if it's truly indicative of a winning edge. On the other hand, if you create a system with a 56 percent win rate based on a sample size of five hundred games over the past five years, you would have much more confidence in that system because it's pooling a massive set of data. A good rule of thumb is to look for a sample size of at least one hundred games.

The third characteristic is consistent year-to-year results. In order to ensure the biggest return on investment possible, you want a system that has proven to be successful year in and year out over the course of multiple seasons. When looking for this, you want to see a graph that looks like an upward slope, slowly but surely improving each and every season.

For example, say you built an NBA system that has produced an impressive 62 percent cover rate and +25 units won this past season. However, you backtest that same system since 2010 and it shows a win rate of 47 percent with –50 units. Even though the most recent season was highly profitable, it might just be that it got lucky and had a good year, while all other years have been consistent losers. With consistent year-to-year results, you can ensure that a betting system is truly predictive of a profitable trend and not just highlighting a fluky year.

On the flip side, maybe you create a system that has +50 units won since 2010. However, further analysis shows that it produced an incredible three-season run of +75 units combined from 2010–2012, but every season since it has consistently lost 5–10 units. It would still have a great historical record on the surface, but that doesn't tell the whole story. Maybe the sportsbooks caught up to a certain trend and now all the value is gone. Or maybe there was a rule change that canceled out the edge from previous seasons.

FACT

In 2012, Nate Silver rose to national prominence after correctly predicting the winner of forty-nine out of fifty states in the 2012 presidential election. In his book *The Signal and the Noise: Why So Many Predictions Fail—but Some Don't*, Silver uses elections, baseball, the 2008 financial crash, weather forecasts, and climate change to explain how predictive models work. Silver makes the case that good models pool large data sets from a variety of sources over a long time, whereas bad models buy into media hype, rigid ideologies, and inaccurate polling, and over-emphasize random fluctuations—missing the signal amongst the noise.

Beware of Overfitting

The biggest overall issue to avoid with betting systems is making sure they're not overfitted. Bettors can tinker with past results all day to create a system that produces a high win percentage and an impressive return on investment. However, if that system isn't truly indicative of a trend, the results and records are meaningless.

For instance, you could pore over pages and pages of NHL box scores and find out that on the first Monday of every month, home underdogs coming off a win against a non-conference opponent have had an incredible 80 percent win over the past two seasons. On the surface it might seem like a profitable system, based on the stellar win rate. But is it truly sustainable and indicative of a profitable trend? Probably not. That's because there is no rhyme or reason behind why teams in that specific situation do well.

If you overfit a system, the results become arbitrary. Chances are the system is just random, in which case the impressive win rate might just be a fluke. It doesn't have a sound theory or reason behind it. As a result, the system doesn't instill enough confidence in a bettor to follow it moving forward. It might even be the case that a bettor ignored or overlooked different historically profitable data in favor of an overfitted win rate.

Let's see if we can think our way through a winning hockey betting system. Hockey is one of the most grueling and physically taxing professional sports. So when hockey players get extra time off between games, they play much better because they are able to rest, nurse injuries, and get their legs back. Hockey also has the least beneficial home-field advantage of any sport. This is because the boards along the ice provide a barrier from the fans and drown out the crowd noise, which mitigates the home team's advantage and benefits the visitor. Additionally, favorites perform better than underdogs because they are the better team, which is universal to all sports, not just hockey. When a favorite plays a team that missed the playoffs the previous year, they tend to do even better because the opposing team is used to losing. By combining all of these elements, you can create a "Well-Rested Visiting Favorite" NHL betting system.

After crunching the numbers, we find out that, yes, this system is incredibly profitable. Since 2005, visiting favorites who have had at least three days off and who are playing teams who missed the playoffs the previous season have gone 458–248 (64.9 percent), winning +92.06 units. This means a $100 bettor taking each one would have profited $9,206. This would be an example of a winning betting system. The theory makes sense and the results back it up. A bettor would be confident following this system in the future because it's truly indicative of a winning edge.

FACT

Since 2005, the under has gone 499–495 (50.2 percent), losing –22.41 units in Games 1 through 4 of the NBA playoffs. However, in Games 6 and 7, the under has gone 95–66 (59 percent), winning +23.75 units. Why is there such a big discrepancy between the first four games and the last two? Because if a series reaches Game 6 or 7, the players are exhausted and have tired legs, which means they are more likely to miss shots, leading to fewer points. Also, the two teams are evenly matched and fighting for their playoff lives. So they will dig in and play better defense, which benefits the under. This is an example of a profitable NBA system bettors can exploit late in a playoff series.

Keep an Open Mind

One of the biggest keys to building a betting system is having an open mind. Never buy into widely held beliefs, because often conventional wisdom is wrong. Think your way through the nuances of each particular sport. What situations provide the most benefit to teams? What edges are universal across the board, no matter who the team is? Think about the variables that all teams must deal with, like scheduling, rest, home versus road, favorite versus underdog, division versus non-division. Does a high total benefit a favorite or an underdog? How about a low total? How do teams typically perform coming off a win or a loss, or after a big rivalry game? How does weather affect points scored?

The beauty of betting systems is that the possibilities are endless. All it takes is an idea. Sometimes you can have a fantastic idea that you're excited about and feel like has a massive edge, but then you run the numbers and find out it's a losing bet. Other times you randomly stumble upon a profitable trend when you weren't looking for it. The key is to always keep searching. Keep watching games and looking for trends. Never rest on your laurels and just accept the status quo. Keep digging. Keep testing new theories. The worst that can happen is that you find out something isn't profitable. But even this is a benefit because knowing that it's a losing bet allows you to lay off the situation next time it occurs, saving you from a future lost bet.

FACT

In his 1953 essay "The Hedgehog and the Fox," philosopher Isaiah Berlin says that almost all people are either hedgehogs or foxes. Hedgehogs relate everything to one central school of thought, and foxes see the variety of things. The title comes from a verse from the Greek poet Archilochus, who said, "The fox knows many things, but the hedgehog knows one big thing." Berlin wrote about how the Russian writer Leo Tolstoy was a fox but wanted to be a hedgehog and it tormented him. In betting terms, the best forecasters and system builders are foxes.

How to Create a Betting System

Unless you already have theories ready to test, it's almost impossible to just sit down and create a winning betting system off the top of your head. An easier way to go about it is to take it day by day. Each morning, flip back to yesterday's box scores and try to re-create the situation that a winning team was in, or better yet, re-create a certain situation that you may have overlooked.

For example, say you were leaning on the Padres as a +150 underdog at home against the Dodgers last night but decided to lay off because you didn't like the pitching matchup and the game wasn't heavily bet enough. Then you wake up and see the Padres won 4–1. A casual bettor would kick themselves and then turn the page and erase it from their memory. But a smart bettor wouldn't just brush it aside. Instead, she would use the missed opportunity as a learning experience. Spend some time digging deeper into the matchup and the betting data to see what you might have missed. Maybe it turns out that the Padres just got lucky. Or maybe teams in that particular situation win at a high rate, but you ignored one key piece of information.

QUESTION

Is there an easier way to create betting systems other than poring over box scores and inserting data into spreadsheets?

Yes, there is. *Bet Labs* is a web-based platform where bettors can access a full database of archived games from all the major sports since 2003. Bettors can use more than four hundred different filters to test theories and build data-driven systems. It saves countless hours of work and streamlines the process considerably.

After dissecting the betting data more closely, you see that the Padres closed with 25 percent bets and had reverse line movement +152 to +147. You could then begin to build a betting system based on divisional underdogs at home getting at least 5 cents of reverse line movement. To your surprise, you crunch the numbers and find out that teams in this spot have turned a consistent profit since 2005. Then you get to thinking, what if you only look at bigger underdogs that are +145 or higher? You layer in the moneyline range of +145 or more and the system improves even further.

You may have missed a profitable opportunity, but now you ensure that you won't miss it again the next time it pops up.

On the flip side, just as you could look back to yesterday and re-create winning situations from the night before, you could also backtest losses. For example, say you took the over 11 in the Diamondbacks at Rockies game because the public was heavy on the under and you saw a steam move on the over. The D-backs ended up winning 3–1 and you lost your over bet. You review the data and notice that the wind was blowing in at six miles per hour. You research how the total does when the wind is blowing in at Coors Field and find out that the under has performed extremely well over the past ten seasons. There's nothing you can do to take back your lost over bet from the night before, but at least now you are aware of the trend and can make sure you never make the same mistake again.

Always Look to Improve

Once you've created a profitable system, cultivate it. Look for ways to tweak or improve it. Maybe a small adjustment one way or the other can make it even more profitable. It's also important to monitor how rule changes or changes to the league could affect your betting system.

For instance, maybe you created a fantastic college basketball over/under system that focuses on unders in big conference games with high totals. It's been one of your most consistent winning systems in any sport. However, in 2015–16, the NCAA decided to change the shot clock from thirty-five seconds to thirty seconds in an attempt to increase scoring. As a result, the five-second decrease allowed more possessions for both teams, leading to less dribbling, more shots, and an increase in overs. As a result, your fantastic under system is no longer profitable.

FACT

In 2002, Haralabos "Bob" Voulgaris rose to fame as one of the most successful NBA bettors on the planet. He found an incredible edge betting on halftime totals. He noticed that oddsmakers would just take the game total and cut it in half, not accounting for team's specific tendencies, the matchup, the coaching, and how teams committed extra fouls in the fourth quarter. He made millions betting first- and second-half totals. But then the oddsmakers caught up to the trend and changed how they set halftime lines. As a result, Voulgaris's edge was lost.

In the end, bet systems are beneficial for one simple reason: if a team has present-day value but also fits a historically profitable situation from the past, it increases edge and makes you much more confident in your bet.

Return on Investment

To gauge the efficiency of a betting system, bettors use a variety of metrics. This includes wins versus losses, win percentage, and units won. But the best and most popular metric is return on investment, also referred to as ROI.

Return on investment tells you how profitable a system is. To calculate ROI, divide how much money a system has made versus the cost of the investment. The result takes the form of a percentage. If a system has a positive ROI, that means it's been a good system that has made bettors money. If a system has a negative ROI, that means it's been a losing system that has cost bettors money.

For example, say you have a betting system that is based on five hundred games played. You risked $100 on every game and you won +25 units playing the system. To calculate the ROI, you would multiply your profit (25 units) by the amount you risked on each bet ($100), then divide that by the total bets made (500) multiplied by the amount you risked on each bet ($100). Basically, we are trying to take the net profit and then divide it by the total cost of the investment.

It might sound confusing. This is what it would look like written out:

(25 units × $100) / (500 games × $100)

This comes out to 0.05, which translates to 5 percent. This means the particular system has a return on investment of 5 percent.

In other words, for every $100 we risk on this system, we can expect a profit of $5.

The reason why return on investment is the best way to measure the performance of a system is because some systems could have a losing win-loss record but still turn a profit. This happens with moneyline systems based on underdogs who provide positive odds with plus-money payouts. For example, a system could have a 48 percent win rate, which on the surface looks like a losing system, but because the system is betting on underdogs who are always +110, +120, +130, +140, or more, you can still generate a positive return on investment despite a losing record.

QUESTION

What is considered a good return on investment for a successful sports bettor?
Generally speaking, to be considered a sharp or successful sports bettor you would need to produce a positive ROI of at least 2 percent. Some of the sharpest professional bettors reach an ROI of 5 percent. That would be considered the equivalent of winning about 55 percent of your games. Only the sharpest bettors in the world reach an ROI of 10 percent. That is almost unheard of. It would be like winning 60 percent of your bets. A good number to strive for as a bettor: 2 percent.

CHAPTER 9

Making a Pick

You've grasped the basic fundamentals of betting. You've set realistic expectations, removed all bias, and learned the contrarian/sharp action philosophy. Your bankroll management plan is set. Now you're staring at a bunch of games and you're ready to make a pick. What are the first things you should look for? How do you analyze the betting data and locate value? What is the checklist you should go through to make a smart bet? Most of us can't afford to spend countless hours a day watching game film and breaking down every stat and head-to-head matchup under the sun. However, we can all learn how to read the sports betting marketplace. If you pay close attention, it will tell you where the value is.

Check Off All the Boxes

When looking to make a pick, bettors should run through the same basic checklist in their head regardless of the sport. Sure, some sports are different than others, but the overall premise remains the same. You want to be as selective as possible and only bet games that check off the four major boxes: number of bets, betting percentages, line movement, and bet signals. Historical data is the fifth box to check off. It's not a requirement, but an added bonus or cherry on top. The two most important boxes are betting percentages and line movement. That will tell you where the public is and where the sharps are, the two biggest things you need to know.

Don't think of it as handicapping games. Your goal shouldn't be to pick out a winner for every single game. Instead, think of it as searching for games that fit the model we're looking for: against the public, with the house, and with the professional bettors. The goal is to only bet games that meet those requirements. Some days you might find ten games that fit the model, some days you might find five, some days you might not have any. Never force it. Let the board do all the talking.

FACT

In the old days of betting, lines would vary greatly between different sportsbooks, sometimes by 2 points or more. Professional bettors exploited this fact by picking out the sportsbooks offering the best numbers and placing their bets at that particular sportsbook. But then in the mid-1990s, everything changed when Don Best Sports Corporation created the "Don Best Screen," also known as the live-odds page. This screen showed all the lines from all the different books in real time, so bettors could monitor the entire market and see what lines each sportsbook was offering. This forced the sportsbooks to set and adjust their lines more carefully, which caused the entire market to meld their odds closer together with fewer outliers.

Number of Bets

Before you start breaking down all the betting data, you must first understand how popular the game is relative to other games being played that day.

You need to know how much action the game is getting and if there is any contrarian value to be had. To do this, compare the number of bets to other games on the board. If the ticket count is high, that means the game has potential for good contrarian value that can be exploited. If the ticket count is low, you should avoid the game because, although the subsequent data is correct, it doesn't present much contrarian value. There just isn't enough public to bet against. It might be the case that, if the number of bets is low, you are betting against mostly sharp bettors who know more about the game than you do, and you don't want to do that.

The biggest key to going contrarian is focusing on the most heavily bet games of the day. As a result, you only want to get down on games with the highest number of total tickets, which means heavy action from public players. By isolating the most heavily bet games of the day, you place yourself in the strongest position to bet against the public. Look for primetime games, nationally televised games, rivalry games, and games between popular teams with lots of star players.

Betting Percentages

Once you've located a heavily bet game with a high number of tickets, the next question you must answer is this: who is betting this game and what side are they on? Where is the public? Where are the sharps? Are they on the same side or on different sides?

QUESTION

Should I only bet on teams that are receiving 35 percent or less bets?
As long as the game is heavily bet and one team is getting a minority of bets, that's the ultimate goal. If the side is getting 38 percent or 43 percent but also has sharp action, that doesn't mean you have to lay off. Don't concern yourself too much with the specific 35 percent cutoff point. That's just a benchmark. Your goal is to be below it, but if you are a few percentage points higher it doesn't mean you must automatically bypass the game. Just remember that you always want to be on the less than 50 percent side first, and the lower that the percentages are, the better.

First look at the betting percentages to find out where the public is. For football and basketball, this means focusing on the percentage of spread bets (SPD). You are looking for lopsided situations where the public is betting heavily on one side, creating value to bet against them. Typically, this means 65 percent or more bets on one side, with 35 percent or less on the other. You want to be on the 35 percent or less side because that means you are going against the highest percentage of average Joes and capitalizing on the most amount of public bias.

Compare Bets to Dollars

Once you've located a heavily bet game with lopsided percentages, the next step is to start figuring out where the sharps are. Remember, we don't just want to bet against the public, we also want to be with the professional bettors. To do this, look at the dollar percentages. The key with betting and dollar percentages is using them in tandem. You never want to focus on one and ignore the other, or vice versa. You want to compare and contrast them. Depending on how close or far apart they are, that will tell you where the sharp money is.

The goal is to look for situations where a team is getting a higher share of dollars compared to bets. This means that the bigger, sharper wagers are in their favor. If a team is getting a much lower percentage of dollars compared to bets, that's an automatic red flag. It means that the team is getting mostly $5 average Joe bets.

For example, if an NFL team is getting 30 percent of spread bets and 45 percent of spread dollars, that's a good thing. It means the team is both contrarian and has smart money on their side. If a team is getting 30 percent of spread bets but 60 percent dollars, that's even better. The wider the bet versus dollar discrepancy, the stronger the sharp action. The biggest key is that a team is getting at least 1 percent more dollars than bets.

However, if an NFL team is getting 30 percent of spread bets but 15 percent of dollars, that's a bad thing. Sure, you are still contrarian based on the betting percentages, but you don't have any smart money in your favor. You are checking off one box, but not the rest.

Just remember this one key phrase: low bets, higher dollars.

ALERT

Line Movement

We all know you can't judge a book by its cover. But when it comes to betting, you can judge most games based on how the line moves. Depending on which way the line moves, by how much, and at what time, bettors can get inside the heads of the sportsbooks and discover which side is providing value. A line can only move three ways: up, down, or remain stagnant. In a vacuum, this movement (or lack thereof) is somewhat meaningless on its own. However, when you compare the line movement to the betting percentages, you can uncover the mystery and identify which side is providing value.

If a team is getting a majority of bets and the line moves toward them, there isn't much value to be had. That's considered normal, standard movement. For example, if an NFL team is getting 70 percent of spread bets and moves from –7 to –7.5, that's standard operating procedure. The sportsbooks are adjusting the line to compensate for heavy lopsided action. By moving the line further toward the popular side, they are hoping to entice betting on the unpopular side so they can balance their risk.

When it comes to reading line movement, you always want to look out for "fishy" movement, or line movement that doesn't make sense on the surface. If a team is getting a minority of bets, but the line moves in their direction, that's critically important and indicates sharp action in their favor. If a team is getting a vast majority of bets but the line remains frozen and doesn't move further in their favor, that's notable as well. Always look out for line movement that makes you scratch your head. Ask yourself: why did the sportsbooks move the line away from the popular side? Why didn't they adjust the line further toward the popular side?

Having access to sports betting analytics provides bettors a huge advantage. But if you don't have access to live odds or other real-time tools, just concentrate on where the public is and how the line moves. Those are the two biggest factors to focus on.

ESSENTIAL

If a game has relatively split betting percentages but the line movement is massive toward one side, it may not have as much contrarian value, but that's still a great indication of sharp action. In a vacuum, if the betting percentages are roughly even, the line shouldn't move at all. For example, if a team is getting 48 percent or 53 percent of bets but goes from –6 to –7 on the spread or +140 to +120, it's clear that sharp action caused the movement. It may not be contrarian, but that is definitely the sharp side.

Bet Signals

Bet signals are the final step to making your pick. They will show you whether or not sharps have gotten down hard on the game, what side they took, what number they hit, and what time they triggered the move. If you've broken down the game correctly, you will see bet signals on the same side you are leaning. You can test your skills by first looking at the percentages and line movement and then seeing if the bet signals back it up.

If the bet signals are on the same page as the betting and dollar percentages and line movement, you are good to go. If you see conflicting signals that go against the rest of the data, lay off. If you see steam and reverse line moves on both sides of a game, lay off as well. That means sharps have differing opinions on the game. You want the sharps to be fully united on one side. If you don't see any signals, that's also a red flag. It means no sharps were confident enough to get down on the game. Ideally, you are looking for at least one bet signal or multiple bet signals all on the same side that line up with the percentages and movement.

In the end, this is what you're looking for in that contrarian, sharp sweet spot: a heavily bet game with lots of public action in which one team is getting a minority of bets, but a higher percentage of dollars, and which has line movement and bet signals in their favor.

If you've checked off the four major boxes, then you can move on to all the supplementary data. Check the weather to see if it could affect your bet on a total. Check the umpires and officials to see if they favor the home team, road team, the over, or the under. Check the matchups to see how each team lines up against each other. If they're all in agreement, that makes you even more confident in your play.

However, if you see a piece of supplementary information that goes against your pick, don't automatically lay off or bet the other side. One very important thing to remember: professional bettors have all the information you are looking at and much more. They have dissected every inch of the game. They know every detail and who it favors, including details you may have never considered. So if they're getting down on one side, it means they've already considered all the factors. And if a piece of supplementary information goes against the pick, it means the professionals aren't worried and still feel confident in the game. There's a reason this information is considered supplementary. It's already baked into the cake. Follow the percentages and line movement. Those are the most important things to focus on.

ESSENTIAL

If a game only checks off one or two boxes, don't automatically bet the game or dismiss the game. Instead, circle that game and keep an eye on it. Monitor how the betting data develops over the next few hours. Come back to it later in the day, closer to game time, and see if you can check off more boxes. Maybe the team became more contrarian or had a late reverse line move. Or maybe the percentages evened out. Always remember, the market is fluid and constantly changing.

In the end, anything can happen. That's betting. You can break down the perfect play that checks off all the boxes and it still may lose. However, don't let that deter you. You still made the right call. Stick to the blueprint and always remember: you're playing the long game.

Historical Data

Adding the historical data component isn't a requirement. But if a game fits a valuable historical trend and matches a profitable betting system, that makes you that much more confident in your bet. Consider it a luxury or an extra box to strive to check off. Before you place your bet, do some research on the situation of the team you're betting on. If they're on the road, coming off a loss, and playing on *Monday Night Football*, look up how teams in that situation have performed over the past five to ten seasons. If you're looking to bet a total, check to see which direction the wind is blowing and make sure it lines up with the side you're betting on. See if there is an edge to either side, because it could either solidify your bet or make you question your bet if the discrepancy is glaring.

ESSENTIAL

All the major boxes need to be checked off in order for you to make your pick. Think of it this way: you are a lawyer building a case. You need to have all your facts and information lined up together to present the strongest case possible to the judge and the jury. If you've built a compelling case and all the boxes are checked off, you can feel confident in making the play. If your case is weak and not everything lines up in the same direction, you should lay off the bet.

Bet Favorites Early and Underdogs Late

By now, we know the betting public is psychologically biased toward betting "winning teams" and always wants to back "the better team" in nearly every game. As a result, average Joes put the overwhelming majority of their money down on favorites. Because casual bettors make up the vast majority of the market, sportsbooks are forced to adjust their lines if the betting is overwhelmingly in favor of one side so they can limit their risk.

Bettors can take advantage of this tendency by always remembering one key phrase: bet favorites early and underdogs late.

If you are looking to bet on a favorite, you want to bet them as early as possible, typically as soon as the line is released. Why? Because the public will bet on the favorite the vast majority of the time, which means in most cases the line will close further toward the favorite. As a result, the earlier you bet the favorite, the better odds you will receive.

Anticipate Line Movement

For example, say powerhouse Michigan opens as a 21-point favorite against winless Appalachian State. The public immediately gravitates to Michigan because not only are they a great team, but they're at home and playing a cellar dweller. The public loves Michigan to win in a blowout and cover the 21-point spread. As a result, 80 percent or more of the early bets are coming down on Michigan.

This means that the oddsmakers have huge liability on Michigan. If Michigan covers, they will get cleaned out because they will have to pay out winning tickets to everyone who bet Michigan.

In order to limit their liability, the oddsmakers will move the line toward Michigan, first from –21 to –21.5 By moving the line toward Michigan, the sportsbooks are hoping to entice bettors to grab Appalachian State at a better number of +21.5. If the sportsbooks aren't able to entice any underdog bets on Appalachian State +21.5, then they might move the line even further to +22. When it's all said and done, maybe Michigan closes at –23.

ESSENTIAL

As contrarian bettors, the majority of our bets will be on underdogs. This is because we are betting against the public and the public is almost always on the favorite. As a result, the vast majority of the time you should wait as late as possible to place your bet. Let the public continue to hammer the favorite, providing you better odds. Also, let the number of bets build up as high as possible, which increases the contrarian value.

Now apply this movement to favorites in general. In this case, if you liked Michigan, you would have wanted to bet them early at –21. If you waited, you would have missed out on critical points and had to lay a worse number, from –21.5 to –23. Conversely, if you liked Appalachian State all along, you would have been smart to wait it out and let the public hammer the favorite, providing you free points and additional value. If you bet Appalachian State early you would have only gotten +21, but if you waited you would have gotten +23.

Now let's say Michigan wins the game 42–20. If you bet Michigan early at –21 or –21.5, you have covered your bet. If you bet them at –22, you pushed. If you bet them late at –22.5 or –23, you have lost your bet. On the flip side, if you bet Appalachian State early at +21 you would have lost, +22 you would have pushed, and +22.5 or +23 you would have covered.

The same logic can be applied to betting the moneyline. For example, say the New York Yankees open –135 against the Minnesota Twins (+120). More than 75 percent of bettors are taking the Yankees, so the oddsmakers move the line from Yankees –135 to –145. In the end, maybe the Yankees close at –150. Conversely, the Twins move from +120 to +130 and then close at +135. If you had bet the Yankees early, you would have saved yourself 15 cents. Meanwhile, if you waited on the Twins, you could have padded your potential payout.

Picking the right side isn't the only thing when it comes to betting. It's also about getting the best possible odds. The better odds you get, the more likely you are to win your bet. This always comes down to timing and trying to anticipate and read the market.

ALERT

Betting favorites early and underdogs late isn't a 100 percent fool-proof strategy. There will always be instances when the line moves away from the favorite and toward the underdog. Maybe it's because of injuries, the weather, or sharp action coming in on one particular side. However, in the vast majority of cases, the line will move further toward the favorite and away from the underdog, which is why it's a good rule of thumb to bet favorites early and underdogs late.

How to Judge the Value of Your Bet

One of the most common misconceptions in betting is that if a bet wins, it was the right bet. On the other hand, if a bet loses, the most obvious reaction is to think it was the wrong bet. Often you'll hear people say, "The right side is the winning side, the wrong side is the losing side." It's easy to see why people think this way; however, wins and losses don't determine whether a bet was right or wrong. A smart bet is determined before the game begins based on the data. The outcome is irrelevant. To better determine if a bet was right or wrong, bettors use implied probability, expected value, and closing line value.

Implied Probability

Implied probability is crucially important toward bettors' understanding of the relative likelihood of their bets actually winning. It takes the moneyline of a given bet (–110, +135, etc.) and converts that number into a percentage illustrating how likely the event in question is to happen. In a more useful sense, it also tells bettors how often they'd need to win a bet of a certain moneyline in order to break even.

For the arithmetically curious, here's how the conversion works. Note that it's different for minus-money odds and plus-money odds.

Minus-money odds, where x is the moneyline, including the negative sign:

Implied probability = $x / (x - 100)$

Plus-money odds, where x is the moneyline:

Implied probability = $100 / (x + 100)$

This concept is useful in every aspect of betting, from standard single-game bets to futures. Before taking the Dodgers at –350 in a game against the Padres, for example, it's vitally important that bettors understand they've just claimed the Dodgers have at least a 77.78 percent chance of winning that one game. Before placing a bet on the Patriots to win the Super Bowl at +275—that's where the team was listed prior to the 2017 season—bettors must realize that they're giving one team a 26.67 percent chance to win a championship in a thirty-two-team league.

Being able to complete that thought process brings us right into our next concept.

Expected Value

Stemming from the idea of implied probability, expected value is pretty much what it sounds like: a measure of how much a bettor can expect to win (or lose) on a given bet.

Let's start with an easy one. Say you're betting on a coin flip: a 50/50 outcome. If I offer you +105 odds on heads, you'll take the bet. Why? Because if we calculate the implied probability of a bet at +105 odds, it comes out to:

$$100 / (105 + 100) = 100 / 205 = 0.4878$$

This comes out to an implied probability of 48.78 percent. In other words, in order to break even betting at +105 odds, you would need to win 48.78 percent of the time. Anything above that number means you're turning a profit. Obviously the true probability of the coin landing on heads is 50 percent, so you'll win this bet at a higher rate than the rate at which you'd need to win to break even. This is a positive expected value (or +EV) situation, because you can expect to make money on this deal.

If I'd instead offered you −105 odds—sportsbooks actually offer this bet for the Super Bowl coin toss—you (hopefully) wouldn't take that bet. Those odds imply a higher win rate (51.22 percent) than the true 50 percent win rate, so you'd expect to lose money on this deal. In other words, it's a −EV situation.

Bettors should only place bets on what they believe to be +EV situations: when the true probability is higher than the implied probability.

Of course, in sports betting, the true probability isn't a given number, as it is in a coin flip. We don't get to know, for example, that the Packers have exactly a 63.7 percent chance of beating the Lions prior to the game—and that's a good thing. If that probability *were* actually calculable, sportsbooks would simply set lines with juice centered around that number, and every bet, regardless of which side it was on, would be a −EV situation—like the Super Bowl coin-toss bet.

FACT

Expected value is used mostly by professional bettors who run their own numbers and come up with their own lines on a game. They will compare their odds to the sportsbooks' odds. If the sportsbooks odds are better than their own odds, that would be a +EV situation that the professional bettor would look to capitalize on. For example, if a professional thinks an underdog should be +3 but the sportsbooks are offering +4, that would be a +EV bet taking the underdog at +4. However, if the sportsbooks lines were worse than the sharp bettor's own odds (think +2 instead of +3), that would be a −EV situation and a bet they would stay away from.

Instead, oddsmakers use their best judgment, which gives sports bettors the opportunity to take advantage of lines that they believe to be misrepresentations of the teams involved. But because there's no given exact probability, it can be hard to label given bets as +EV or −EV.

For this reason, the best way to measure the value of a bet is by comparing it to the closing line.

Closing Line Value

When sportsbooks offer a game to bettors, they set a line that they believe to be an accurate representation of the two teams involved. But they aren't fixed to that opening line.

Up until game time, the oddsmakers weigh the bets they've received on the game, along with any new information that has come out relating to the players, weather, officials, or any other factors that could affect the outcome of the game, and adjust their lines accordingly. If news of a key player's injury is released, that team will certainly lose some value (i.e., they'd move from −5 to −3, or −160 to −145). If weather forecasts change and some heavy rain or wind comes into play, the total may increase or decrease depending on how oddsmakers feel that change will affect the teams' ability to score. And of course, if sharp bettors all load up on one side, oddsmakers will realize they've put out an inaccurate line and quickly adjust it to limit their liability from sharp players.

Regardless of the reason, lines can change dramatically between the time they open and the game's start time. Once that time comes around, though, oddsmakers will have settled on a number that incorporates all of the new information to produce the most accurate number possible.

The final line available before a game actually begins is referred to as the closing line, and it serves as a reference point for bettors to judge their overall betting skill level and grade their individual bets. By comparing the number they bet to the number at which the line closes, bettors can determine the amount of value their wager holds.

For example, say you bet the Chiefs as a 3-point favorite against the Chargers. But later the line changes to Chiefs −2, and stays there for the remainder of the time it's available. The Chiefs go on to win the game by two touchdowns, so you've won your bet comfortably. All is well, right? Not exactly.

Since you laid 3 points on a team that closed as a 2-point favorite, you paid more for the Chiefs than what they were really worth. And although it worked out in this particular game, over the long term that lost point will significantly dent your profits.

That's why sharp bettors determine the quality of their bets by comparing them to the closing line, not whether they win or lose. If you were to take the Chiefs at –3 against the Broncos and the line instead closed at Chiefs –3.5, then we can label that as a good bet because it beat the closing line by a half point. In other words, it has a half point of closing line value.

Always Try to Beat the Closing Line

Believe it or not, the slight edge you gain by beating the closing line is actually enough to turn a losing bettor into a profitable one.

From 2005–2017, if you'd bet on every NFL favorite, you would have gone 1,859–1,860–111 against the spread. Yes, in a sample of over 3,800 games, only one win separates favorites and underdogs (another example of how good the oddsmakers are at setting lines). Essentially, we're back to talking about coin flips. Because of the juice, though, that 50 percent win rate would have lost you –78.5 units.

But let's say you beat the closing line, on average, by just a half point on all those spread bets on the favorite. Those 111 pushes would become wins, and it's probably safe to assume that there were about 111 half-point losses that would become pushes.

Your record is now 1,970–1,749–111, a 52.9 percent win rate that puts you just over the point of profit (assuming the standard vig of –110).

Closing line value also applies to moneylines. Let's say you're a $100 bettor—meaning your unit size is $100—and you make, on average, five bets per night, or 150 bets per month.

Now further assume that you, on average, beat the closing moneyline by just 1 cent per bet (i.e., you bet the Cardinals –134 and they close –135, or you bet the Pirates +121 and they close +120).

While it may seem meaningless at the time, you're actually making up to an extra dollar on all of your winning bets. In the case that you win on an underdog bet, you've won a full extra dollar. In the Pirates example, you'd have won $121 instead of $120.

When you win on a favorite, you earn an extra fraction of a dollar, with the amount coming closer to the full buck as you approach even money. In the Cardinals example, you'd win an extra 56 cents by betting –134 instead of –135.

By the end of a month, depending on your win rate and diversification of favorites and underdogs, you've likely made anywhere between a half unit and one full unit, just from a 1-cent edge on the closing line.

So whether it's on a point spread or moneyline, don't be fooled into judging your bets based simply on the outcome. Understand that a winning bet that doesn't beat the closing line isn't as skilled as a losing bet that does, and that ultimately, beating the closing line is the best way to ensure a positive expected value and a long-term profit.

QUESTION

If you beat the closing line ten times in a row, but lose all ten bets, are you still considered a sharp bettor?
Yes. All bettors go through short stretches where they get extremely lucky or unlucky. Luck comes and goes, but skill is sustainable. If you're beating the closing line but losing the bets, that means you're breaking down the games correctly and are on the right side, but you aren't getting any breaks. This is why sharp bettors don't worry too much if they're in a cold spell. As long as they're beating the closing line, they know they're on the right track and it's only a matter of time until their luck turns.

Now that we've learned how to make a smart pick and how to judge the value of our bet, the next step is to actually place the bet. This can be a tricky process for first-time bettors, but once you learn your options and how to execute each one, it becomes very easy.

CHAPTER 10

How to Place a Bet

You've crunched all the numbers, finished your analysis, checked off all the boxes, and arrived at a smart and valuable pick. Now the final step is actually placing your bet. Generally speaking, you have two options: you can either bet the game in person at a sportsbook anywhere it's legal, or place your bet through an online, offshore sportsbook. If you're betting in person, what do you say? How do you physically place your bet? What are some tips on how to conduct yourself inside a sportsbook? If you're betting through an online account, how do you set up your account? What sites are the best sites to use? Are they all the same? Or are some different or better than others? How do you shop for the best line to ensure that you get the best odds possible? When you win, how do you cash out? Knowing the ground rules and what options are available to you is a critically important component of being a successful long-term bettor.

Betting at a Sportsbook in Person

The first time you walk into a sportsbook can be overwhelming and a bit intimidating. It's loud, the lights are bright, and the walls are covered with huge TV screens showing countless games across all sports. There are dozens, if not hundreds, of bettors cheering on all different kinds of bets. You will notice massive LED scoreboards that display countless team names along with the odds on each team. A long line of patrons will be waiting to place their bets at the cashier, which is referred to as the "ticket window" or just plain "window" for short. You don't want to be "that guy" in the front of the line who has no idea what to do and is holding everyone else up.

Betting in a brick-and-mortar sportsbook like those in Las Vegas is not all that different from placing a bet on your phone or laptop. You find the bet you want, figure out how much you want to put on it, and then place your bet. Instead of making a few clicks, you just have to do a little more legwork.

When you enter a sportsbook, the first thing you should do is try to find a seat. This may seem trivial, but depending on the day and popularity of the sports in season, seats may be hard to come by. Finding a good spot isn't just important for a good view to watch the game after you place your bet, but it also gives you a chance to review your options and gives you a makeshift workspace or workstation as you go through your bets for the day. Consider it your mini-office inside the sportsbook.

Even though we are living in an increasingly paperless world where almost everything is digital and found online, paper can be your best friend at the sportsbook. Each sportsbook prints off all of their offerings before the day starts, which displays all the games you can bet on and the lines for each game. These are known as "betting sheets." As soon as you walk in, grab a sheet for each sport that you are interested in betting on. You should have them at the table when you sit down. You can always ask for more sheets at the ticket window. Even though the lines have likely moved since the sheets were printed, the betting sheets still come in handy. By comparing the lines from earlier in the day to the current and updated lines on the LED scoreboards, you can see how the odds have moved. The betting sheets also allow you to jot down notes on particular games.

Know the Amount You Want to Bet, the Game Number, and the Bet Type

For every game you can bet on, the sportsbooks list a number to the left of each team, along with their odds. This is called the game number. In the betting community, it's also referred to as the "NSS number," "ID number," "rotation number," or "Vegas rotation number." The numbers are unique to each team and are universal across almost all sportsbooks. The two teams playing each other will have two different numbers, but they will both be in a row. It could be anything from 965 and 966 to 417 and 418. Once games are completed, the sportsbooks will recycle the game numbers and use them to identify new, upcoming games.

In order to place a bet, you must know the game number ahead of time. If you want to bet $100 on the Vikings to win the Super Bowl, you don't want to walk up to the ticket window and say "One hundred dollars on the Vikings." The person at the counter doesn't know if you want the Vikings in their game this weekend, to win the Super Bowl, or to win the NFC North. This is why it's important to grab the betting sheets when you first enter the sportsbook. Keep them handy at all times. Bring the betting sheet with you while you're waiting in line so you can have the correct game number ready to go. A good piece of advice is to use the golf pencils the sportsbooks supply and circle the game numbers you are going to bet.

FACT

Some sportsbooks allow bettors to bet on credit. This means that the bettor doesn't have to pay for the bet in cash at the window. It's like a loan, with the sportsbook expecting you to pay it back in a certain amount of time. Anyone can apply for a sportsbook line of credit, but not everyone is eligible. You have to provide extensive personal and financial information. If you fail to repay the credit, your overall credit will be ruined and you could face jail time. Typically, credit is only offered to "high rollers" who the sportsbooks trust.

When you're ready to place your bet, find the shortest line you can and wait your turn. Make sure you bring your betting sheet with your bets and games numbers circled. And of course, have your wallet ready. Keep in mind that sportsbooks typically only accept cash, so don't expect to hand the cashier a credit card or conventional check. Always use cash. It's the best, easiest, and usually the only acceptable form of payment.

When you get to the front, a friendly attitude never hurts. You may be having a great vacation and are super excited to place your first bet, but the person on the other side of the desk, also known as the "ticket writer," is working his regular day job. Say hello to the cashier and then tell him how much you want to bet, the game number, and the bet type for each one of your bets.

For example, if you want to bet $50 on the Falcons as a 7-point favorite, know the game number next to the Falcons and tell the cashier, "Fifty dollars on 137 spread." Then hand him the $50 in cash. If you want to bet $25 on the Orioles as a +130 moneyline underdog, tell the cashier, "Twenty-five dollars on 635 moneyline," and hand him the $25 in cash.

ESSENTIAL

Each sportsbook has a different set of rules and policies, but most will offer bonuses and freebies when you place your bets. There is almost zero downside to getting a player's card from the sportsbook (consider this a rewards card or loyalty card). It can earn you some free play in the casino or maybe some free food or hotel discounts. When you are actually placing your bets, many sportsbooks will offer free drink tickets. There is often a minimum amount you have to bet, but feel free to ask the ticket writer for drink tickets if you are looking to partake in some drinking activity.

Double-Check and Hang On to Your Tickets

Once you tell the ticket writer the amount, the game number, and bet type, don't walk away. Wait for the cashier to give you a receipt for your bet, which is popularly referred to as the "ticket" or "bet slip." Once you receive the receipt, stay at the window and carefully review the ticket. Is the game number correct? Is the amount correct? Is the bet type correct? If there is an issue or you notice something that is incorrect, immediately give the ticket back to the cashier and ask him to amend it. Once you walk away from the window, there is no turning back. If you notice a mistake after you've left the window, the sportsbook will not fix the bet. All sales are final. The only power you have is when you're at the window.

Once you make sure the ticket is correct, you can walk away from the window and sit down to watch the games and cheer on your bets. Always hold on to your betting tickets. The worst thing that can happen is you win your bet, but you lost your betting ticket and have no way to cash your bet. If you are planning to leave the sportsbook and go out on the town and party all night, head up to your hotel room and leave the tickets in a safe place. Always guard the betting tickets with your life. You don't have to stay in the sportsbook all day. You can leave at any time and then cash the winning ticket the next morning.

ESSENTIAL

If you're planning a trip to Las Vegas, one of the best times to go is during March Madness for the opening rounds of the NCAA Tournament. This is considered the Super Bowl of betting, with countless games being played throughout the day for a two- to four-day stretch. The excitement and intensity are unparalleled. Some of the best and most popular Vegas sportsbooks include the Westgate Las Vegas SuperBook, the Wynn Las Vegas, Caesars Palace, The Venetian, The Palazzo, the Bellagio, South Point, Red Rock, The Mirage, and The Cosmopolitan.

How to Cash In Your Winning Bets

To cash in your tickets, you'll head to the exact same window at which you placed your bet. Hand over your winning tickets, and the sportsbook will scan each one and then give you your total. If you aren't sure whether your bet won or lost, go ahead and hand it over as well. If it's a loser, it will get scanned and shown as a zero on the cash register. There's no harm in asking. You have nothing to lose. It's good etiquette to tip the ticket writers on winning bets, just as you would for a waiter or blackjack dealer after a good hand. Another option is to mail in your tickets later. The back of every ticket will have an address with instructions on where to mail your ticket.

The sportsbook will then mail you your winnings. Many bettors mistakenly pass up bets they like because they won't be around to collect their winnings. Don't worry, sportsbooks pay out bets 365 days a year.

That's the basics of betting at the ticket window inside a sportsbook. Follow these steps and you won't feel like such a novice, even if it's your first time. Even if you aren't sure about something, you can always ask the staff. Before you know it, you'll be a veteran in no time.

Betting Through an Online Sportsbook

In the old days, if you wanted to place a bet you only had two options to choose from. You could either travel to Las Vegas, walk up to a sportsbook, and place a bet in person. Or you could bet through a local bookie. If you didn't have access to either, you were out of luck and had no other way to place a wager.

But today the industry has evolved. The biggest game changer was the rise of the Internet in the early 1990s. This revolutionized sports betting by giving birth to dozens of online sportsbooks, also referred to as offshore sportsbooks because they are prominently based throughout the Caribbean in places like the Panama, Curaçao, Bermuda, and Costa Rica.

Now bettors don't have to be in Vegas or meet up with a bookie to place a wager. They can bet a game from the comfort of their own home (or anywhere else) as long as they have access to the Internet. Because online accounts still operate in an unregulated, quasi-legal arena, all bettors should first check to see which books are available to them based on which state they live in.

ESSENTIAL

A bookie, which is short for *bookkeeper*, is someone who operates an underground sportsbook. They are often referred to as "locals" because they are located in close proximity to bettors. While many bettors still use bookies, new bettors should avoid bookies at all costs. If you win, you could be prosecuted for not paying taxes. Also, a bookie could go missing at any point and never pay you your winning bets. If you lose big, the bookie can threaten or intimidate you into paying your lost bets.

In recent years, online accounts have exploded in popularity. First, they are the easiest, most accessible way to bet. Second, you don't have to go through the shady process of meeting up with a bookie. Yes, some bookies are reliable and run legitimate enterprises, but just like touts, they can be dangerous and scary. Last, offshore books provide an element of anonymity that many bettors desire.

However, not all online sportsbooks are created equally. They differ immensely, not only in terms of the lines they offer, but also how much they are willing to accept in terms of wager size and, most importantly, what kind of clientele they cater to. Knowing which sportsbooks and what kind of sportsbooks are available to you is hugely important in order to successfully shop for the best line.

Setting Up Your Online Sportsbook Account

In order to bet online through an offshore sportsbook, you need to first create and fund your account. This can be a rigorous and time-consuming process. However, once you've created your account you can place bets anywhere and take advantage of the convenience of online and mobile betting.

To create your account, go to the sportsbook's website and go through the application process. Usually you will see a big "Join" tab in the top right corner of the homepage. It will ask you to provide your name, email, address, birth date, phone number, social security number, and whatever you'd like your password to be.

The next step is to fund your account. The quickest and most common payment method is with a credit card or debit card, in which case the funding is nearly instantaneous. Some books will accept conventional checks as well, but that takes longer to get going. Many books will also accept cash via Western Union or MoneyGram. Sportsbooks will also set a minimum deposit number, which could be anywhere from $25 or $100, depending on the sportsbook.

There are dozens of online sportsbooks and they do not operate with a universal set of rules when it comes to making deposits. As a result, bettors should double-check the fine print for each individual sportsbook. If you ever have a question, a good idea is to go to the sportsbook's website and see if they have a "live chat" feature so you can speak directly to a representative and get further clarification. Also be sure to ask if they have any promotions or bonuses available. Typically, sportsbooks will offer free plays or bonuses on deposits that meet a certain amount. They might also offer a refer-a-friend bonus.

FACT

Over the past few years, cryptocurrency, also known as crypto, has become a widely popular payment method among sports bettors, with many sportsbooks now accepting crypto. The biggest advantage is that crypto, like Bitcoin, Ethereum, or Litecoin, is almost instantaneous and the sportsbooks do not require a fee to use them. Bettors can also more easily deposit and withdraw their crypto with just a click of a mouse or tap of a finger. One of the most popular and well-regarded Bitcoin sportsbooks is *Nitrogen Sports*. They were founded in 2012 and are based in San Pedro, Costa Rica. They accept US players and deal exclusively in Bitcoin.

Be Careful Cashing Out

When it comes to cashing out, many sportsbooks intentionally set up a series of hoops that bettors need to jump through before receiving their payouts. They're doing this for a reason: they want you to keep your money with them. Simply put, they're hoping that the process is so extensive and frustrating that you give up and leave your money in your account. Be ready to provide extensive documentation, including PIN numbers, banking information, address, social security number, phone number, email, and more.

Once you've completed these tasks, sportsbooks will then demand withdrawal service fees. These can range from $10 to $20 with a Western Union or MoneyGram payout, or up to $50 for cashier's checks. Some books have fees that are even higher. It's also important to note that sportsbooks will set minimum and maximum withdrawal thresholds, which are based on each payment method. Depending on the sportsbook, a minimum withdrawal could be $100 or more, with a maximum of $1,500 or more.

Regardless of which sportsbook you have an account at, the most important thing to remember is this: don't cash out every cent and drain your account to zero. You are playing the long game. Always be patient and never put short-term gain over long-term sustainability. We all want instant gratification. When we're doing well, we all want to take our money out and enjoy the spoils of our victories. However, don't just take the money and run. If you know how to make smart bets, that's the most important thing. It means you'll be able to profit over the course of the long haul. The smartest thing to do is sit back and let your bankroll continue to build, then cash out once a year or so. That way you can avoid the service fees and maximize your payouts.

Three Types of Sportsbooks

Generally speaking, there are three categories of sportsbooks: square, sharp, and reduced juice. Knowing the differences between all three is key in order to maximize your chances of winning and place yourself in the strongest position possible in terms of getting the best odds.

Square Sportsbooks

Square sportsbooks cater almost exclusively to casual bettors who bet for fun. Because average Joe recreational bettors are their target audience, square sportsbooks will shade their lines toward public favorites, home teams, and overs, knowing that these are the teams public players will bet on the most often.

As a result, square sportsbooks provide great odds for value-minded contrarian bettors who are willing to take unpopular sides, specifically underdogs, road teams, and unders. For example, say the mighty Warriors are hosting the lowly Hornets. A bigger, market-setting sportsbook might post the line at Warriors –10 with a total of 215. However, a square sportsbook knows that the public will bet the Warriors and the over no matter what, so they post Warriors –11.5 with a total of 217. Savvy contrarian bettors could take advantage of these shaded lines by betting the Hornets and the under at artificially inflated odds. They could get 1.5 additional points on the spread and 2 additional points on the total simply by betting the game at a square sportsbook.

Because square sportsbooks shade their numbers, they do not originate their own lines. Instead, they wait for the bigger, market-setting sportsbooks to release their odds, then they follow suit. Square sportsbooks will not move their lines until the bigger sportsbooks move. They are basically copycats.

When a square sportsbook doesn't take in any big bets but moves their odds just because the bigger books moved, this is referred to as "moving on air."

Square sportsbooks come with major limitations that bettors should be aware of. First, because they cater to public players, they have low betting limits, meaning bettors can only wager small amounts. So while a market-setting sportsbook might have a limit of $5,000, a square book might have a limit of $500.

Additionally, square sportsbooks will shade their lines against individual bettors who win at a high rate. So the Warriors might be listed at −11.5 at a square book for a bettor who wins 40 percent of her games. But for a bettor who wins 55 percent of his games, he might be listed at −12.5. If a sharp bettor continues to win at a high rate, he might even be kicked out of a square book, meaning the square book would no longer accept his action.

ESSENTIAL

The most popular square sportsbook is *Bovada*. Established in 2011, *Bovada* is located in Quebec, Canada, and only accepts US bettors. Their minimum deposit is $25 and their minimum bet amount is $1. They are known for having a variety of prop bets and parlay options. Other popular square sportsbooks that accept US bettors include *Sportsbook, BetUS, MyBookie,* and *GTBets*.

Sharp Sportsbooks

Sharp sportsbooks originate their own lines. They are the first ones to release their odds. They set the market and then other sportsbooks will follow their lead. Sharp sportsbooks don't care what other sportsbooks are offering in terms of odds. They also aren't concerned with shading their odds based on how the market is being bet. They don't follow the crowd; rather, the crowd follows them.

The biggest difference between square and sharp sportsbooks is that sharp sportsbooks have incredibly high limits. This means that they accept large wagers. Depending on the particular sportsbook, they might accept bets of $5,000, $10,000, $20,000, or more. Because of their high limits, sharp sportsbooks are the preferred sportsbooks for professional bettors.

Since sharp sportsbooks cater to professional bettors and high rollers, they also move their lines quickly when the market gets steamed or takes in a huge bet from a big player. Once they move their odds, the entire market will copy them and move in the same direction.

ESSENTIAL

The sharpest offshore sportsbook is *Pinnacle*. Founded in 1998 and located in Curaçao, *Pinnacle* is typically the first offshore sportsbook to release lines and has the highest limits of any offshore sportsbook. Unfortunately, *Pinnacle* does not accept US bettors. The next sharpest books that accept US bettors include *Bookmaker* (also known as *CRIS*), *5Dimes*, *BetOnline*, *Heritage Sports*, *JazzSports*, *Bet Buckeye Sports*, and *BetGrande*.

Reduced Juice Sportsbooks

In addition to sharp and square sportsbooks, there are also reduced juice sportsbooks, which are popularly referred to as "RJ sportsbooks." These sportsbooks are somewhat rare and relatively unknown to public bettors, but they're the best-kept secret and favorite type of sportsbook for serious, experienced, and professional bettors.

By now, we know that standard juice on any given game is –110. This is also referred to as "10-cent juice" or "0-cent lines," meaning you are paying the house 10 cents on $1 as a fee for them accepting your bet.

Reduced juice books are one of the most powerful tools and key advantages for professional players because they offer lines well below the standard juice. Instead of having to lay –110, these books will offer –105 or –107.

It may not seem like a big difference, but it can drastically improve your performance over time by increasing your payouts and limiting your losses.

In order to overcome the standard –110 juice and break even, bettors must win 52.38 percent of their bets. However, if that same bettor were to use –107 juice, they would only need to win 51.7 percent of the time. If the bettor used –105 juice, that required win rate would fall to 51.2 percent.

When *Pinnacle* was founded in 1998, it revolutionized the betting industry by becoming the first offshore sportsbook to offer reduced juice. Instead of –110, *Pinnacle* offers –105 or –104. Unfortunately, *Pinnacle* stopped accepting US players in 2007 after the Unlawful Internet Gambling Enforcement Act was passed. For US bettors who don't have access to *Pinnacle*, the next best reduced juice book would be *5Dimes* or *Heritage Sports*.

In order to maximize value, aim to have an account at one of all three types of sportsbooks: square, sharp, and reduced juice. By having access to all three, you set yourself up to get the best numbers possible, which makes a massive difference over the long haul and can greatly improve your return on investment.

Shop for the Best Line

One of the biggest mistakes a new bettor can make is only betting through one sportsbook. This is a bad idea because it forces you to take whatever odds your particular sportsbook is offering. You have no wiggle room or other options to choose from. You are at the mercy of your sportsbook. Instead, you should open up multiple accounts at several different sportsbooks so you can shop for the best line, get better numbers, and take advantage of better prices.

You might love your one sportsbook, feel comfortable with it, and not want to jump through the hoops of having to open up another account. However, don't let that stop you. You are forfeiting massive value and limiting yourself greatly by not doing so. Ideally, you should have at least three different sportsbook accounts.

Why is having multiple accounts so important? So you can shop for the best line, also referred to as "line shopping." Think of it this way: if you're going to buy a car, are you automatically going to buy the car at the dealership down the street? Of course not. You're going to shop around, compare prices, check out other dealerships, and look for the lowest and best price possible. With sports betting, you want to do the same exact thing.

Shopping for the best line is especially critical when it comes to betting spread and total sports like football and basketball because just a half point can be the difference between a win and a loss.

For example, let's say you've crunched the numbers and decided that the Heat are a smart bet. You only have an account at one sportsbook and they're offering Heat +4.5. However, a second sportsbook is posting Heat +5 and a third book is posting Heat +5.5. Because you only have access to the first sportsbook, you are forced to play the Heat +4.5. However, if you opened up multiple accounts and had access to multiple sportsbooks, you could jump on the Heat +5 or, even better, +5.5. By taking the time to open up multiple accounts, you just got an extra half point or full point for free.

It may not seem like a big deal, but getting better numbers, even if the difference is small, can make a world of difference in the long run. It can turn losses into pushes, losses into wins, and pushes into wins. Shopping for the best line can also help for moneyline sports like baseball and hockey. It allows bettors to maximize their payouts when they win and limit their losses when they lose.

Shopping for the best line should always be the last thing you do before placing your bet. Never place a wager without first seeking better numbers. You may not always find them, but be sure to always make the effort. When you cover by a half point instead of pushing or losing, you'll be glad you shopped around.

Sports betting is hard enough to begin with, so every edge you can give yourself makes a difference. Shopping for the best line and getting the best number possible is the mark of a successful long-term bettor. If you can consistently get an extra half point on spreads, you can increase your win percentage by up to 2 percent over the long term. By consistently getting better prices on moneylines, spreads, and totals, while also paying the lowest juice possible, you can drastically increase your payouts and limit your losses.

CHAPTER 11

How to Bet Baseball

Baseball is arguably the most profitable sport for sharp bettors. Unlike football and basketball, where the majority of bets are based on the point spread, baseball is a predominantly moneyline sport. This means that bettors only need to pick who will win the game, not who will cover the spread. The baseball schedule is also the longest of any sport, with over 2,400 regular-season games per season. With so many games every single day for more than six months, baseball bettors are provided seemingly endless opportunities to maximize their edge. By avoiding big favorites and focusing on divisional underdogs with plus-money payouts, bettors can win at a sub-50 percent rate but still make money. Baseball is also one of the best sports for reverse line movement, betting against the public, betting on bad teams after wins, and betting totals based on variables like wind and umpires.

Action versus Listed Pitcher

Before diving into how to bet baseball, bettors must first understand a unique and critically important nuance of baseball betting. In football, quarterbacks are the most important players on the field and have a massive effect on not only the lines, but also the outcome of your bet. In baseball, the equivalent is the starting pitchers.

In baseball, it's common to see a starting pitcher get scratched because of an injury, pushed back for an extra day of rest, or in some cases, get traded. Scratched means that the pitcher was scheduled to start the game, but something happened and he is no longer pitching. This causes the game to come off the board and reopen at a drastically different number. Off the board (OTB) means that the sportsbooks take down the odds and no longer allow bettors to bet on the game. Once the replacement pitcher is announced, the sportsbooks will reopen the line at a different number based upon the new starting pitcher.

As a result, baseball bettors are afforded two options when placing their bet: they can either bet "action" or "listed pitcher." If you bet action, that means your bet is locked in no matter what happens to either team's pitcher. If you bet "listed pitcher," that means both starting pitchers must start the game in order for your bet to count. If either starting pitcher changes, the bet is voided, which means it's canceled and you get your money back.

For example, say you bet on Clayton Kershaw and the Dodgers early in the day as −140 favorites against the Cardinals (+130). But then an hour before game time, Kershaw is scratched with a late injury (and replaced by a much worse pitcher). The sportsbooks would take the game off the board and then might reopen the line at Dodgers +110 and Cardinals −120, based on the pitching change.

If you had bet "action" on the Dodgers −140, you would still be locked into your bet at that same exact price, despite the pitching change. So instead of being able to bet Dodgers +110 at their new line, you would be forced to stick with your −140 bet, which means you got awful odds on the Dodgers. However, if you had bet "listed pitcher" on Dodgers −140, your bet would be voided.

Not all scratched pitchers can affect your bet negatively. Sometimes it can work in your favor. For example, in the instance listed above, say you bet the Cardinals "action" at +130. You would then be locked into that juicy plus-money payout. So even though the Cardinals reopened at –120 after the Kershaw scratch, you would still keep your +130.

ESSENTIAL

All baseball bets will automatically default to "action." Bettors must select the "listed pitcher" option on their own in order to ensure their bets are dependent on the starting pitchers. Some sportsbooks will also offer listed pitcher for each specific team. This allows bettors to lock in their bet only if the pitcher they care about starts the game. If the other pitcher is scratched, the bet still stands.

However, this can be a dangerous game, not only for moneyline bets but for totals and run-line (spread) bets as well. Sometimes it's a gift, sometimes it's a curse.

The worst thing that can happen is you spend all day researching a game, lock in a play at a great price, then see all your hard work go to waste when a pitching change takes place.

Instead of hoping a pitching change works in your favor, you should avoid action bets and always bet listed pitcher. It gives you more control over your bet. Remember, you can always re-bet the game if you still value at the new post-scratch price.

Avoid Big Favorites and Heavy Public Favorites

Sportsbooks know that casual bettors love betting favorites. As a result, oddsmakers will shade their lines toward favorites, specifically targeting the most popular public teams. By backing these big favorites, you are playing right into the sportsbooks' hands by consistently getting overvalued, overpriced odds. In baseball, a big favorite can be defined as a team that is –150 or higher on the moneyline.

Since 2005, favorites of –150 or higher have gone 7,345–4,258, which translates to a 63.3 percent win percentage. On the surface, that sounds pretty impressive. However, because bettors are forced to pay such a steep price, betting these big favorites would have lost bettors –215.72 units. This means that a $100 bettor taking every single one would be down $21,572 since 2005. As a result, you should avoid big favorites at all costs.

Favorites have also been a losing bet when they're receiving heavy public support. This is defined as favorites getting 70 percent or more of moneyline bets. Since 2005, these teams have gone 7,637–5,258 (59.2 percent). Again, a great record, but because of the overpriced lines and laying a big minus number, they've lost a whopping –390.67 units. A $100 bettor taking every one since 2005 would be down more than $39,000.

Sure, heavy favorites will win the majority of their games, but they don't present any real value to bettors, especially when the public is loading up on them in overwhelming fashion. Remember, if you risk 1 unit on a –170 favorite and they win the game, you only win +0.58 units based on the heavy favorite price. However, if they lose, you lose your 1 unit. Conversely, if you risk 1 unit on a –260 favorite and they win the game, you are only winning +0.38 units. And if they lose, you lose your 1 unit. Basically, with big favorites you are getting small payouts if they win, but losing big if they lose. So despite the impressive win rate, you aren't making any money, you're losing. Simply put, the juice isn't worth the squeeze.

FACT

On August 23, 1989, Pete Rose received a lifetime ban from baseball for betting on games while he played for and managed the Cincinnati Reds. At the time, a *Gallup/Newsweek* poll showed that 19 percent of Americans viewed the ban as "too tough," 10 percent said "too lenient," 41 percent said "about right," and 30 percent said "don't know." The *Dowd Report*, which investigated Rose's gambling habits, found that Rose wagered a minimum of $10,000 per day on baseball games between 1985 and 1986.

Take Advantage of Divisional Underdogs

By now, we know that in order to turn a profit betting spread sports like football and basketball, bettors must win 52.38 percent of the time in order to break even (assuming –110 standard juice). However, if baseball bettors avoid big moneyline favorites and consistently focus on valuable plus-money underdogs (think +120, +130, +150), they can win at a below 50 percent clip but still finish the year with positive units won. This is the beauty of baseball and a big reason why sharp bettors love it so much. When underdogs lose, you only lose what you risked on the game. But when they win, you enjoy valuable plus-money payouts.

However, this doesn't mean you can blindly bet every single underdog and still turn a profit. The key is to focus on divisional underdogs. This means taking the underdog when two teams in the same division play each other (think Red Sox versus Yankees). In baseball, teams within the division play each other nineteen times per year, which translates to about 8.5 percent of all games over the course of a 162-game season. Because divisional teams play each other so often, it breeds increased familiarity. Both teams know each other's tendencies and aren't surprised by anything. They know the opposing players (specifically the opposing pitchers), the stadiums, and the scouting reports like the back of their hand. This familiarity levels the playing field and benefits the underdog.

Since 2005, divisional underdogs have gone 6,557–8,555 (43.4 percent). This sounds like a terrible losing record, but because of the plus-money payouts it's produced +59.23 units. Meanwhile, underdogs playing outside the division have gone 7,701–10,620 (42 percent), losing –573.60 units. This means a $100 bettor taking every divisional underdog would have profited $5,923 since 2005, while a $100 bettor taking every underdog outside the division would have lost an absurd $57,360. As a result, bettors should target divisional underdogs over non-divisional underdogs.

Focus On Road Divisional Underdogs with High Totals

Divisional underdogs become even more profitable if we layer in two more filters. First, focus on road divisional underdogs. Just like all other sports, public baseball bettors overvalue home-field advantage. This heavy bias creates increased value on road teams in the form of inflated lines. Since 2005, road divisional underdogs have gone 4,340–5,815 (42.7 percent), producing +123.12 units. This means a $100 bettor would have profited $12,312.

If we layer in games featuring high totals, road divisional underdogs get even better. When betting on any kind of underdog, regardless of home or road, division or non-division, you always want to make sure the game has a high total. High totals benefit underdogs in baseball. If there are more runs expected to be scored in a game, it leads to more variance and wacky things happening, which benefits the underdog. A high total can be defined as an over/under of 8.5 or more.

Since 2005, road divisional underdogs with a high total of 8.5 or more have gone 2,606–3,400 (43.4 percent), producing +148.24 units. This means that a $100 bettor would have profited $14,824 since 2005 betting every single one.

Bet Against the Public

Betting against the public is a core philosophy that applies across the entire betting marketplace. However, each sport has its own sweet spot. For some sports it might be teams getting less than 40 percent of bets, for others it might be teams getting less than 35 percent or 25 percent of bets.

In baseball, the most profitable contrarian threshold is teams getting less than 20 percent of moneyline bets. This isolates the most lopsided games in which the public is betting heavily on one side and completely dismissing the other, leading to inflated contrarian value. Since 2005, teams getting less than 20 percent of bets have gone 1,265–1,878 (40.2 percent), producing +70.98 units. Blindly taking every team getting less than 20 percent of bets has been profitable, with a $100 bettor earning $7,098 since 2005.

ESSENTIAL

One of the best times to bet against the public is *Sunday Night Baseball*. Every Sunday night, there is one late game during the MLB season, typically starting at 8 p.m. ET. It is the most heavily bet game of the day and offers great contrarian value. Since 2005, teams getting less than 40 percent of bets on *Sunday Night Baseball* have gone 96–110 (46.6 percent), winning +15.42 units. If they're also receiving reverse line movement of at least 1 cent, they improve to 51–32 (61.4 percent), winning +32.32 units.

One way to improve these results is to focus on underdogs coming off a win. This allows savvy contrarian bettors to capitalize on public bias that says a team got lucky last game and can't possibly win again. Since 2005, underdogs getting less than 20 percent of bets that won their previous game have gone 619–851 (42.1 percent), earning +86.19 units. By simply focusing on teams coming off a win, you've improved the return on investment for sub-20 percent teams substantially.

Reverse Line Movement

When betting baseball, or any other sport, you always want to be on the sharp side and align yourself with the professional bettors. Reverse line movement is a clear indication that sharp bettors have taken a side. It's a dead giveaway that smart money is moving the line.

Reverse line movement allows bettors to increase the betting against the public threshold. The presence of heavy sharp action can compensate for not being as contrarian. In other words, a team doesn't have to receive less than 20 percent of bets. They can receive a higher percentage of bets and still be profitable as long as the team is also receiving heavy sharp action from professional bettors.

Since 2005, teams getting less than 35 percent of bets (both underdogs and favorites) have gone 7,385–10,298 (41.8 percent), losing –125.55 units. As you can see, despite being contrarian, you are losing big in the end. A $100 bettor would be down more than $12,500 since 2005. However, if we layer in reverse line movement of 1 cent or more, teams getting less than 35 percent of bets improve to 3,479–4,386 (44.2 percent), producing +58.13 units (think Pirates receiving 30 percent of bets and moving from +140 to +139). Contrarian teams are not profitable on their own, but if sharps bet on them and cause the line to move in their direction, they are.

However, not all reverse line movement is created equally. The bigger the reverse line movement, the more valuable the team becomes, but it indicates heavy sharp action. As a result, bettors should always keep an eye out for huge line moves because that signals big, smart money. Instead of looking at teams receiving less than 35 percent bets with 1 cent reverse line movement, let's raise it to 10 cents or more reverse line movement (think Pirates receiving 30 percent of bets and moving from +140 to +130). Since 2005, these teams have gone 1,740–2,093 (45.4 percent), earning +105.48 units. Underdogs in this spot have gone 1,442–1,864 (43.6 percent), winning +84.41 units, and favorites have gone 298–229 (56.5 percent), winning +21.07 units. Both underdog and favorite are profitable.

If we raise the reverse line movement from 10 cents or more to 20 cents or more (Pirates receiving 30 percent of bets and moving from +140 to +120), the sample size shrinks but the win-loss record improves to 585–689 (45.9 percent), earning +57.64 units.

The moral of the story is to always look for sharp action in the form of reverse line movement when betting against the public.

FACT

Since 2005, road divisional underdogs receiving less than 30 percent of bets with reverse line movement in the most heavily bet games (receiving at least the daily average number of bets) have gone 339–411 (45.2 percent), winning +118.00 units. A $100 bettor taking every one of these teams since 2005 would have profited $11,800. This is considered the Holy Grail baseball betting system. It combines betting against the public with sharp action in the most valuable spots unique to baseball. Bettors should always search for games that fit this model.

Bad Teams after Wins

Public bettors love betting favorites, especially when they're hot and coming off a win. However, when bad teams win a game, the public automatically thinks they're bound to lose their next game. After all, they're bad for a reason, so if they get lucky and win a game, it must be a fluke. They're destined to revert back to form and lose their next game.

On the surface it makes sense, but it just isn't true. It's another example of the gambler's fallacy. The truth is that bad teams coming off a win are supremely undervalued, which provides an excellent buy-low opportunity for contrarian bettors. This is another way to bet against the public without even looking at the betting percentages.

In baseball, a bad team is defined as a team that has a win percentage of .400 or less, meaning they win 40 percent or less of their games. When these teams lost their previous game, they've gone 2,804–3,475 (44.7 percent), losing −95.28 units. However, when these teams won their previous game, they've gone 1,500–1,648 (47.6 percent), winning +162.93 units. It's night and day for bad teams after a loss versus after a win.

Why is this system so simple and profitable? Because it has a sound theory behind it. When bad teams lose a game, it can create a downward spiral, leading to more and more losses. However, when they win a game, they gain much-needed confidence and can carry that momentum into the next game. Combine that with the heavy public bias against them and they become even more valuable. A $100 bettor taking every bad team off a win has profited $16,293 since 2005.

American League Teams in Interleague Play

Baseball has two leagues: the American League and the National League, with fifteen teams in each. For decades, teams in different leagues would only play each other in the World Series. However, in 1997, the MLB created interleague play, with teams playing one rivalry-based interleague series per year, all on the same weekend. Starting in 2005, interleague series became more frequent, with multiple series throughout the season. Nowadays, an American League East team will play all four National League East teams, and vice versa. Each season, the divisional matchups rotate.

ESSENTIAL

The best time of year to bet against the public is during the MLB play-offs. This is due to the increased public betting during the postseason. The games are more popular, they're all in primetime, and the ticket counts skyrocket, which leads to increased contrarian value. Since 2005, teams receiving less than 50 percent of bets have gone 228–196 (53.8 percent), winning +64.11 units. Home teams receiving less than 50 percent of bets have performed even better: 108–63 (63.2 percent), earning +39.30 units.

Because of the larger interleague sample size, bettors are provided additional opportunities to take advantage of these unique matchups.

Since 2005, when interleague play expanded, the American League has held a distinct advantage over the National League. This is due to the fact that American League teams have much stronger rosters because they include the designated hitter, while National League teams do not.

Since 2005, American league teams have gone 2,047–1,715 (54.4 percent), producing +129.95 units. This means that betting $100 on every AL team in interleague play would have produced a profit of $12,995. Bettors should also keep an eye out for interleague games and remember to lean on American League teams.

Windy Unders

When avoiding big favorites and focusing on valuable underdogs, baseball bettors can win at a sub-50 percent rate but still turn a profit based on the plus-money payouts. However, the same cannot be said for betting on totals. Because you have to pay the juice on totals, bettors need to win at the same 52.38 percent rate in spread sports in order to break even. As a result, bettors need to be extra careful when betting totals, making sure that a potential over/under play checks off all the boxes and fits a historically profitable trend.

All MLB stadiums are different, with unique dimensions and wind patterns. When it comes to betting windy unders, the absolute best stadium is Wrigley Field, the home of the Chicago Cubs. When the Cubs play a day game at Wrigley and the wind is blowing in from any direction (left, center, or right), the under has gone 248–186 (57.1 percent), winning +47.19 units. If the total is 8 or higher, the under improves to 264–96 (63.1 percent), winning +59.55 units. You should always target windy under at Wrigley Field. They don't call it the Windy City for nothing.

No single factor has a greater impact on totals than the wind. You should never bet an over or an under without first knowing which direction and how hard the wind is blowing.

When the wind is blowing in, it benefits unders greatly. It's pretty simple: if a batter hits a home run that would normally land in the first row of the seats, on a windy day when the wind is blowing toward home plate, the ball will instead be knocked down and turn into a warning track out. The wind will take away potential homers and turn them into outs, leading to fewer runs scored.

Since 2005, when the wind is blowing in, the under has gone 1,065–877 (54.8 percent), winning +118.42 units. If the wind is blowing in harder at five miles per hour or more, the under improves to 819–659 (55.4 percent), winning +105.61 units. Bettors should always look to bet unders when the wind is blowing in. It's one of the easiest and most straightforward betting systems for baseball totals.

Windy Overs

Just as the wind blowing in benefits unders, when the wind is blowing out, it benefits overs. Instead of a ball being caught on the warning track, the wind pushes the ball into the first row of the stands.

Since 2005, betting every single over has led to an awful record of 15,667–16,193 (49.2 percent), losing an astounding –1,091.28 units. This is because public bettors love overs so the oddsmakers will shade the total toward the over, forcing public bettors to take overpriced odds.

However, the one saving grace to betting overs is when the wind is blowing out. In these situations, the over has gone 2,831–2,646 (51.7 percent), winning +78.95 units. If the wind is blowing out at eight miles per hour or more, the over improves to 1,037–919 (53 percent), earning +77.82 units. Bettors should avoid overs because they are incredibly overpriced and overvalued. One of the only exceptions is when the wind is blowing out.

FACT

One of the best stadiums for betting overs is Coors Field, home of the Colorado Rockies. This is due to the high altitude of the stadium, located a mile above sea level. The thin air leads to lower density, which causes baseballs to travel on average 5 percent farther at Coors Field than at other stadiums. This leads to more home runs and runs scored, benefiting overs. In the later summer months, when the temperature heats up, overs perform even better at Coors. Since 2005, if the total is 10.5 or less in August and September, the over has gone 156–103 (60.2 percent), earning +45.65 units.

Unders in Domes or Closed-Roof Stadiums

Another thing to keep in mind when betting totals is whether the game will be played inside or outside. Always check to see if the game is being played in a dome or a stadium with a retractable roof that is closed.

Watch out for stadiums like Tropicana Field in Tampa Bay, Safeco Field in Seattle, Rogers Centre in Toronto, Chase Field in Arizona, Minute Maid Park in Houston, and Marlins Park in Miami. When playing in a dome or a closed-roof stadium, the conditions are perfect, which provides a great advantage to the pitcher. Also, the lack of wind ensures that the ball won't carry as far. As a result, this is a huge benefit to unders.

Since 2005, when a game is played in a dome or closed-roof stadium, the under has gone 1,705–1,526 (52.8 percent), earning +74.19 units.

Contrarian Unders for Winning Teams

One of the most profitable betting systems for totals is contrarian unders for winning teams. This is when two winning teams go head to head and the under is receiving 35 percent or less bets. A winning team is defined as any team with a win percentage of .510 or higher, which means they're winning 51 percent of their games or more. The theory is sound and simple: when two good teams play each other, they tend to play tighter, lower-scoring games because they're so evenly matched. This leads to more low-scoring games and benefits the under.

FACT

One of the most popular baseball prop bets among public bettors is the Grand Salami. Each day, the oddsmakers set a total for the combined amount of runs scored across the entire league for that particular day. Bettors can then bet on whether or not the total runs will be over or under the given numbers. An average Grand Salami is usually between 120 and 140, depending on the number of games that day. The Grand Salami is considered a "fun" bet, but incredibly hard to handicap. Unless you have a clear edge, you should avoid it just as you would parlays.

Since 2005, when two winning teams play each other the under has gone 3,570–3,177 (52.9 percent), winning an astounding +196.13 units. If you add in contrarian value, which means the public is heavy on the over and the under is getting 35 percent or less bets, the under improves to 1,246–1,015 (55.1 percent), winning +186.96 units. You should always target unders when two good teams play each other, especially when you can bet against the public as well.

Unders with Reverse Line Movement

Public bettors love betting overs. As a result, unders are a smarter betting strategy overall. However, the key is also to focus on situations where the public is betting the over heavily and the total falls. Think of it this way: the Blue Jays are playing the Astros and 75 percent of bets are taking the over, yet the oddsmakers drop the total from 8.5 to 8. Why would they drop the total to give public over bettors a better number? No, they're not being nice or charitable to public bettors. They dropped the total because they took in sharp action from respected players on the under 8.5, forcing them to drop the total.

ESSENTIAL

In the rare instances that the public is betting heavily on an under, it creates unique contrarian value to bet on the over. Usually this happens when two great starting pitchers are going head-to-head, with the public expecting a low-scoring 2–1 game. It also happens if the public sees a super-high total and automatically thinks it's bound to go under. The key is looking for contrarian overs with reverse line movement of at least a half run: this means that even though the public is on the under, the total rises. Since 2005, if the over is getting less than 40 percent of bets but the total rises at least a half run, the over has gone 177–131 (57.5 percent), winning +41.87 units.

Since 2005, if 30 percent or less bets are on an under and the total falls a half run or more, the under has gone 762–711 (51.7 percent), or +29.54 units. If you isolate the most heavily bet games (at least one times the daily average) that are receiving 30 percent or less under bets and the line falls a half run or more, the system improves dramatically to 357–267 (57.2 percent), or +80.96 units.

Remember, if the public is heavy on an over and you see the line fall, that's a dead giveaway that sharps are on the under. This means the under is a smart bet.

Know the Umpires

One factor that constantly gets overlooked by casual baseball bettors is the home plate umpire. Umpires are human. They all have different tendencies, which savvy bettors can target and exploit.

Some umpires are more susceptible to criticism than others, which means some cave under the pressure of a home crowd when forced to make a big call at a pivotal point in the game. Others thrive off the hate of a home crowd, which benefits the away team. Some umpires make a point of leveling the playing field, giving added breaks and benefits of the doubt to underdogs.

Conversely, some umpires have tight strike zones. This leads to more walks, more men on base, and more runs scored, which benefits overs. Meanwhile, others have a wide strike zone, which leads to more strikeouts, fewer walks, and more batted balls in play, which benefits unders.

Umpires should never be a primary box to check off when betting a game, but bettors should always be aware of who the umpires are. Depending on their tendencies, they could strengthen a potential play or make you lay off a bet you weren't too confident in to begin with.

For example, since 2005, home teams have gone 257–166 (60.8 percent) and produced +51.68 units when Lance Barksdale is the home plate umpire. This means that a $100 bettor taking every home team would have profited $5,168 with Barksdale calling balls and strikes. Meanwhile, away teams have lost –63.45 units with Barksdale behind the plate. As a result, bettors should always be aware of Barksdale when deciding whether to place a bet on a home or away team. If a bettor is targeting a home team, knowing Barksdale is calling balls and strikes would solidify the bet. But if they're targeting an away team, maybe they reassess the data or lay off.

When betting totals, combining the umpire information with the weather and wind direction can make a big difference. The goal is to look for situations where they're on the same page. For example, maybe the wind is blowing in and a top "under" ump is behind the plate.

These are little things that experienced bettors should always factor in before placing their bet. Think of umpires as a cherry on top. They won't make or break a pick, but they can bring added value to a play if they line up on the same side as the other data.

FACT

The greatest betting scandal in sports history took place in 1919, when Shoeless Joe Jackson and the Chicago White Sox intentionally threw the World Series against the Cincinnati Reds in exchange for money from the famous gambler Arnold Rothstein. Players received between $5,000 and $35,000 for fixing the games. Eight White Sox players were banned from baseball for life. To this day, they are popularly referred to as the Black Sox. After the trial, Major League Baseball created the position of commissioner to try to restore the integrity of the game.

Embrace Volume Betting

One of the biggest keys to being a successful long-term bettor is remaining disciplined with your bankroll and limiting your plays to the most valuable games of the day. Making too many picks is the quickest and easiest way to chip away at your bankroll (think ten or more plays per day). One bad night could wash away all your hard-earned winnings.

That being said, if there's one sport where volume betting can lead to increased profits, it's baseball.

More closely, say you have a betting system that has a return on investment of 2 percent. For the sake of argument, let's also say that you bet 20 percent of all games. This means that if there are ten games in a given day, you are betting on two of them. In baseball, 20 percent of a 2,430 regular-game season translates to 486 total bets over the course of a year. In football, 20 percent translates to only fifty-one bets, since an NFL regular season has only 256 games overall.

In both situations, a 2 percent ROI leads to the same return on invest-ment. However, the sheer volume of baseball wagering, due to the massive number of total games per season, leads to a much higher amount of units won and, therefore, a much higher profit. More closely, using the example above, making 486 total MLB bets at a 2 percent ROI would result in +9.72 units (486 × 0.02) for a full season. But for the NFL, this would result in just +1.02 units (51 x 0.02). Baseball would net more than nine times the profit because of the much larger sample size, despite the ROIs being the same.

To put this into perspective, let's say a bettor was risking $100 per bet in both the MLB and NFL with that same 2 percent ROI. The MLB bettor risking $100 on every game ($100 × 9.72 units) would finish the year with a profit of $972. Meanwhile, the NFL bettor risking the same $100 per game and same 2 percent ROI would only net $102. This is why volume betting is unique to baseball. It can help lead to much bigger returns, despite having the same ROI as other sports.

Prepare Yourself for Volatility

Baseball's massive schedule and long season provide excellent value for high-volume bettors. However, there are drawbacks that baseball bet-tors should be aware of. The biggest potential pitfall to betting baseball is the fact that there are massive swings. Baseball bettors can go on an epic month-long hot streak but also endure month-long cold spells. No sport experiences greater volatility.

If you are betting on 20 percent of all games in an MLB season, you are making 486 total bets. In the NFL, betting 20 percent of all games means making fifty-one bets. As a result, one MLB season is like betting nine or ten seasons of NFL betting. If you bet NFL for ten straight years, you might have four great seasons, three awful seasons, and three mediocre seasons.

Basically, you are wrapping nine or ten NFL seasons into one baseball season. As a result, the baseball roller coaster ride will provide huge ups and downs. The key to betting baseball is patience. Stay the course and think long term. It's an incredibly long season. When you're red hot, don't get arro-gant and double down, because it could turn on a dime the other way. On the flip side, when you're cold, don't lose hope and give up. You're never as hot or as cold as you think.

CHAPTER 12

How to Bet the NFL

When it comes to gambling, the NFL is the undisputed king. No sport garners more attention and action from public bettors. According to the UNLV Center for Gaming Research, Nevada sportsbooks have taken in more than $30 billion in football bets since 1992. Meanwhile, Nevada sportsbooks have taken in $81 billion on all sports combined since 1984. This means that football accounts for nearly 40 percent of all money wagered in Las Vegas. With the rise of daily fantasy sports and the expansion of legalized betting, football betting will only get more and more popular in the years to come. In this chapter, you will learn the importance of key numbers, what type of underdogs to target, how to exploit public perception, how to capitalize on the bye week, how to take advantage of weather when betting totals, and much more.

Key Numbers for Spread

Football is predominantly a spread sport. This means that the vast majority of wagers are based on the point spread, not the moneyline. Instead of having to pick who wins the game, you are picking which team will cover the spread.

Before diving into high-level NFL betting strategies and concepts, you must first understand the importance of key numbers. In order to do this, we must learn how scoring works in the NFL.

It might seem obvious, but the most common methods of scoring are by kicking field goals (3 points) and scoring touchdowns (6 points plus the extra point, also known as the PAT, or "point after touchdown"). The only other scoring methods are by a safety, when an offensive team is tackled inside their own end zone, and a 2-point conversion, when a team scores from the 2-yard line following a touchdown. These account for 2 points each, but safeties and 2-point conversions are very rare. As a result, the vast majority of NFL scoring is based on multiples of three (3, 6, 9, 12, and so forth) and seven (7, 14, 21, 28, and so forth).

Because the scoring rules are based on multiples of three and seven, it means that most games are decided by some combination of these numbers. As a result, they are considered key numbers.

The most common margin of victory in the NFL is 3 points. Since 2003, 15 percent of all NFL games finished with one team winning by exactly 3 points over the opponent. This makes "3" the most important key number.

The second biggest key number is 7. Since 2003, 9.2 percent of games ended with one team winning by exactly 7 points. This means that nearly a quarter of all games land on 3 or 7, making them the two most important key numbers.

To put this in perspective, let's say the Giants are playing the Eagles. The Giants score two touchdowns (14 points) and kick two field goals (6 points). The Eagles score two touchdowns (14 points) and kick one field goal (3 points). This would mean that the Giants won the game 20–17, with the game landing on the key number of 3.

On the other hand, maybe the Giants score three touchdowns (21 points) and the Eagles score two touchdowns (14 points), with neither team kicking any field goals. This would mean a 21–14 win for the Giants, with the margin of victory landing on the key number of 7.

After 3 and 7, the next most important key numbers are 6 (6 percent of the time since 2005), 10 (5.8 percent of the time), and 4 (5.2 percent of the time). It's also interesting to note that only 3.8 percent of games end with one team winning by exactly 1 point.

Always keep key numbers in mind and place your bets accordingly. Depending on which side you're betting on, you always want to make sure you're "off" a key number. It can be the difference between a win, a loss, or a push.

For example, say you're looking at a game with a spread of 3. If you like the favorite, you want to get "off" the key number of 3 and try to get –2.5 instead. Why? Because three is the most common margin of victory. If you bet the favorite –3 and they win by three, you push your bet. But if you bet the favorite at –2.5 and they win by three, you win your bet because you got off the key number.

FACT

After the 2014 season, the NFL changed the rule for extra points. Instead of kicking the extra point from the 2-yard line, they pushed the extra point back to the 15-yard line. Extra points used to be considered automatic, but since they are now farther away, it's led to more missed kicks. In the three years before the rule change, kickers made 99.5 percent of their extra points. In the three years since, that number dropped to 93.9 percent. This has had an effect on key numbers. With the rule change, the key number of 6 has increased from 5.53 percent to 8.09 percent (because with more missed extra points, teams come away with 6 points instead of 7). The other changes: 5 points is more common (2.87 percent to 5.06 percent), while 10 points is less common (6.12 percent to 4.68 percent), and 4 points is less common (5.37 percent to 4.3 percent).

Always Get the Hook

Now flip the scenario and say the spread is 3 points and you want to bet on the underdog. You shop for the best line and do everything you can to get the +3.5. That extra half point is critically important. If the game lands on 3, you push your +3 bet, but with the +3.5, you win. In betting circles, the extra half point is called the hook. It can turn potential pushes into wins. When betting on underdogs, always try to get the hook.

The same thought process applies to any games with a spread of 7 points, the second biggest of the key numbers. If you were looking to bet on the favorite, you would want to get off the key number of 7 and bet the favorite at −6.5. That way if the favorite wins by seven, you cover and win your bet. If you bet the favorite at −7, you push.

ESSENTIAL

Key numbers also exist for totals, but they aren't nearly as prevalent as key numbers for spread. Since 2003, the most common key number for totals is 41, with 3.9 percent of games landing on 41. A total of 41 is commonly represented by a final score of 21–20, 24–17, 27–14, or 28–13. The next most common key numbers for totals are 37 and 44, each happening 3.8 percent of the time. Other key numbers include 43 (3.7 percent) and 51 (3.6 percent). Since the 2014 extra point rule change, 43 has become the most common key number, at 4.0 percent of all games. You should approach total key numbers the same way you approach spread key numbers: always look for the hook, especially when betting unders (get −41.5 instead of −41).

If you were looking to bet the underdog, you hold out for the +7.5. By getting the hook, you win your bet if the game lands on the key number of 7.

Isolating the other key numbers of 10, 6, and 4 means that if you're looking to bet an underdog with the spread at any of these numbers, you want to get the hook and take the underdog at +10.5, +6.5, and +4.5 (so if it lands on 10, 6, or 4 you cover). Meanwhile, if you're looking to bet the favorite in this situation you want to bet them at −9.5, −5.5, and −3.5 (so if it lands on 10, 6, or 4 you cover and win your bet).

Always ask yourself if you're near a key number. If you are, how can you get off that key number so you can maximize your chances of winning?

Home-Field Advantage Is Real, but Overvalued

Public bettors love betting home teams across all sports, but especially in the NFL. Average Joes see massive stadiums filled with 60,000 to 80,000 die-hard screaming fans and are automatically inclined to bet the home team. There's no denying it, home-field advantage does exist, specifically in terms of crowd noise. When a home team is on offense, the home crowd will quiet down so the quarterback can hear the play call in his helmet from the offensive coordinator, and then bark out the signals to his teammates or call an audible. But if the opponent is on offense, the home crowd will scream at the top of their lungs and make as much noise as possible so the opposing quarterback can't hear the play call or communicate with offensive teammates.

Home-field advantage is real, and the sportsbooks take it into account when setting a line. The oddsmakers typically award 3 points for home-field advantage. Think of it this way: the Broncos are playing the Patriots and the two teams are equally matched, with no clear favorite or underdog. If they were playing on a neutral-site stadium, the sportsbooks would open the spread at 0 (pick or pick'em).

However, if the game was played in Denver with the Broncos as the home team, Denver would be a 3-point favorite. If the game was played in New England and the Patriots were the home team, New England would be a 3-point favorite.

While home-field advantage is real, it's also overvalued by the betting public. The public places added emphasis on home-field advantage, but in reality it's already been built into the line. As a result, public bettors who love betting home teams are almost always getting overpriced odds that have already been shaded by the sportsbooks.

Also keep in mind, when betting the spread, the home team needs to cover the number, not just win the game. Since 2003, home teams have gone 2,172–1,618, winning 57.3 percent of their games. However, when it comes to covering the spread, they've gone 1,812–1,884 (49 percent). Because of the losing record and paying the juice, home teams have lost −151.87 units. This means that if you bet $100 on every home team since 2003, you would have lost $15,187.

FACT

Just as home teams are overvalued, road teams are undervalued. The public is automatically inclined to bet against road teams, thinking they're unlikely to waltz into a hostile environment and escape with a cover. This creates value for contrarian bettors to capitalize on public bias and zig when average Joes zag. Road teams also enjoy shaded numbers in their favor. Since 2003, road teams have gone 1,884–1,812 against the spread (51 percent), losing –10.43 units. They may not be profitable, but they've performed much, much better than home teams. They've only lost about 10 units while home teams have lost nearly 152 units. This doesn't mean bettors should avoid all home teams and bet all road teams. However, it's important to keep these high-level trends in mind when breaking down a game.

Divisional Underdogs

Betting on only underdogs or only favorites has been a losing proposition for NFL bettors. Since 2003, underdogs have gone 1,860–1,859 ATS (50 percent), losing bettors –84.66 units. Meanwhile, favorites have gone 1,859–1,860 (50 percent), losing –78.52 units. The fact that favorites and underdogs have produced nearly identical records tells you how good the oddsmakers are at setting lines.

However, if we focus on divisional underdogs versus non-divisional underdogs, we start to see a massive discrepancy and can isolate a profitable edge. Divisional underdogs are underdogs that are playing against an opponent within their division (think Packers playing the Bears; both are in the NFC North). Non-divisional underdogs are underdogs playing an opponent outside of their division (think Jaguars from the AFC South playing the Bengals of the AFC North).

Since 2003, divisional underdogs have gone 709–683 ATS (50.9 percent), losing –7.5 units. On the surface that doesn't sound very impressive. However, compare that to non-divisional underdogs and you'll see a massive discrepancy. Since 2003, non-divisional underdogs have gone 1,151–1,176 ATS (49.5 percent), losing –77.16 units. Translation: divisional underdogs have lost slightly, while non-divisional underdogs have lost big.

Why do divisional underdogs perform better than non-divisional underdogs? Just as in baseball, it's all about familiarity. There are four teams in each NFL division, and each team plays their divisional opponents twice, once at home and once on the road. This happens every year. As a result, divisional teams are most familiar with each other, knowing each other's tendencies, stadiums, opposing coaches, and individual player matchups. This familiarity levels the playing field and benefits the underdog.

Road Divisional Underdogs

We know that the public loves betting home teams and the sportsbooks shade their lines with this public bias in mind. So what is the divisional underdog breakdown on the road versus at home? If you guess it would be night and day, you'd be correct.

Since 2003, divisional underdogs on the road have gone 474–420 ATS (53 percent), producing +31.62 units. You aren't breaking the bank with road divisional underdogs, but you're beating the magic number of 52.38 percent and slowly building your bankroll over the course of the long haul. A $100 bettor would be up $3,162 betting each one since 2003.

Meanwhile, home divisional underdogs have produced a polar opposite record. Since 2003, they've gone 234–255 (47.9 percent), losing –32.08 units. As a result, you should target road divisional underdogs over home divisional underdogs.

Underdogs Low Totals, Favorites High Totals

In baseball, underdogs with high totals (8.5 or more) are more profitable than underdogs with low totals (8 or less). The more expected runs scored in a baseball game leads to more variance, leveling the playing field and benefiting the underdog. However, the exact opposite is true in the NFL.

In the NFL, underdogs with low totals are more profitable than underdogs with high totals.

Before getting into the how and why and breaking down the results, first we must define what a "high" and "low" total mean in NFL betting. In years past, a low total was considered to be around 42 or less. A super-low total would be considered anything less than 40 points. With the rise of fantasy football and subsequent rule changes to benefit offensive players and drive up scoring, a low total is now considered to be around 44 or less.

A high total would be considered anything in the mid-to-high 40s. A super-high total would be 50 or more.

Since 2003, underdogs with a total of 42 or less have gone 785–764 against the spread (50.7 percent), losing –14.09 units. When the total is 46 or higher, they've gone 517–556 ATS (48.2 percent), losing –63.58 units. As you can see, both are losing, but underdogs with low totals have cover at more than a 2 percent higher rate and have lost nearly 60 fewer units.

Why do low totals benefit underdogs in the NFL? Because unlike in baseball, with fewer expected points scored, this generally means it will be a tighter, lower-scoring game, making it harder for the favorite because they need to score more points in order cover the spread. On the flip side, a higher total means more points are expected to be scored, which makes it easier for the favorite to cover the spread.

Since 2003, favorites with a low total of 42 or less have gone 764–785 ATS (49.3 percent), losing –52.86 units. However, if the total is 46 or higher, favorites have gone 556–517 ATS (51.8 percent), winning +18.7 units. The higher the total, the more it benefits a favorite.

Just think of it this way: when betting on underdogs, you want to look for situations where the total is low. When betting on favorites, you want a higher total.

Betting Against the Public

Betting against the public is a sound strategy in the NFL because it's such a popular sport with a heavy amount of public action. However, it's just a starting point. You can't just bet every team getting less than 50 percent of bets. Just like other sports, you have to isolate the most lopsided games on the board. The more contrarian you get, the more profitable fading the public becomes.

Since 2003, teams getting less than 40 percent of spread bets have gone 1,168–1,183 ATS (49.7 percent), losing –77.55 units. So despite being contrarian, they are still a losing bet. A $100 bettor taking every team getting less than 40 percent of the bets would be down $7,750 since 2003.

However, if you drop the threshold from less than 40 percent of bets to less than 35 percent of bets, you cut your losses nearly in half. Since 2003, teams getting less than 35 percent have gone 847–842 ATS (50.1 percent), losing –40.50 units. Still a losing record, but the results are improving.

If you take it a step further and look at teams getting less than 30 percent of spread bets, you see the cover rate improve a full percentage point and the units lost nearly disappear. Since 2003, teams getting less than 30 percent of spread bets have gone 543–520 ATS (51.1 percent), losing only –6.39 units. While this system is still in the negative, the losses are greatly diminished. It's more or less a wash. You are losing less than a half unit per year.

FACT

Underdogs receiving 20 percent or less spread bets have provided excellent value for contrarian bettors. These are considered the most lopsided games of the year, when the public is all over the favorite and completely dismissing the underdog. Since 2003, underdogs getting 20 percent or less spread bets have gone 113–90 against the spread (55.7 percent), winning +17.53 units. This is popularly referred to as the 80/20 Rule. It doesn't happen often, typically less than five times per year, but it produces consistent year-to-year winning results.

Now let's drop the threshold another 5 percent. Here's where the results get interesting.

Since 2003, teams getting less than 25 percent of spread bets have gone 282–238 ATS (54.2 percent), winning +29.78 units. We aren't just slightly in the green, we're turning a real profit. This means that a $100 bettor taking every team getting less than 25 percent of spread bets would have profited nearly $3,000 over the past fifteen years. That breaks down to a profit of about $200 per year.

In other words, the optimal threshold for fading the public is teams getting less than 25 percent of spread bets. Betting against the public improves even more if you target underdogs getting less than 25 percent of spread bets in games that also feature low totals of 42 or less. These teams have gone 120–92 against the spread (56.5 percent), winning +22.83 units since 2003.

Underdogs Off a Blowout Loss

Recency bias plagues public bettors. If a team played awful the week before, public bettors will be quick to bet against them the following week. On the other hand, if a team looked great and posted a resounding victory the previous week, the public will automatically be inclined to bet on them in their next game.

In the same vein, bettors fall in love or out of love with teams depending upon whether or not they covered for them the previous week. If an average Joe bets on the Cardinals as a 3-point favorite and the Cardinals win by 10, the bettor will look to bet the Cardinals the very next week because they came through for him. On the flip side, if that same public bettor bet the Cardinals –3 and they lost by 7 points, that bettor will be mad and upset at the Cardinals and won't want to bet on them the next week because they burned him and lost him money.

The sportsbooks know how this psychological public bias works, and they shade their lines based on public perception. As a result, opportunistic contrarian bettors willing to buy low on bad teams and sell high on good teams increase their chances of winning because they're afforded artificially inflated odds.

The public doesn't usually bet on underdogs, but they're more inclined to back them if they're coming off a win. Basically, average Joes think that if an underdog played well the previous game, they'll carry over the momentum and their chances of covering the next game are higher. The sportsbooks will take advantage of this by shading lines toward the underdogs, giving public underdog backers a worse number.

Since 2003, underdogs coming off a win have gone 614–627 against the spread (49.5 percent), losing –37.51 units in their next game. However, underdogs coming off a loss have gone 1,044–1,003 against the spread (51 percent), losing only –10.74 units.

Although underdogs coming off a loss are still a losing bet, they cut the losses substantially compared to underdogs coming off a win. Translation: underdogs coming off a win are overvalued by the public.

However, it's important to remember that not all losses are created equal. The bigger the loss, the heavier the public bias will be against that losing team in the following week. If an underdog keeps a game close and only loses by a few points, the public will be less inclined to bet against them the following week. But if an underdog gets absolutely crushed, the public will automatically bet against them the next week.

This creates massive value for contrarian bettors to buy low on underdogs coming off blowout losses.

Since 2003, underdogs coming off a loss of 14 or more points have gone 432–391 against the spread (52.5 percent) in their next game, winning +18.81 units. If they're also on the road, they improve to 255–216 against the spread (54.1 percent), winning +24.9 units.

If the underdog is coming off a blowout loss of 21 or more points, they've gone 236–200 against the spread (54.1 percent) in their next game, winning +22.81 units.

The ultimate value spot is underdogs coming off a blowout loss of 20 points or more. In the following week, these teams have gone 266–218 against the spread (55 percent), winning +33.38 units.

While the public won't want to touch underdogs off a big loss with a ten-foot pole, sharp bettors know it's smart to buy low on these situations.

FACT

Since 2003, underdogs getting less than 25 percent of spread bets coming off a loss have gone 197–155 against the spread (56 percent) in their next game, winning +31.31 units. If they lost their last game *and* failed to cover, they've been even better, going 155–113 against the spread (57.8 percent), winning +33.76 units. If these teams are also playing at home, they improve to 119–81 against the spread (59.5 percent), winning +32.06 units. In this unique case, contrarian bettors can take advantage of public bias, buy low on an underdog off a loss and failed cover, and capitalize on home-field advantage.

Take Advantage of Reverse Line Movement

Reverse line movement is a universal sharp money indicator across all sports. However, unlike baseball, where reverse line movement is based on the moneyline, reverse line movement in football is based the spread. In football, not all reverse line movement is created equally. Its profitability depends on whether it's coming in on an underdog or a favorite, and also by the size of the reverse line movement.

Since 2003, NFL teams getting less than 40 percent of bets have gone 1,168–1,183 against the spread (49.7 percent), losing –77.55 units with a –3.2 percent ROI. However, when you layer in reverse line movement of a half point or more, teams getting less than 40 percent of bets improve to 419–402 against the spread (51 percent), losing only –4.9 units. By adding reverse line movement, you erase almost all of your losses and get back to almost even money. This is another example of betting against the public being strengthened when it also has sharp action.

However, it's important to note that we see a huge difference between favorites and underdogs when it comes to reverse line movement. Since 2003, underdogs getting less than 40 percent of bets with at least a half point of reverse line movement have gone 347–346 against the spread (50.1 percent), losing –16.86 units. However, favorites getting less than 40 percent of bets with at least a half point of reverse line movement have gone 69–54 against the spread (56.1 percent), winning +11.18 units.

Think of it this way: the Saints are a 7-point favorite against the Buccaneers. The Saints are only getting 35 percent of bets, yet the line moves from New Orleans –7 to –7.5. This situation has earned a $100 bettor $1,118 since 2003.

If the favorite is getting less than 40 percent of bets and receives a full point of reverse line movement (think Saints 35 percent, move from –7 to –8), the results are even better: 58–41 against the spread (58.6 percent), winning +13.64 units. These two examples would be considered "Fade the Trendy Underdog" plays. Although the public was heavy on the Buccaneers, the line moved further to New Orleans. Betting on the Saints would be the smart play for sharp bettors.

Big Reverse Line Movement on Underdogs

While these reverse line move plays on a favorite are highly profitable, they don't come around too often. So how can we take advantage of reverse line movement on underdogs?

Let's start with contrarian underdogs in general. Since 2005, underdogs getting less than 40 percent of bets have lost big: 1,040–1,050 against the spread (49.8 percent), losing –64.67 units.

If we add in at least a half point of reverse line movement, underdogs getting less than 40 percent improve to 347–346 against the spread (50.1 percent), losing only –16.86 units. So by adding in some sharp action, we shave off nearly 50 lost units. With a full point of reverse line movement, underdogs getting less than 40 percent improve slightly but are still a losing play: 200–201 against the spread (49.9 percent), losing –11.99 units.

It's not until underdogs get at least a full point and a half of reverse line movement that they cross from the red into the green: 130–116 against the spread (52.8 percent), winning +7.26 units. Think of the Jets being a 7-point underdog to the Patriots. The public is loading up on the Patriots, yet the line moves from Jets +7 to Jets +5.5.

Although rare, underdogs getting less than 40 percent of bets with a full 2.5 points of reverse line movement perform even better (think Jets 35 percent, going from +7 to +4.5). That spot has produced a record of 44–30 against the spread (59.2 percent), winning +11.58 units.

Think of it this way: you only need a half point of reverse line movement if it's coming in on a favorite. That's because the public rarely bets heavily on an underdog, so when they do, you only need a small amount of sharp action in order to strengthen the play. However, if the team is an underdog, you need much more reverse line movement in order to turn a profit, at least 1.5 points or more.

Contrarian Underdogs with Inflated Lines

While reverse line movement is a top sharp money indicator, it isn't the only way to capitalize on line movement. Bettors can also take advantage of inflated lines. This means that the public is pounding one side in overwhelming fashion, causing the line to rise, which provides extra "free" half points or full points to contrarian bettors willing to go the other way.

Since 2003, if an underdog is getting 30 percent or less spread bets and the line moves away from them at least a half point, they've gone 279–238 against the spread (54 percent), winning +26.96 units.

Think of it this way: the Bills are a 7-point underdog against the Chiefs. You see 73 percent of bets are hammering the Chiefs, pushing Kansas City from –7 to –7.5. Opportunistic contrarian bettors willing to back the Bills just got a free half point of inflated line value, simply because the public is overvaluing the Chiefs. This situation has earned a $100 bettor nearly $2,700 since 2003.

If we drop the contrarian threshold to 25 percent or less bets with at least a half point inflated, underdogs improve to 163–125 against the spread (56.6 percent), winning +30.71 units.

When focusing on heavy contrarian underdogs (30 percent or less bets), savvy bettors should wait for the public to hammer the favorite so they can inflate the line and get an extra half point or more.

Early Season Underdogs

Blindly betting underdogs has been a losing proposition. Since 2003, underdogs have gone 1,860–1,859 ATS (50 percent), but because of the juice they've lost –84.66 units. However, that doesn't tell the whole story. You need to know *when* to bet underdogs, specifically what time of year.

In October, November, December, and January, underdogs have gone 1,462–1,489 ATS (49.5 percent), losing –96.06 units. However, in September they've turned a profit, going 398–370 ATS (51.8 percent), winning +11.4 units. September is the only month in which underdogs have been in the green. This is due to the fact that underdogs are starting the season fully healthy and are optimistic about having a good year, whereas later in the season, injuries set in and teams begin to give up. Also, early in the season, the defenses are usually ahead of the offenses, which leads to lower-scoring and tighter games, which benefits underdogs.

Another key is focusing on September underdogs who missed the playoffs the year before. Early in the season, public bettors don't have much data to go off of, so they instead look back to the previous season. If they remember a team being awful the previous year, they will be even more inclined to bet against them, which creates added value for contrarian bettors to buy low in these situations.

If they missed the playoffs the year before, September underdogs improve to 314–283 against the spread (52.6 percent), winning +16.79 units. Meanwhile, if they made the playoffs the year before they've gone 84–87 against the spread (49.1 percent), losing –5.39 units.

September is also the best time of year for divisional underdogs, especially when they're contrarian. Since 2003, divisional underdogs in September have gone 153–123 against the spread (55.4 percent), winning +22.79 units. If they're getting less than 40 percent of spread bets, September divisional dogs are even better: 91–55 against the spread (62.3 percent), winning +31.7 units.

FACT

Week 1 is the best week of the season to bet on underdogs who are getting big points. This is largely due to recency bias. The betting public sees a terrible team that they expect to get blown out, but because it's early in the season and underdogs are fully healthy, this is when they present the most value. Since 2003, underdogs getting at least 6.5 points have gone 32–18 against the spread (64 percent) in Week 1, winning +12.21 units.

Favorites Off a Bye

In the NFL, every team gets one bye week per season. This means that the team gets a full week off to rest and rejuvenate without having to play a game. Bye weeks vary based on the scheduling and the team. Some teams get bye weeks early in the year (starting after Week 4), while others get their bye week later in the year (as late as Week 12).

Savvy bettors can take advantage of the bye week by targeting favorites who are coming off the bye. Typically, favorites are better coached and have better players. When the players have a chance to rest and rehab injuries and the coaching staff has a full two weeks to prepare for the next opponent, it aids the favorite in their next game off the bye.

Since 2003, favorites coming off their bye week have gone 138–91 against the spread (60.3 percent) their next game, winning +40.98 units. A $100 bettor betting every favorite off the bye has won more than $4,000 since 2003.

Favorites off a bye and on the road are even better: they've gone 56–25 against the spread (69.1 percent), winning +28.39 units. Part of this has to do with the public overvaluing home-field advantage, which creates added contrarian value for road favorites off the bye.

Home favorites off a bye have been a great bet as well, going 81–66 against the spread (55.1 percent), winning +11.65 units.

Unfortunately for underdogs, the bye week does not help them. Since 2003, underdogs coming off the bye have gone 92–107 against the spread (46.2 percent), losing –19.94 units.

Before placing an NFL bet, always check to see which teams are coming off a bye. You should remember to target favorites and avoid underdogs.

FACT

The most famous NFL betting contest in the world is the Westgate SuperContest, based out of the Westgate Las Vegas SuperBook. For sports bettors, this is considered the Super Bowl of handicapping. It typically costs $1,500 to enter. Contestants pick five games against the spread each week. The prize money is determined by the number of entries, with the top 100 contestants receiving payouts. In 2017, more than 2,500 handicappers entered the contest. The winner, Briceton Branch Jr., won $1.3 million.

Divisional Unders

When it comes to betting totals, blindly betting overs or unders have both been a massive loser for bettors. Since 2003, overs have gone 1,890–1,886 (50.1 percent), losing –82.58 units. Meanwhile, unders have been even worse, going 1,886–1,890 (49.9 percent), losing –106.72 units. On the surface, the win-loss records don't seem awful, but it's because you always have to pay the juice with totals that make them a boon for the books and a death knell for public players.

However, one specific edge that bettors can exploit is divisional unders. When two teams from the same division play each other, we know the familiarity benefits the underdog. It also benefits the under. A big reason for this is because the familiarity allows the defenses an advantage over the offenses. They know what to expect and few things surprise them. As a result, games between two divisional teams lead to tighter games and more unders.

Since 2003, when two teams in the same division play each other, the under has gone 746–667 (52.8 percent), winning +37.51 units. When two teams outside of the division play each other, the under has gotten absolutely demolished, going 1,140–1,223 (48.2 percent), losing –144.23 units.

It might seem obvious, but if the total is higher, divisional unders perform even better. Since 2003, when the total is 43 or more, divisional unders have gone 416–338 (55.2 percent), winning +55.36 units. If the total is 45 or higher, divisional unders improve to 284–218 (56.6 percent), winning +50.46 units with a 10 percent ROI.

When looking to bet a total, always target unders in divisional games and avoid unders in non-division games.

Windy Unders

Just as wind speed and direction can greatly affect baseball totals, it can also have a huge impact on NFL totals, specifically when it comes to unders.

If the wind is blowing at five miles per hour or more, unders have gone 1,112–1,049 (51.5 percent), winning +1.67 units with a +0.1 percent ROI. If you increase the wind speed to ten miles per hour or more, unders skyrocket to 418–335 (55.5 percent), winning +58.7 units. This means that a $100 bettor taking every one would have made nearly $6,000 since 2003.

Why is wind so important when betting unders? Because it makes it much harder on the offense. When the wind is swirling, it's harder to throw the ball. Long passes can get caught in the wind and blown off course, leading to more incompletions, which stops the clock and makes it harder to move the ball downfield. It also negatively affects the kicking game, causing field goals to go wide right, wide left, or come up short. But most of all, when it's harder to throw the ball because of swirling winds, it forces teams to run the ball more often. This chews up the clock and makes the game go by faster, leading to fewer offensive possessions and fewer points scored.

The key with windy unders is making sure the total has a line freeze or inflated line. This means that the total either stayed the same or rose at least a half point. In these situations, you are taking advantage of public over bias that has either kept the line from falling (getting worse), or handed out a free extra half point or more to contrarian under backers.

Since 2003, unders with five-mile-per-hour wind or more with either a line freeze or total that rises at least a half point have gone 580–484 (54.5 percent), winning +64.99 units.

If the wind is blowing at ten miles per hour or more and the total has remained frozen or risen at least a half point, the under has gone 206–136 (60.2 percent), winning +57.77 units.

Another element to layer in is a high total. Obviously, the higher the total, the easier it is for an under to hit. If the wind is blowing at five miles per hour or more, has a line freeze or inflated line, and the total is 44 or higher, the under has gone 292–225 (56.5 percent), winning +51.61 units. If the wind is ten miles per hour with a line freeze or inflated line and a total of 44 or higher, the under improves to 98–57 (63.2 percent), winning +35.53 units.

Always remember, wind is your best friend when betting an under.

If a game is played in a dome or closed-roof stadium, it benefits an over. The artificial turf provides a slick, fast track, which allows offensive players to cut on a dime and get a leg up on the defense. It also provides perfect conditions for quarterbacks and kickers. Since 2003, the over has gone 434–408 (51.5 percent) in domes, winning +5.68 units. If the game is played indoors between two non-division opponents, the total is 45 or less, and the total stays the same (line freeze) or falls (deflated line), the over has gone 100–74 (57.5 percent), winning +21.34 units. If the total is 42 or less, the system improves to 55–29 (65.5 percent), winning +23.40 units.

Cold Overs

Cold, inclement weather creates added intrigue for public bettors, which provides inflated value for savvy bettors who don't buy into the hype. For years it's been a widespread public belief that freezing temperatures in November, December, and January benefit unders. The thought process is simple: it's cold out, players' fingers are numb, the ball is slick, and it's harder for offensive players to throw the ball, catch the ball, stay warm, and stay loose, which leads to less offense and lower-scoring games.

However, this just isn't the case. Since 2003, when the temperature is less than 40 degrees, the under has been a losing bet, going 204–223 (47.8 percent), losing –29.32 units. On the flip side, when the temperature is less than 40 degrees, the over has gone 223–204 (52.2 percent), winning +8.65 units. Not much of a profit, but still a winning bet.

If we target non-division overs when the temperature is less than 40 degrees, the over is a stellar 138–99 (58.2 percent), winning +32.07 units. This is due to the fact that two teams outside the division are unfamiliar with each other, which benefits the offense and leads to more points.

If the game is played at freezing temperatures (31 degrees or lower), the over improves to 106–79 (57.3 percent), winning +21.53 units.

The ultimate cold weather over spot is 31 degrees or lower in a non-divisional game. In these situations, the over has gone 68–32 (68 percent), winning +32.37 units.

By targeting cold weather overs (specifically in non-division games), bettors can take advantage of public bias and also get artificially inflated numbers. The oddsmakers know casual bettors will want to bet on cold weather unders, so they shade their lines toward unders, giving contrarian over backers better numbers and increased value.

Survivor Pools

One of the most popular betting rituals for NFL bettors is survivor pools, also known as survivor tournaments, eliminator challenges, or suicide pools. This is when a group of people enters the same contest and all pick one team each week, with each member trying to "survive" for as long as possible. If your team loses, you are eliminated from the competition. The trick is that you can't pick the same NFL team twice, so you can't just keep picking the best teams in the league over and over again. Rules can be adjusted for different sports, but generally speaking those are the rules for any survivor pool.

The common strategy for most players is to look at the spreads for that week and pick the team that is the largest favorite. If you have already used that team, then move on to the second-largest favorite, and so on. This may seem like a sound strategy at first glance, but if you are following the masses with your picks you are putting yourself at a disadvantage.

A key piece of information that you should be using in survivor pools is the percentages that each team is being picked in a given week. These percentages are readily available on sites like *ESPN* and *Yahoo*. These percentages will not match up completely to the percentages in your league, but there should be a good correlation between the two.

With this information at your disposal, you can now avoid the most popular picks of the week and separate yourself from the rest of the field. This is the best way to improve your chances of winning the pool, which is the ultimate goal. Many players think that surviving as long as possible is the goal, but it isn't. Being eliminated in Week 3 pays out the same amount of money as being eliminated in Week 10. The goal is to win the entire pool, so differentiation is key. Just like regular betting, you want to incorporate a contrarian philosophy.

Let's say the 49ers are 7-point favorites and 65 percent of survivor picks are taking them this week, according to the major sites you have researched.

Meanwhile, the Packers are 6.5-point favorites but are only receiving 12 percent of survivor picks. Even though the 49ers have a better chance of keeping you alive in your pool this week, the Packers give you a higher expected value over the course of the season. If the 49ers get upset, then 65 percent of entries are eliminated, greatly increasing your odds of taking the whole pot. Secondly, it gives you a chance to differentiate later in the season if the 49ers do win, as you will still have San Francisco as an option while a majority of players will not.

Most decisions won't be cut and dried. There are factors to take into account, including saving teams for later, the size of your pool, and analyzing your opponent's options, but for the most part if you differentiate yourself from the rest of the pack, you will increase your odds of being the last one to survive.

CHAPTER 13

How to Bet College Football

If the NFL is the undisputed king of betting, college football is the crown prince. Many of the same NFL betting strategies cross over to college; there, as in NFL betting, the popular bet types are the spread and total. However, there are also major differences that bettors should be aware of. First off, NFL players are professionals, while college players are student athletes. This means the level of competition can be greatly skewed, with a lack of parity between big-name schools and small schools. The NFL has only thirty-two teams, while college has 130 Division I-A teams. The NFL plays mostly on Sundays, while college football is played on Saturdays. The NFL plays a sixteen-game regular season, while college teams play roughly twelve regular-season games. In this chapter, you will learn how to take advantage of road teams, short road underdogs, favorites after the bye week, windy unders, hot overs, betting against the public in bowl games, and much more.

Home-Field Advantage Is Incredibly Overvalued

Just like in the NFL, home-field advantage in college football is real but also overvalued. In fact, it's even more overvalued. Public bettors love betting home teams, but especially in college sports. This inflated bias has everything to do with the age and inexperience of the players. In professional sports, the players are grown men. They're older, more mature, and more experienced. They are less likely to fall victim to a deafening crowd slurring obscenities at them. They won't be intimidated. They might lose the game or get blown out, but it won't be solely because of the hostile environment of playing on the road.

However, the same can't be said for college players. They aren't professionals. They're 18–21-year-old kids taking the leap from high school to college. They're now playing in front of 70,000 to 90,000 screaming fans. Many of them have never experienced anything like it before. Sure, it's great when you're at home and everyone is cheering you on. But what about when you're a visiting team and enter the chaos and insanity of a hateful road crowd? Conventional wisdom says college student athletes will have more nerves, get easily distracted, lose their composure, and fold under pressure. While all of this sounds plausible, there's just one problem: the data proves this isn't the case.

eV FACT

In college football, oddsmakers typically reward 2.5 points for home-field advantage. However, the discrepancies can vary between 1 point and 4 points depending on the team, stadium, and how often they cover at home historically. To determine the exact number, oddsmakers weigh past results over the last three to ten seasons. If a team consistently beats the spread at home, the number will be closer to 4 points. If they rarely cover at home, it will be closer to 1 point. Since 2005, the two best home teams against the spread are Oklahoma (47–31 ATS, 60.3 percent, +13.56 units) and Wisconsin (49-35 ATS, 58.3 percent, +12.14 units).

Home teams win the majority of their games. Since 2005, home teams have gone 5,226–3,641, which translates to a win percentage of 58.9 percent. However, it's a completely different story when it comes to covering the spread. Since 2005, college football home teams have gone 4,631–4,868 against the spread (48.8 percent), losing an astonishing –484.46 units. This means a $100 bettor taking every home team on the spread has lost nearly $50,000 over the past thirteen years. The oddsmakers know that the public loves betting home teams, so they set and shade their lines accordingly. This forces public players to take overpriced, inflated numbers.

On the flip side, road teams have been a losing bet as well, but not nearly at the level of home teams. Since 2005, road teams have gone 4,865–4,630 against the spread (51.2 percent), losing only –12.98 units. They're essentially a wash, losing less than one unit per season. Bettors should keep these trends in mind. This doesn't mean you should take every road team and avoid all home teams, it just means that one provides much more value than the other and you should keep that in the back of your mind when selecting a play.

Road Underdogs with Low Totals

Blindly taking all underdogs or all favorites has cost bettors big-time over the years. But underdogs have been slightly better against the spread. This makes sense, as public players gravitate toward favorites, which makes them overvalued. Since 2005, underdogs have gone 4,878–4,848 against the spread (50.2 percent), losing –222.21 units, while favorites have gone 4,848–4,878 against the spread (49.8 percent), losing –284.90 units.

Since underdogs have performed slightly better, let's see if we can layer on a few additional filters and identify a profitable trend. We notice that underdogs perform better on the road compared to at home. This is another way to capitalize on public bias, since recreational players love to bet on home favorites. Road underdogs have gone 3,248–3,110 against the spread (51.1 percent), losing –30.94 units. Still losing overall, but you shave off nearly 192 lost units by focusing on road underdogs instead of all underdogs.

The next step is to add in a low total. As in the NFL, low totals benefit underdogs because if fewer points are expected to be scored, that leads to tighter, closer games and makes it harder for the favorite to cover the spread. It's also important to note that college football features much higher totals than in the NFL. You routinely see totals in the 60s or 70s in college, while high NFL totals are in the high 40s, low 50s range. As a result, a low total in college is much higher than a low total in the NFL.

If the total is 55 or less, road underdogs have gone 1,837–1,707 against the spread (51.8 percent), winning +36.99 units. If the total is 50 or less, road underdogs perform even better: 1,062–933 against the spread (53.2 percent), winning +73.72 units. If the total is 45 or less, road underdogs improve to 424–353 against the spread (54.6 percent), winning +49.73 units.

ESSENTIAL

Underdogs perform much better in conference games than they do in non-conference games. Just like divisional underdogs in baseball or the NFL, the heightened level of familiarity between the opponents levels the playing field and benefits the underdog (teams play conference opponents once every season). Additionally, these conference showdowns are considered "rivalry" games and often the biggest games of the year for both teams. Since 2005, road underdogs with low totals of 45 or less playing conference opponents have gone 284–224 against the spread (55.9 percent), winning +45.7 units.

Short Road Underdogs

One of the simplest, most consistent, and best-kept secrets in college football is betting road underdogs with small or "short" spreads. These situations allow bettors to take advantage of public bias toward home favorites. The key is the small spread. The road underdog must be getting 4 points or less. This means the road underdog is either a pick'em, +1, +1.5. +2, +2.5. +3, +3.5, or +4.

Since 2005, road underdogs getting 4 points or less have gone 600–508 against the spread (54.2 percent), winning +64.57 units. To put this in comparison, underdogs getting more than 4 points have gone 2,642–2,593 against the spread (50.5 percent), losing –92.66 units.

Why are short road underdogs so profitable? First, the public wants to bet home favorites anyway. But then they see the low spread and think it will be even easier for the favorite to cover. The home favorite only has to win by a touchdown or less? Sign me up! Also, you have to take into account home-field advantage. Typically the oddsmakers will award 2.5 points for home-field advantage. So if a road underdog is getting 3 or 4 points, it means the teams are evenly matched. On a neutral field, the game would be a pick'em. If a road underdog is getting less than 3 points, it means that the road underdog would be considered the favorite on a neutral field. As a result, grabbing the points, and not laying them, would be a smart bet.

QUESTION

We know that short road dogs cover at a high rate. But how often do they win the game?
Since 2005, if you bet every short road underdog +4 or less on the moneyline instead of the spread, you would have gone 532–598 (47.1 percent), winning +84.64 units. If the win percentage is below 50 percent, how can you be making so much money? Because when you bet the moneyline instead of the spread, you're betting the short underdogs at plus-money prices like +115, +125, +135, +145, and +155. As a result, you're only winning 47.1 percent of the time, but because of the juicier payouts, you're turning a bigger profit with moneylines versus spreads.

Betting Against the Public

Betting against the public is a sound strategy for college football bettors. However, because there are so many games each week, typically sixty or more on any given Saturday, this means that public bettors have many different games to choose from. As a result, the number of bets can vary widely based on the matchup. A game between two small schools like Toledo and Western Michigan might get 5,000 bets, while a game between powerhouses like Michigan and Ohio State might get 40,000 bets. As a result, you can't just blindly bet every team getting a minority of bets in college football. The key is being extra selective and only going contrarian in the most heavily bet games of the day, the games with the highest number of public bettors. Go where the public is.

Since 2005, teams with less than 35 percent of spread bets have gone 2,447–2,528 against the spread (49.2 percent), losing –207.04 units with a –4.1 percent ROI. In other words, blindly taking all contrarian teams has been a huge losing bet. However, if we focus on only the most heavily bet games, contrarian teams perform much better against the spread.

Teams getting less than 35 percent of bets in games receiving at least the daily average number of bets have gone 978–954 against the spread (50.6 percent), losing –26.21 units. Simply getting rid of the small conference games that don't attract much action improves contrarian betting dramatically, saving bettors more than 180 lost units.

If we isolate the most heavily bet games of the day, those receiving at least 2.5 times the daily average number of bets, teams getting less than 35 percent of bets become profitable: 114–90 against the spread (55.9 percent), winning +18.38 units. This means that if the average game that day is receiving 5,000 bets, these games are receiving at least 12,500 bets.

If we focus on only conference underdogs getting less than 35 percent of bets in the most heavily bet games (at least 2.5 times the daily average number of bets), we achieve the ultimate contrarian spot. These teams have gone 66–42 against the spread (61.1 percent), winning +20.89 units since 2005.

ESSENTIAL

Bettors should keep an eye out for contrarian home teams in heavily bet games. Typically, public bettors will always bet home teams, so in the rare instances where they load up on a road team, it provides rare contrarian value on home teams, especially in heavily bet games. Since 2005, home teams getting less than 45 percent of spread bets in games receiving at least 2.5 times the daily average number of bets have gone 130–97 against the spread (57.3 percent), winning +26.36 units. This is one of the few situations where home teams are undervalued.

Favorites after the Bye Week

Just like in the NFL, college teams receive one bye week per year. This means that one week during the season, they don't have to play a game. This off week provides teams much-needed rest and an opportunity to mentally recharge, reset, and rehab injuries. Bye weeks do not benefit all teams equally. We see a massive difference between favorites and underdogs coming off the bye in college football.

Since 2005, favorites coming off the bye have gone 384–356 against the spread (51.9 percent), winning +8.53 units. They aren't a huge moneymaker, but they're profitable. Conversely, underdogs coming off the bye have been a losing bet, going 373–386 against the spread (49.1 percent), losing −33.32 units. If we focus on favorites and add a few additional filters, they perform even better off the bye.

If the favorite is playing at home after the bye, they've produced a record of 260–218 against the spread (54.4 percent), winning +27.99 units. This is night and day compared to on the road, where they've gone 115–127 ATS (47.5 percent), losing −17.26 units.

If the home favorite coming off a bye is ranked (this means they're ranked anywhere between one and twenty-five), they've gone an incredible 80–57 against the spread (58.4 percent), winning +18.82 units.

Why does the bye week disproportionately benefit favorites over underdogs? Because favorites have better players and are typically better coached than underdogs. The two-week break provides extra time for coaches to game-plan against the upcoming opponent. If the team is at home, they perform even better because players don't have to worry about traveling. Being ranked is the cherry on top. It means they are one of the top twenty-five teams in the country, so you know they've been playing well all season.

Contrarian bettors will almost always be betting on road teams and underdogs. Taking home favorites off the bye week is one of the few instances where home favorites provide value.

QUESTION

Does reverse line movement work in college football?
Yes, it does, but you have to pick your spots and focus on the most heavily bet games. A prime spot to take advantage of reverse line movement is contrarian home teams with the line moving in their favor. Since 2005, home teams receiving 35 percent or less spread bets with at least a half point of reverse line movement in games receiving at least 1.5 times the daily average number of bets have gone 161–113 against the spread (58.8 percent), winning +40.07 units. Think of a home team getting 30 percent of bets but going from −3 to −3.5 or +3 to +2.5. If the average game is receiving 10,000 bets that day, this game would be receiving at least 15,000 bets.

Fade Home Favorites after Low-Scoring Games

We know that the public loves betting home favorites. But what happens if the home favorite is coming off a low-scoring game?

Since 2005, home favorites who scored less than 10 points in their last game have gone 157–229 against the spread (40.7 percent), losing –80.77 units. If you faded teams in this spot (meaning you bet on the road underdog against the home favorite who scored 9 points or less their previous game), you would have won +59.92 units.

Why is this such a profitable spot? Because public bettors automatically assume the home favorite will bounce back and cover the next game. However, that's not the case. Home favorites feel added pressure in front of their home crowd and the offensive woes that plagued them the previous game create a "hangover" effect that can carry over to the next game.

ALERT

The top college football teams are ranked one through twenty-five by the Associated Press and a poll conducted by the coaches. The rankings are updated each week based on how teams perform. One way to take advantage of rankings is to look for games where two ranked teams go head-to-head. In these situations, the favorite has gone 312–260 against the spread (54.5 percent), winning +36.32 units since 2005. If the favorite is also contrarian—getting less than 50 percent of spread bets—they improve to 122–89 against the spread (57.8 percent), winning +27.27 units.

Conference Unders

When it comes to betting totals, overs have been a massive losing bet for public bettors. Once again, the public loves betting overs, but the books shade the total toward the over, forcing public bettors to take overpriced, inflated lines. Since 2005, overs have gone 4,695–4,874 (49.1 percent), losing an astounding –455.44 units. This means that a $100 bettor taking every over has lost more than $45,000 over the past thirteen seasons.

Unders have also been a losing bet, but not nearly as bad as betting overs. Since 2005, unders have gone 4,874–4,737 (50.7 percent), losing –121.27 units. It may not be profitable, but it saves bettors more than 330 lost units.

The key with betting unders is focusing on conference matchups. Unlike the NFL, where there are two conferences with three divisions in each conference, college football has eleven major conferences. The most well-known conferences are the SEC, ACC, Big Ten, Big 12, and the Pac 12. These are considered the "Power Five" conferences, with the biggest and best teams in college football.

Just as NFL games between divisional opponents lead to more unders, the same can be said in college football for unders between conference opponents. The same logic applies: because teams in the same conference play each other once every season, this leads to increased familiarity. Conference teams know each other very well, which creates rivalries and ultimately benefits the defense, leading to lower-scoring games.

Since 2005, we've seen a massive difference between conference unders and non-conference unders. When two teams in the same conference play each other, the under has gone 3,226–3,047 (51.5 percent), winning +19.22 units. If the game is between two teams from different conferences, the under has gone 1,646–1,687 (49.4 percent), losing –139.28 units.

If the game is heavily bet and receiving at least the daily average number of bets, conference unders improve to 341–319 (51.7 percent), winning +39.11 units.

Bettors should also focus on how the total moves when it comes to conference unders. If the total rises a half point or more (think 45 to 45.5 or 46), conference unders have been a losing bet: 1,381–1,350 (50.6 percent), losing –38.39 units. However, if the total falls a half point or more (think 45 to 44.5 or 44), the under has gone 1,474–1,348 (52.2 percent), winning +53.80 units. If the total falls 3 points or more (45 to 42), the under improves to 430–370 (53.8 percent), winning +39.51 units. Why is it important to target conference unders that fall? Because the public is always biased toward betting overs, so if you see the line fall, that typically means sharp bettors took the under.

Remember, overs are incredibly overvalued and should largely be avoided. When looking to bet a total, focus on conference unders that also feature sharp action that causes the line to fall.

Bettors should always target unders when two teams with stellar rushing offenses go head-to-head. Running the ball (instead of throwing it) aids the under because the clock continues to tick after each running play, causing the game to go by more quickly. This leads to fewer possessions and fewer points being scored. Since 2005, if the two teams playing each other average 215 rushing yards per game or more, the under has gone 214–164 (56.6 percent), winning +38.57 units.

Windy Unders

When it comes to windy unders, college football is even better than the NFL. If professional quarterbacks and kickers have trouble playing in the wind, you can bet that less talented and less experienced college players struggle even more.

Since 2005, if the wind is blowing at five miles per hour or more, the under has gone 3,074–2,869 (51.7 percent), winning +48.49 units. If we increase the wind even further, we find an amazing edge. Since 2005, if the wind is blowing at ten miles per hour or more, the under has gone 991–829 (54.5 percent), winning an incredible +112.44 units. If the wind is twenty miles per hour or more, the under has gone 63–35 (64.3 percent), winning +25.68 units.

This is one of the simplest and most profitable college football betting systems. Just as in the NFL, the wind makes it harder for quarterbacks to throw the ball, leading to more incomplete passes and fewer touchdowns. However, college quarterbacks are much less accurate and have weaker arms than professional quarterbacks, so they struggle even more throwing into the wind. Also, when you can't throw, you run the ball instead, which chews up the clock, leading to fewer possessions and touchdowns.

Another component to factor in: college kickers are much worse than professional kickers. They struggle to consistently kick field goals in perfect weather. If you layer in wind, forget about it. Another advantage to windy unders in college is the fact that there are so many more teams and stadiums all across the country, so there are more opportunities to bet windy unders and take advantage of inclement weather.

Always remember to check the wind before betting a college football total. If you see winds of at least five miles per hour or more, bet the under. If wind speeds are ten miles per hour or more, even better.

ESSENTIAL

Bettors should always target the under when military academy teams are playing each other. This means Army versus Navy, Army versus Air Force, or Navy versus Air Force. These schools play a totally different style of offense. It's much less complex. They rarely throw the ball and almost always run it instead. This chews up the clock and leads to extremely low-scoring games. Since 2005, the under has gone 30–8 (78.9 percent), winning +20.63 units when two military schools go head-to-head. It only happens three times a year, but bettors should always take the under when it arises.

Hot Overs

College football typically begins a week or two before the NFL, so many games are played in hot summer weather in late August and early September. One way bettors can take advantage of this is by targeting the over when it's hot out.

Since 2005, when the temperature is 80 degrees or higher at game time, the over has gone 732–686 (51.6 percent), losing –0.68 units. This might not seem impressive, but you have to remember that betting all overs, regardless of the temperature, has resulted in –455.44 units. So by targeting hot games you wash away almost all –455.44 lost units.

The magic number is 85 degrees. When the temperature is 85 degrees or higher, the over has gone 305–252 (54.8 percent), winning +34.81 units. When the temperature is 90 degrees or higher, the over has gone 81–57 (58.7 percent), winning +19.23 units.

Why does the over do well in hot weather? Because defensive players are forced to run around and defend against the offense, which makes them tired and short of breath, providing an advantage to the offense.

Another way to improve hot overs is to focus on non-conference games, which means targeting the over when two teams in different conferences play each other. Because teams in non-conference games aren't very familiar with each other, this benefits the offense because the defense doesn't know what to expect. This leads to more points being scored.

When the temperature is 85 degrees or higher and the two competing teams come from different conferences, the over has gone 226–156 (59.2 percent), winning +54.97 units.

Before placing your college football total bet, always be sure to check the weather first. If the forecast calls for temperatures in the mid-to-high 80s, remember that the over is a smart bet, especially in non-conference games.

Bowl Games

The goal of every college football team is to make a postseason bowl game. These are mini Super Bowls that only the top regular-season teams are invited to play in. They take place mostly in December and early January. There are more than forty different bowl games, with usually one or two bowl games per day for a full month-long stretch. They are all nationally televised games and provide unique value to contrarian bettors.

One of the easiest ways to take advantage of bowl games is by betting against the public. Why? Because bowl games are incredibly popular and much more heavily bet than regular-season games. A regular-season game might get 15,000 bets, while a bowl game gets 50,000 or more. Many casual bettors may not place a bet all season long, but they'll bet on their alma mater if they're in a bowl game. Once the regular season ends, there is typically a two-week or month lead-up until the bowl game. This allows media hype to build and public opinion to drive a narrative, which is typically toward the favorite.

Since 2005, bowl game teams getting less than 50 percent of spread bets have gone 243–205 against the spread (54.2 percent), winning +24.92 units. The more contrarian bowl teams are, the most profitable they become. Teams getting less than 40 percent of bets have gone 136–94 against the spread (59.1 percent), winning +34.45 units. Teams getting less than 30 percent of bets are rare, but incredibly profitable. They've gone 35–20 against the spread (63.6 percent), winning +13.44 units.

Another variable to remember is that all bowl games are played on a neutral field, which means there is no true home team. This helps level the playing field, which benefits underdogs.

Since 2005, underdogs have gone 239–218 against the spread (52.3 percent), winning +8.6 units in bowl games. Meanwhile, favorites have lost –31.89 units.

If an underdog is being dismissed by the public, they become even more profitable. Underdogs getting less than 50 percent of spread bets have gone 187–160 against the spread (53.9 percent), winning +17.10. If they're getting less than 35 percent of bets, they've gone an incredible 82–50 ATS (62.1 percent), winning +27.79 units.

Another way to take advantage of contrarian underdogs is to look for bowl games with short spreads. This means the oddsmakers are expecting a close game. If an underdog is getting less than 35 percent of bets and spread is between 1 and 6.5 points, underdogs have gone 50–30 ATS (62.5 percent), winning +17.38 units.

If a bowl game underdog is getting 40 percent or less bets and the total is less than 55, underdogs have gone 70–39 ATS (64.2 percent), winning +27.15 units.

The only profitable spot for bowl game favorites is when they're contrarian. This creates a "Fade the Trendy Underdog" scenario for bettors. Favorites getting a majority of bets (51 percent or more), have gone 160–187 ATS (46.1 percent), losing –34.59 units. However, if they're getting less than 50 percent of bets, they improve to 56–45 ATS (55.5 percent), winning +7.82 units.

Long story short: bowl season is the best time of year to go contrarian. Bettors should always target teams getting less than 50 percent of bets. If they're getting less than 40 percent of bets or less than 30 percent of bets, even better. Only take favorites if they're getting a minority of bets. And remember, underdogs have greater value.

ESSENTIAL

Another bowl game edge is focusing on teams who failed to cover at a high rate during the regular season. This means that bettors who bet on them ended up losing their bets. As a result, those same bettors remember the team letting them down and costing them money, so they will automatically be biased against them and look to fade them. Since 2005, teams who covered at a 33 percent or less rate during the regular season (only covered in a third or less of their games), have gone 33–21 ATS (61.1 percent) in bowl games, winning +11.14 units.

CHAPTER 14

How to Bet the NBA

After football, the next most popular sport to bet on is basketball. According to the UNLV Center for Gaming Research, Nevada has taken in nearly $20 billion in basketball betting since 1992. That amounts to roughly 25 percent of all money bet on sports in Nevada. Basketball is a high-scoring sport, so the most popular bet types are the spread and the total.

Unlike the NFL, where games are played once a week, the NBA plays an eighty-two-game schedule with five to ten games per night. This provides more betting opportunities for casual bettors and professionals alike. Because the NBA is the second-most heavily bet sport behind football, this leads to increased contrarian value and inflated lines. You can turn a profit by betting against the public, focusing on road underdogs, taking advantage of contrarian unders with reverse line movement, betting against home teams in back-to-backs, fading teams that are tanking, and much more.

Home-Court Advantage Is Overvalued

Casual bettors love betting home teams across all sports. And basketball is no different. Once again, this leads to sportsbooks shading lines toward home teams, causing home teams to be overvalued, with public bettors unknowingly betting overpriced odds.

In the NBA, home-court advantage is typically 3 points. Depending on the arena, it could be as many as 4 points or as few as 2 points. Additionally, the schedule can have a big impact on home-court advantage. The NBA is unique in that there are many back-to-backs during the season. This means teams are playing two games on consecutive nights. Because of strenuous travel and little rest, home-court advantage can be mitigated based on the schedule. If a home team is playing on the second night of a back-to-back and the opponent had the previous day off, the home team won't enjoy much of a home-court advantage.

NBA home teams have won 59.4 percent (9,799–6,709) of their regular-season games at home since 2005. On the surface, this sounds like an impressive record. However, because the vast majority of basketball betting is based on the point spread, winning the game doesn't matter. It's all about whether or not a team covers the spread. Unfortunately for home teams, they win most of the games, but do not cover.

FACT

In 2014, NBA Commissioner Adam Silver wrote an op-ed in *The New York Times* titled "Legalize and Regulate Sports Betting." This marked the first time that a commissioner of a major professional sports league came out in favor of legalized betting. "Sports betting should be brought out of the underground and into the sunlight where it can be appropriately monitored and regulated," he wrote. It is known to be a watershed moment in the push to legalize betting in America.

Since 2005, NBA home teams have gone 7,971–8,282 against the spread (49.1 percent). Because of the losing record and having to pay the juice, this translates to –715.10 units. This means that if you bet $100 on every home team from 2005 to 2017, you would have lost $71,510.

On the flip side, just as home teams are overvalued, road teams are undervalued. Since 2005, road teams have only won 40.6 percent of their games (6,709–9,801), but they've covered 50.9 percent of them (8,272–7,971). However, this doesn't mean they've been profitable to bet on the spread. Because bettors have to pay the juice, road teams have lost –65.67 units. It might be a losing record, but it's much better compared to what you would have lost betting on home teams (–715.10 units).

Contrarian Road Underdogs

With sportsbooks shading their lines to exploit public bias, betting against the public is a smart strategy in the NBA. However, you can't just bet on every team getting a minority of bets. You have to be selective and pick your spots. Because the public loves betting home teams and favorites, this means that road underdogs are the most valuable teams to bet on.

Since 2005, NBA teams getting 40 percent or less spread bets have gone 4,882–4,774 against the spread (50.6 percent). Unfortunately, despite the slightly winning record, bettors have lost –136.86 units because of the juice. However, we notice a massive discrepancy between home teams and road teams. Home teams receiving 40 percent or less spread bets have gone 2,694–2,755 against the spread (48.4 percent), losing –205.28 units. But road teams getting 40 percent or less spread bets have gone 2,183–2,013 against the spread (52 percent), winning +69.71 units. Once again this speaks to how overvalued home teams are and how undervalued road teams are.

If we go a step further and only look at road underdogs receiving 40 percent or less bets, they improve to 2,166–1,992 against the spread (52.1 percent), winning +74.53 units.

The ultimate contrarian spot is road underdogs receiving 30 percent or less bets. Since 2005, they've gone 573–484 against the spread (54.8 percent), winning +63.08 units. However, we must remember that not all spreads are created equal. Just like small road underdogs in college football, small road underdogs in the NBA provide the most value. Since 2005, road underdogs receiving 30 percent or less bets who are getting 6 points or less have gone 214–150 against the spread (58.8 percent), winning +54.51 units. These teams are also worth betting on the moneyline. If you bet them to win instead of cover, they've gone 163–214 (43.2 percent), but because of the plus-money payouts they've produced +57.26 units won.

ESSENTIAL

The best time of year to bet on contrarian road underdogs is early in the season. In October, November, and December, road underdogs getting 35 percent or less spread bets have gone 482–384 against the spread (55.7 percent), winning +78.66 units since 2005. From January 1 on, they've been a break-even bet, going 800–767 against the spread (51.1 percent), losing –5.07 units. Early in the season, road underdogs are much more competitive because they're healthier and give a full effort. Later in the year if they're out of the playoff race, teams can begin to tank and not try as hard.

Buy Low Off a Loss

Another way to take advantage of road underdogs is buying low on teams coming off a loss. This allows savvy bettors to capitalize on public recency bias. If a road underdog lost their previous game, public bettors would be more inclined to bet against them, expecting an easy win and cover by the home favorite. This makes them even more valuable to bet on. Since 2005, road underdogs coming off a loss have gone 3,174–2,978 against the spread (51.6 percent), winning +50.72 units. If the road underdog is coming off a win, they've been a terrible bet, going 2,413–2,416 against the spread (50 percent), losing –107.60 units.

Bettors should pay particular attention to road underdogs coming off a blowout loss. If a road underdog lost the previous game by 10 or more points, they've gone 1,587–1,423 against the spread (52.7 percent) in the next game, winning +90.14 units. If they lost the previous game by 15 or more points, they've been even better: 941–823 against the spread (53.3 percent), winning +75.19 units. Always buy low on teams who lost and lost badly in their previous game. They are the most undervalued teams for contrarian bettors.

ESSENTIAL

Public bettors love betting favorites, especially really big favorites. If they see a "great" team playing a "terrible" team, they'll expect a blowout and easy cover. However, historically, big contrarian underdogs have been extremely profitable to bet on. Since 2005, underdogs receiving 30 percent or less spread bets that are getting 10 points or more have gone 299–233 against the spread (56.2 percent), winning +52.45 units. These big contrarian underdogs have been profitable both at home and on the road. At home they've gone 105–86 against the spread (55 percent), winning +13.9 units. On the road, they've been even better, going 193–147 against the spread (56.8 percent), winning +37.55 units.

Taking Advantage of Inflated Lines

The optimal threshold for betting against the public in the NBA is 30 percent. Since 2005, NBA teams getting 30 percent or less spread bets have gone 2,052–1,916 ATS (51.7 percent), winning +32.25 units.

While taking all teams getting 30 percent or less bets is profitable, a key cherry on top is looking for contrarian spots that also feature inflated lines. An inflated line is created when the public bets one side overwhelmingly, causing the oddsmakers to adjust the line further toward the popular side. This benefits contrarian bettors immensely because it provides a better number for savvy bettors willing to back the unpopular side.

To put this in perspective, say the Lakers are 10-point favorites (–10) against the Hawks. The Lakers are receiving 75 percent of spread bets, forcing the oddsmakers to adjust the Lakers from –10 to –11. The lopsided public betting on the Lakers created an inflated line of 1 point for Hawks bettors. Instead of betting the Hawks at +10, you can now bet Hawks +11. You just got a free extra point, purely because of public bias. Smart money didn't move the line. Sharp bettors didn't bet the Lakers. The line move was caused by the public overvaluing the Lakers.

Since 2005, NBA teams receiving 30 percent or less spread bets with an inflated line of a half point or more (think the Hawks get 25 percent of bets but move from +10 to +10.5) have gone 1,087–959 against the spread (53.1 percent), winning +74.76 units. If the line is inflated 1 point or more (Hawks

25 percent and move from +10 to +11), teams 30 percent or less improve to 685–563 against the spread (54.9 percent), winning +89.52 units.

If the inflated line is 2 points or more (Hawks 25 percent and move from +10 to +12), teams receiving 30 percent or fewer bets have gone 224–160 against the spread (58.3 percent), winning +53.79 units.

When betting against the public in the NBA, targeting teams receiving 30 percent or less is the starting point. The next step is to sit back and allow the lopsided betting to move the line, providing contrarian bettors extra value in the form of free points and better odds.

QUESTION

What if a team is getting 40 percent of bets and moves from +10 to +11. Would that be considered an inflated line?
Unfortunately not. Inflated lines only work in the most lopsided games. Since 2005, teams receiving between 31 percent and 49 percent of bets with an inflated line of 1 point or more have gone 1,551–1,626 against the spread (48.8 percent), losing –143.34 units. So despite being contrarian and having the line get better, these teams haven't been profitable. This is because the line movement may not be a direct result of public bias. It could be sharp action moving the number, in which case you wouldn't want to bet against it.

Contrarian Unders with Reverse Line Movement

After the spread, the second most popular NBA bet type is the total. Just as public bettors love betting home teams and favorites, they also love betting overs. The bookmakers know this, so they'll shade totals toward overs, forcing public bettors to take overpriced numbers.

Since 2005, the over has bankrupted public bettors and been a windfall to the sportsbooks, going 8,103–8,225 (49.6 percent), losing –527.57 units. Betting every under isn't a winning strategy either; however, it does cut the losses significantly—by more than half. Unders have lost –250.70 units.

The key with betting unders is making sure they're contrarian and also receiving sharp action. You want to find the sweet spot where you can both bet against the public and place yourself with the professional bettors who win at a high rate. This means focusing on unders that are receiving 40 percent or less spread bets with reverse line movement. In other words, the public is betting heavily on the over, but the total falls because the sportsbooks took in an overload of professional action and smart money on the under.

Think of it this way: the Celtics are playing the Knicks. The total opened at 210 and 70 percent of bets are taking the over. Normally in situations like this, the oddsmakers would raise the total from 210 to 211 to compensate for the lopsided over betting. However, you see the line fall from 210 to 209. This means professional bettors bet the under, causing reverse line movement.

In these situations, when the under is receiving 40 percent or less bets and the total falls at least a point, the under has gone 1,519–1,227 (53.6 percent), winning +129.64 units. This means that if you bet $100 on every single one since 2005, you would have made $12,964.

Contrarian unders with reverse line movement are one of the simplest and best NBA betting systems for totals.

FACT

On July 31, 2018, the NBA and WNBA signed a deal with MGM Resorts to be its official gaming partner. It marked the first-ever partnership between a sports betting company and a major professional sports league. The deal was for three years and $25 million. MGM agreed to provide the NBA and WNBA with gaming data so the league could monitor for suspicious activity. In return, the NBA gave MGM its official scoring and statistical data, which MGM could then use to strengthen its odds, specifically for live or in-game betting.

Divisional Unders

In the NBA, there are six divisions, with five teams in each division. Teams in the same division play each other four times per year. This increased familiarity leads to a better understanding of the opponent, which inevitably benefits the defense, leading to lower-scoring games and more unders. Since 2005, when two teams in the same division play each other, the under has gone 1,668–1,536 (52.1 percent), winning +57.5 units. On the flip side, unders between non-divisional opponents have gone 6,557–6,569 (50 percent), losing –308.29 units.

If we add a betting against the public angle, divisional unders perform even better. This allows us to take advantage of public bias on the over. Since 2005, when the under is getting 40 percent or less bets, divisional unders have gone 910–790 (53.5 percent), winning +82.83 units.

The cherry on top for contrarian divisional unders is also having reverse line movement. This means sharp bettors have bet the under, causing the total to fall. Since 2005, divisional unders receiving 40 percent or less bets with at least a full point of reverse line movement have gone 314–219 (58.9 percent), winning +81.25 units.

Remember: unders always perform better when the two teams are from the same division. If the under is also contrarian and has sharp action, even better.

FACT

In July of 2008, former NBA referee Tim Donaghey was sentenced to fifteen months in prison for participating in the NBA's worst gambling scandal. Donaghey was a gambling addict who fell deep in debt. To pay his debts, he provided tips and inside information to the mafia and the bookies. During the games, he would make incorrect calls that benefited one side over the other and affected the point spread. He received between $2,000 and $5,000 from the bookies for every pick he helped win. Donaghey claimed that other referees threw Game 6 of the 2002 NBA finals between the Lakers and Kings so the NBA could extend the series to seven games and generate more TV revenue. In Game 6, the Lakers attempted eighteen more free throws than the Kings. The Lakers won the game and went on to win the NBA title.

Bet Against Home Teams on Back-to-Backs

Bettors should always be aware of NBA teams playing on the second night of a back-to-back. These situations are extremely valuable because teams are tired from playing the previous night. As a result, it provides an edge for the opponent. Since 2005, teams playing their second game in consecutive days have gone 3,778–3,824 against the spread (49.7 percent), losing −218.00 units.

To take advantage of this trend, you should look for situations where a home favorite is playing on the second night of a back-to-back and played the previous night on the road. This means that they had to travel, in addition to being tired. Also, because they're a favorite, the public will be inclined to bet on them, which means they're overvalued. The last ingredient is making sure the opponent is from the same conference. Teams in the same conference play each other at least three times per season. This leads to increased familiarity and levels the playing field, which benefits the underdog, just like divisional underdogs in baseball or football.

Since 2005, if you bet against home favorites in the second night of a back-to-back who were on the road the previous game and are now playing a conference opponent, you would have gone 507–423 against the spread (54.5 percent), winning +62.11 units.

Always remember, home favorites on the second night of a back-to-back are overvalued. It's a good idea to bet against them, especially if they were on the road the previous night and are now playing a conference opponent.

ALERT

One of the rare instances when it's profitable to bet on home teams is when they're contrarian underdogs receiving big reverse line movement. Since 2005, home underdogs receiving less than 40 percent of bets with at least 1.5 points of reverse line movement have gone 132–88 against the spread (60 percent), winning +36.49 units (think of a home underdog getting 35 percent of bets and moving from +10 to +8.5). If the team is coming off a loss, they've performed even better: 84–51 against the spread (62.2 percent), winning +28.10 units.

Take Advantage of Tanking

Late in the season, NBA bettors need to be aware of tanking. Tanking occurs at the end of the season, when teams who are eliminated from playoff contention start to intentionally lose games so they can increase their chances of getting a high pick in the upcoming draft. You want to bet against these bad teams down the stretch because they have given up on the season.

To take advantage of tanking, wait until around the fifty-five-game mark. That way you can isolate the last portion of the season, when it's clear that teams are out of the race and intent on losing. The key is looking for match-ups when a bad, tanking team is playing a decent or above-average team that is fighting for the playoffs. Those teams are motivated to win in order to make the postseason.

The other key is making sure the tanking team is at home. This allows you to capitalize on public bias, who will overrate home-court advantage. Since 2005, tanking teams (with a win percentage of 39 percent or less) who are underdogs at home against average or above-average teams (with a win percentage of 48 percent or higher) have gone 342–439 against the spread (43.9 percent), losing −114.14 units. That means if you bet against these teams, you would have gone 439–343 against the spread (56.1 percent), winning +75.54 units.

How to Bet the NBA Playoffs

During the regular season, it's profitable to bet on underdogs and road teams because the public overvalues favorites and home teams. However, this isn't the case when it comes to the playoffs. In the postseason, public bettors tend to bet on underdogs at a higher rate. They love to bet on teams getting points, as they think the games will be very close because the teams are so evenly matched. This leads to the overvaluing of underdogs and undervaluing of favorites.

Since 2005, playoff favorites have gone 605–543 against the spread (52.7 percent), winning +33.3 units. On the flip side, underdogs have gone 543–605 ATS (47.3 percent), losing −84.66 units.

It's also important to note that home teams possess a big advantage in the NBA playoffs. This is because home-court advantage gets elevated in the postseason. The crowds are louder than regular-season games, the fans are more engaged, and the stakes are higher, which creates an extra-hostile environment for visitors. Since 2005, playoff road teams have gone 559–589 against the spread (48.7 percent), losing −53.26 units. Home teams have gone 589–559 against the spread (51.3 percent), winning +1.9 units. You're not breaking the bank with home teams, but they are much more profitable than road teams overall.

If we combine favorites, home teams, and add a contrarian angle, we identify a highly profitable playoff trend. Being contrarian is a cherry on top when it comes to playoff betting because postseason games are much more heavily bet than regular-season games. As a result, playoff games receive more public action than regular-season games, which makes betting against the public highly profitable. If the home favorite is receiving 40 percent or less spread bets, they've gone 91–57 against the spread (61.5 percent), winning +29.12 units. This is a "Fade the Trendy Underdog" situation. If the public is dismissing the home favorite and loading up on the road underdog, it creates added value on the home favorite.

Capitalize On Rest

Playoff series can be grueling. The level of intensity is extremely high and players can get tired legs more easily, especially with starting players having just completed a long eighty-two-game season and now playing lots of extra minutes, oftentimes the entire playoff game. As a result, any extra rest during the playoffs can greatly benefit a team, especially home teams.

Typically, playoff games are played every other day or every two days. However, if home teams have three or more days off, they've gone 255–219 against the spread (53.8 percent), winning +23.5 units. If home teams enjoy four or more days off, they've gone an incredible 97–58 against the spread (62.6 percent), winning +34.22 units. The extra days off provide much-needed rest and more time to game-plan and make adjustments. The key is being at home, which means the team doesn't have to travel and is waiting for their opponent in their home building.

ESSENTIAL

Bettors should always buy low on playoff favorites who just suffered a blowout loss. If a team loses by double-digit points in their previous game, the public remembers that and automatically wants to bet against them the next game, thinking that they're due to play poorly again. However, these teams are incredibly undervalued and tend to bounce back in their next game, especially if they're a favorite. Since 2005, favorites who lost their previous game by 10 points or more have gone 126–89 against the spread (58.6 percent), winning +31.45 units.

Playoff Unders

The public loves betting overs, especially in the playoffs. This bias, combined with an influx of public betting and high ticket counts, creates a perfect storm for contrarian bettors to take advantage of postseason unders. Since 2005, postseason overs have gone 561–594 (48.6 percent), losing –56.19 units. On the flip side, unders have won at a 51.4 percent clip, turning a slight profit of +1.34 units.

Just like in the regular season, the key with postseason unders is making sure they're also contrarian and have sharp action. Since 2005, if the under is getting less than 50 percent of bets and the total falls 1 point or more, the under has gone 184–146 (55.8 percent), winning +27.09 units.

Another profitable postseason strategy is targeting unders late in a playoff series. By Game 6 and 7, players are exhausted and their legs are tired. This leads to more missed shots. Additionally, if a series reaches Game 6 or 7, it means one team is facing elimination. This causes both teams to buckle down and put in a maximum effort on defense, leading to fewer points being scored.

Since 2005, the under has gone 499–495 (50.2 percent) in Games 1 to 5, losing –22.41 units. However, in Games 6 and 7, the under has gone 94–66 (58.8 percent), winning +22.81 units.

CHAPTER 15

How to Bet College Basketball

College basketball is very similar to the NBA. Both are bet predominantly on the point spread and the total, and both are great for betting against the public. The biggest difference is that there are over 300 Division I college teams, compared to thirty in the NBA. This means far more betting opportunities. It also means you need to be selective and pick your spots. In this chapter, you will learn how to turn a profit by focusing on several key betting strategies like going contrarian in heavily lopsided conference games, betting against ranked teams, and capitalizing on neutral court unders. You'll also learn how to bet March Madness and fill out a contrarian bracket so you can win your office pool.

Home-Court Advantage Is Overvalued

The public loves betting home teams across all sports. And college basketball is no different. This once again leads to home teams being overvalued by the public. Home-court advantage is real, but it's already factored into the line. Home-court advantage varies greatly in college basketball, more so than any other sport. On average, sportsbooks will award 3 to 4 points for home-court advantage, but it could be as much as 6 or 7 points or as few as 1 or none depending on the team, stadium, and the opponent.

FACT

One of the biggest home-court advantages in college basketball is Cameron Indoor Stadium, home of the Duke Blue Devils. It's one of the loudest and most hostile environments for opposing teams to play in, providing a massive advantage for Duke. The student section is so raucous they've earned the nickname "Cameron Crazies." Oddsmakers award up to 8 points in home-court advantage for Duke, the highest of any team in college basketball.

Since 2005, home teams have won 64.4 percent of their games (26,726–14,579). On the surface, this record is impressive. It means that home teams win nearly two-thirds of their games. However, covering the spread is a different story. Due to home-court advantage being overvalued, oddsmakers shading lines toward home teams, and bettors having to pay the juice, home teams have been a huge loser on the spread, going 20,338–20,956 (49.3 percent), losing –1,709.91 units. This means that a $100 bettor taking every home team from 2005 to 2018 would have lost $170,991.

Betting Against the Public

Betting against the public is a sound strategy in college basketball, but because there are so many games to choose from, bettors need to pick their spots and focus only on the most heavily bet games. Unlike professional basketball, college has dozens of small, unknown schools that don't get much public attention. A game between Siena and Albany is going to be largely ignored by public bettors. As a result, there isn't any contrarian value to be had. You should avoid games between small conference schools. These unpopular, small school games are targeted by professional bettors who have an edge. You don't want to be betting against "the public" in these games, because there is no public.

Instead, focus on the most popular, primetime, nationally televised games. This means games on ESPN between Duke and North Carolina or Kansas and Kentucky. These games are incredibly heavily bet and loaded with public action, which means they provide fantastic contrarian value. Additionally, sportsbooks won't shade lines in small conference games, but they will in the popular games between big schools. This leads to increased contrarian value.

ESSENTIAL

One of the best and easiest ways to bet against the public in college basketball is focusing on lopsided conference games in the biggest, most popular conferences. In college, there are six "superconferences." These include the SEC, ACC, Big East, Big 12, Big Ten, and PAC 12. These are the most competitive conferences that garner the most public attention, making them a prime candidate for contrarian bettors. Anytime two teams from one of these conferences play each other, the team getting less than 25 percent of spread bets has gone 648–526 against the spread (55.2 percent), winning +89.53 units.

Since 2005, teams receiving 25 percent or less spread bets have gone 4,126–4,166 against the spread (49.8 percent), losing –233.20 units. However, if the game is receiving at least the daily average number of bets, teams receiving 25 percent or less bets improve to 1,726–1,645 against the spread (51.2 percent), winning +1.5 units. You aren't breaking the bank, but by simply ignoring the low-bet games, you erase all of your lost units.

The more heavily bet a game is, the more valuable betting against the public becomes. In games receiving at least 2.5 times the daily average number of bets (if the average game that day is receiving 10,000 bets, these games are receiving at least 25,000 bets), teams receiving 25 percent or less bets improve to 277–244 against the spread (53.2 percent), winning +19.61 units. It doesn't happen often, but in games receiving at least 4 times the daily average numbers of bets (average game is 10,000 bets, these games are

40,000 or more), teams receiving 25 percent or less bets are an astounding 47–32 against the spread (59.5 percent), winning +12.29 units.

Contrarian Home Teams in Heavily Bet Games

Because the public loves betting home teams, this means that the majority of contrarian betting value lies on road teams. The one exception is when a home team is being dismissed by the public and the game is extremely heavily bet. In other words, it's one of the most popular games of the day and the public is betting heavily on the visitor. This creates rare contrarian value on the home team.

Since 2005, home teams getting less than 50 percent of spread bets in games with at least 2.5 times the daily average number of bets have gone 146–114 (56.2 percent), winning +24.82 units.

This system is profitable because it allows bettors the unique opportunity to not only bet against the public in the most heavily bet games of the day, but also capitalize on home-court advantage. Another added bonus is that this system generates, on average, about twenty-five system matches per season, which means you will see at least one or two of these situations every week.

If we drop the betting threshold to focus on even more lopsided games, this system becomes more profitable. Home teams getting less than 35 percent of spread bets in games with at least 2.5 times the daily average number of bets have gone 81–56 ATS (59.1 percent), winning +20.78 units. On average, this system will generate about one match per week for bettors.

ESSENTIAL

Another way to bet against the public is to take advantage of recency bias and bet against teams who cover a lot. Public bettors love betting on teams who have won them money recently. They will ride teams on a "cover streak," which leads to the overvaluing of these hot teams. Also, you are counting on regression to take place. These teams are eventually due to not cover. Since 2005, teams receiving less than 25 percent of bets against teams who have covered at least four straight games have gone 287–235 against the spread (55 percent), winning +38.58 units.

Bet Against the Public on Saturdays

College basketball games are played throughout the week, but Saturdays are by far the busiest, with typically seventy-five games or more being played throughout the day. These Saturday games are much more heavily bet than weekday games, because public bettors aren't working and have more free time to watch and bet on the games. As a result, they garner much more public action, leading to higher ticket counts and increased contrarian value.

Since 2005, Saturday teams getting less than 25 percent of bets in games that are getting at least the daily average number of bets have gone 591–503 ATS (54 percent), winning +60.48 units. In other words, if the average Saturday game is getting 10,000 bets, these games are getting 10,000 bets or more. This allows bettors to bypass the less popular, lower-bet games that the public is ignoring, which don't present any contrarian value.

This system gets even stronger if we focus on teams who have failed to cover recently. This means that if public bettors bet on them in previous games, they lost their bets. Conversely, if they bet against them, they won their bets. Public players always remember if a team cost them money or made them money. If a team let them down and lost their bet, they will automatically want to bet against them out of spite. Contrarian bettors can capitalize on this increased public bias by buying low on teams who have failed to cover recently.

If the team getting less than 25 percent of spread bets in a heavily bet Saturday game has failed to cover in their last one to five games, they've gone 324–237 (57.8 percent), winning +72.78 units.

ESSENTIAL

Similar to divisional underdogs in football and baseball, conference underdogs perform better than regular underdogs because of the built-in familiarity and long-standing rivalries. This brings out the best in both teams and levels the playing field, leading to closer games, which benefits the underdog. Since 2005, conference underdogs on the road receiving less than 25 percent of spread bets have gone 983–903 against the spread (52.1 percent), winning +33.44 units. However, if the spread was more than 10 points (+10.5 or higher), conference road underdogs receiving 25 percent or less bets improve to 468–725 against the spread (57.2 percent), winning +74.93 units.

Bet Against Ranked Teams in Conference Play

In college basketball, the best teams are ranked one through twenty-five by the Associated Press and *USA Today*. If a team is ranked in the top twenty-five, their number ranking will appear next to their name on the schedule and on the TV scoreboard. When deciding who to bet on, public players always focus on rankings. If two teams are going head-to-head and one is ranked tenth and the other is ranked twentieth, public bettors will automatically bet the tenth-ranked team because their ranking is better. If a ranked team is playing an unranked team (any team outside the top twenty-five), bettors will immediately bet on the ranked team, expecting an easy win and cover.

The sportsbooks know that public players focus heavily on these rankings, so they'll shade their lines toward ranked teams, forcing public bettors to take a bad number. As a result, this creates added value to bet against ranked teams.

However, this doesn't mean you can just bet against every ranked team. Doing so would have produced a losing record of 4,621–4,570 against the spread (50.3 percent), losing –190.69 units since 2005. The key is only betting against ranked teams in heavily lopsided conference games. This allows bettors to take advantage of public bias and also target rivalry games between two teams in the same conference.

ESSENTIAL

Not all rankings are created equal. The public will be much more inclined to bet on a top-one or top-two team versus a team ranked twenty-fourth or twenty-fifth. Contrarian bettors can take advantage of this by specifically targeting top-five teams. They're the ones receiving the heaviest amount of public bias and shading from oddsmakers, making them the most valuable to bet against. Since 2005, conference underdogs playing a top-five-ranked team have gone 577–484 against the spread (54.4 percent), winning +61.81 units. If they're playing a top-one or top-two team, they improve to 240–191 against the spread (55.7 percent), winning +35.75 units.

Since 2005, conference teams receiving less than 25 percent of bets against a ranked opponent have gone 447–362 against the spread (55.3 percent), winning +62.05 units. Road teams in this spot have performed particularly well, going 124–78 against the spread (61.4 percent), winning +40.17 units.

Neutral Court Unders

In college basketball, teams play in several tournaments throughout the season. At the beginning of the season, they play in tournaments like the Maui Invitational, Myrtle Beach Invitational, or Puerto Rico Tip-Off. At the end of the season, the best teams will play in their conference tournaments and then the Big Dance, otherwise known as the NCAA Tournament or March Madness.

The key with all these tournaments is that they're played on a neutral court. This means they're played in a pre-selected stadium in which neither team is at home or on the road. This provides a massive edge when betting unders.

Since 2005, betting every under on a neutral court has produced a record of 1,570–1,356 (53.7 percent), winning +110.38 units. On the flip side, betting every under on a non-neutral court (in which the home team is playing a true home game in their home stadium) led to massive losses: 19,729–11,9848 (49.9 percent), or –1,414.11 units. In other words, a $100 bettor betting every under on a non-neutral court has lost more than $141,000.

Why do neutral courts benefit unders? Because the players are playing in an unfamiliar environment. They aren't used to the stadiums and don't know the nuances of the courts, the rims, and the shooting backdrop behind the backboard. In addition, because neither team is at home, this means both teams are on the road, so the crowd is divided, with neither side enjoying total support from the fans.

Bettors should always be aware of games played on neutral courts. Typically, you will see a small letter "N" next to the game, denoting "neutral." Always remember, the under has great value in these situations.

ALERT

The best time of year to bet neutral court unders is the first month of the season, in November. This is because the season is young and the players are still learning the offense and learning how to play with new teammates. This leads to less offensive production and lower-scoring games. Since 2005, neutral court unders have gone 1,066–901 (54.2 percent), winning +91.58 units in November. If the total is 145 or higher, November neutral court unders are even better: 404–316 (56.1 percent), winning +59.04 units.

March Madness

March Madness is the highlight of the college basketball season. It's like having multiple Super Bowls every single day for a full month straight. It is one of the most intense and action-packed betting events of the year. It also happens to be the best time of year to bet against the public.

The beauty of March Madness is that every game is extremely heavily bet. A regular average Joe might not bet on a single regular-season game, but because it's March Madness, they'll throw some money down for the fun of it. As a result, the ticket counts skyrocket and the betting market is flooded with public money. Combine the influx of public betting with non-stop media coverage and the overall buzz created by filling out brackets, and you have a perfect storm for contrarian bettors.

Because every March Madness game is heavily bet, this means contrarian bettors don't have to focus exclusively on the most lopsided games of the tournament. As long as a team is getting less than half of the bets, they've turned a profit. Since 2005, March Madness teams getting less than 50 percent of spread bets have gone 462–420 against the spread (52.4 percent), winning +18.36 units. This is the only time of year where blindly going contrarian is profitable.

However, we do notice a difference between underdogs and favorites. Since 2005, betting all March Madness favorites getting less than 50 percent of spread bets has been highly profitable: 127–101 against the spread (55.7 percent), winning +19.27 units. If a favorite is getting less than 40 percent of bets, they've been even better, going 38–27 against the spread (58.5

percent), winning +8.68 units. Buying low on contrarian favorites and "Fading the Trendy Underdog" is incredibly profitable during March Madness.

The magic number for betting against the public with March Madness underdogs is 40 percent. Since 2005, underdogs getting 40 percent or less bets have gone 208–179 against the spread (53.7 percent), winning +18.71 units. The more contrarian we go, the more profitable underdogs become. If the underdog is getting 30 percent or less bets, they've gone 79–63 against the spread (55.6 percent), winning +11.98 units. It doesn't happen often, but if the underdog is getting 20 percent or less spread bets, they've gone an amazing 11–2 against the spread (84.6 percent), winning +8.4 units.

FACT

According to the American Gaming Association, Americans bet more than $10 billion on March Madness in 2018. Of that $10 billion, only 3 percent was wagered legally through Nevada sportsbooks. In March of 2017, Nevada sportsbooks took in $429 million in basketball bets (both pro and college), a new all-time record. Sportsbooks won $41 million of the $429 million bet. Also in 2017, more than twenty-four million Americans participated in NCAA Tournament pools, filling out more than sixty million brackets totaling more than $2 billion in entry fees. With legalized betting spreading across America, these numbers are expected to skyrocket in the coming years.

How to Build a Contrarian Bracket

Every March, the world seems to stop as everyone takes attention away from their job, their family, and their life to focus on the NCAA basketball tournament. While the NCAA would like to close its collective eyes and pretend everyone is enthralled with the sport of college basketball, the real reason for the intrigue boils down to one word: brackets.

While this is a book for those new to betting, even the most novice of bettors has come across a March Madness bracket. Millions of brackets are filled out in offices, homes, and online in hopes of getting all sixty-three games right and obtaining the elusive perfect bracket. While your odds of a perfect bracket are zero, there are ways to improve your odds of taking down your coworkers and earning yourself some bragging rights around the water cooler.

The way most people fill out a bracket is that they start with the matchups in the first round and progress through the games chronologically, just like the actual tournament does. You make selections based on matchups, analytics, gut feeling, or mascots for each game until you have crowned a potential champion.

The problem with this method is that it ignores the fact that almost every scoring format gives you more points the further each team advances. For example, a win in the first round might be 1 or 2 points, while a win in the Sweet 16 or Elite 8 will be 8 or 10 points. This means that the most important team in your entire bracket is the one you pick to win it all. Therefore, they should be your first pick when you are filling out your bracket. You want to decide your champion and then work your way back.

To pick a champion, look at sportsbooks' futures odds and compare them to who the public is picking, using the bracket percentages on big sites like *ESPN* or *Yahoo*. Maybe the sportsbooks are giving Duke, Kansas, and Arizona roughly the same odds of winning the tournament. However, Duke is picked to win it all in 75 percent of public brackets. This means Duke is being overvalued while Kansas and Arizona are being undervalued. As a result, selecting Kansas or Arizona would be a smart pick.

Going contrarian is the best way to increase your odds of winning your bracket pool. But picking all sixteen seeds as contrarian is not a viable strategy. You have to be smart while also going against the public darlings. Once again, go back to the futures betting odds and find the teams that have a good chance to go all the way that aren't getting much love from the general public. Pick these teams to go far and you give yourself a big advantage over the field.

Some other factors to consider are pool size and location. When you are in a pool of only ten people, you don't have to be overly contrarian, whereas if you are in a pool of five hundred, you'll want to follow the steps above. Location can also play a big factor. If you are in a pool in upstate New York, you can surmise that Syracuse is going to get a higher percentage than the general public. If you are in a pool with a bunch of Duke fans, then you'll likely want to have Duke losing earlier than expected to try to gain an edge.

Find teams that have a better chance to reach a round than most people are picking for them and you gain a minor edge. Do that for the entire bracket and you have given yourself a better chance than others in your pool to come out on top when the madness is over.

CHAPTER 16

How to Bet Daily Fantasy Sports

In recent years, conventional sports betting has merged with fantasy sports to create a new phenomenon called daily fantasy sports (DFS). Unlike traditional fantasy leagues, which require you to keep the same roster all season long, DFS allows you to create new lineups every day and then enter them in contests where you can win hundreds, thousands, or even millions of dollars. Essentially, DFS is just like betting, but instead of betting on teams, you're betting on players. In this chapter, you will learn the ins and outs of DFS, including all the different terms, concepts, and strategies needed to create a winning lineup and turn a profit.

The Basics of DFS

Daily fantasy sports haven't been around for decades like traditional sports gambling has. Though there were some archaic formats being played in the 1990s and 2000s, DFS really started to boom in the early 2010s. Major marketing campaigns by DraftKings and FanDuel ensured that anyone who watched TV, used the Internet, or went to a ballgame knew about the new fantasy sports games sweeping the nation.

The beauty of DFS is that you are the general manager of your team. You select who you want to put in your lineup, and you can create new lineups every day. If you pick the right lineup, you could become a millionaire. DFS provides the opportunity for regular people to go from rags to riches, which is a big part of its appeal. For sports fans and regular bettors, it also makes watching a game a lot more fun.

In DFS, each player is given a salary that fluctuates from game to game, with better players costing more than poorer ones. DraftKings and FanDuel are considered the oddsmakers. They set the salaries for each player, similar to oddsmakers setting lines for every team.

The main task for DFS players is to fill out a lineup by selecting players for each position. The one rule is that you have to stay under the salary cap. In the NFL, the DraftKings salary cap is $50,000 and the lineup consists of nine positions: one quarterback, two running backs, three wide receivers, one tight end, one flex player, and defense/special teams.

On an average NFL Sunday, Tom Brady might cost $7,500, Le'Veon Bell $9,400, and Antonio Brown $8,600. You could pick all three to be in your lineup, but then you would only have $24,800 left to spend on the other six positions. You must fill out all the positions in order to submit a lineup.

Once the games begin, players are awarded point totals based on the real-life stats they put in the games. This includes passing yards, rushing yards, touchdowns, points, rebounds, goals, home runs, and so forth. For example, if Brady throws for 300 yards and three touchdowns, he might accrue 50 fantasy points.

The goal of all DFS players is to create a lineup that accumulates as many total points possible. If the players you selected rack up lots of positive stats and your lineup does well, you win real money. This is called "cashing." The amount you win is based upon the tournament you've entered and what place you come in.

FACT

Different Types of DFS Contests

GPPs: Guaranteed prize pools. These generally have the largest fields to go along with the largest prizes. The downside is that only about 20–25 percent of lineups cash. Entry fees range from 10 cents to over $1,000. Most "milly-maker" tournaments have a $20 buy-in. The "milly-maker" is the most popular GPP tournament, short for "millionaire-maker."

Cash: These include head-to-head games between just two competitors, 50/50s in which half the lineups win and half lose, double-ups that pay out twice the buy-in, and other tournaments that pay out a third or more of the entrants.

Multipliers: Tournaments in which the prizes are a multiple of the buy-in fee. For example, a 10x multiplier for a $5 entry would pay out $50. However, fewer than 10 percent of the players would cash in that scenario. The higher the multiplier, the fewer players that cash.

Satellites: These are tournaments in which the top prizes are tickets to other tournaments rather than money. For example, you could win a $5 buy-in and end up with a ticket to a tournament that may cost over $1,000 to buy into. These can also include spots in championships, in which DraftKings and FanDuel host a live, in-person tournament for each major sport at the end of the season to crown a winner. The 2017 DraftKings Fantasy Football World Championship paid out $5 million to the winner.

FACT

In the early 2010s, when DFS started to gain popularity, there was a question about whether or not it was illegal gambling. The answer rested on the fundamental question of skills versus luck. By legal definition, a game based on skill is not gambling, but a game based on luck is. Inevitably, the skill argument won out. Today, DFS is legal in nearly forty states. More broadly, the rise of DFS and social acceptance of DFS helped destigmatize the idea of betting. People saw that DFS was just another form of entertainment, not a deadly sin that ruined sports. This helped open the door to legalized sports betting in 2018.

Important DFS Terms to Know

If you're going to be involved in betting on DFS, here are some words and phrases you should know.

Ownership

Ownership is a crucial element, especially when playing in tournaments. Having a general estimate of what percentage of lineups a certain player will be in allows you to make decisions on who to put in your lineup and how to be contrarian. If you know beforehand that one player has the same exact chance of getting X amount of points as another player, but is going to be owned in half as many lineups, you should always choose the less-owned player.

Players can be over-owned and under-owned based on factors that could range from salary to popularity among casual fans.

Late Swap

Late swapping is a controversial element that varies by company and sport. The late swap feature allows you to edit your lineup after the tournament has begun for games that haven't started. For example, in a baseball tournament that started at 7 p.m. ET, all of the players in 7 p.m. games are locked right away. The players in games at 8 p.m. or 10 p.m. can still be added or removed from your lineup up until those games start. Many players only use late swap to their advantage if someone in their lineup has an injury, but there are other ways it can be used.

Let's say you took a contrarian approach in a tournament and all of your players in the early games played very well. If you had a couple of high-risk players in late games, you could swap them out for safer options.

Salary Change

Much like stocks, players' salaries change on a game-by-game basis. Pay attention to these swings, as they can often create value. In the MLB, NBA, and NFL, players whose salary has dropped a sizable margin over the past month perform better on a salary-based level. This is likely due to overreactions based on fickle statistics that can vary in the short term. The opposite can be said for players whose salaries rise a great deal, as they often tend to underperform based on their new price points. Just like in conventional betting, you want to buy low on bad news and sell high on good news.

Strategize Your Lineup

Not every lineup is created equally. In fact, the approach you should take in cash games is quite different from the one you should take in tournaments. When the goal is to beat one player in a head-to-head or beat half the players in a 50/50, you don't need to be overly risky. You'd win the same amount of money whether your score was slightly above average or elite. When you're trying to win first place in a field of over 100,000 players, you're going to need to take chances and differentiate yourself from the pack.

Contrarian

As is the case with sports betting, a contrarian strategy can be a very successful approach in DFS, especially in GPPs. Though the house is getting a predetermined amount of the cut from every tournament and cash game regardless of who wins or loses, you can gain an edge over the field by going against the grain. Daily fantasy sports have a market environment and can't be played in a vacuum. If you make your lineups without thinking about what everyone else will do, you're not playing the game correctly.

High-Low

This refers to playing a mixture of very expensive (popularly referred to as "studs") and very cheap players (also referred to as "punt plays") in hopes that the studs live up to their expectations and the punt plays all have good nights. This strategy is especially popular in basketball, where injuries can lead to players with minimum salaries being put in the starting lineup.

Multi-Entry

Many GPP tournaments allow you to enter multiple lineups, sometimes more than one hundred. You could enter the same exact lineup dozens of times, play many lineups that are wildly different, or play slight variations of similar lineups, which is the most common strategy. This can be done with lineup builders online that spit out different lineups based on which players you've selected for certain positions. If you've ever seen a screenshot of a DFS player's lineups for one particular multi-entry tournament, the lineups could range from first place or near the top to not cashing at all. This is essentially because they don't put their eggs in one basket and vary their lineups.

Exposure

Exposure is a term used to describe the amount of money you have invested in a certain player on a given night. This could be used to describe a multi-entry contest in which you have fifty lineups, or your entire portfolio for the night, which could include dozens of different contests on multiple sites. If you played twenty total lineups one night worth $100 of entry fees, and $80 worth of those lineups included Mike Trout, your exposure on Trout would be 80 percent—which is quite high. Your success that night would widely revolve around Trout's performance.

FACT

DraftKings was founded in Boston, Massachusetts, in 2012 by Matt Kalish, Paul Liberman, and Jason Robins. Following the 2018 Supreme Court decision to legalize betting, DraftKings announced that it was entering the sports betting marketplace, launching *DraftKings Sportsbook*. It is currently only available in New Jersey, but DraftKings is working to make it available in every state where sports betting is legal.

How to Bet Fantasy MLB

Baseball is the most random of the four major sports because the best players in the game fail more often than they succeed. That said, baseball is perhaps the best sport in which to take a contrarian approach. While LeBron James has a 95 percent chance of putting up 20 points if he doesn't get injured and Aaron Rodgers has a better chance than not to put up 250+ yards passing to go along with a touchdown or two, baseball players, especially hitters, provide no such guarantee.

Stacking

Stacking is a popular approach in which a DFS lineup will consist of several players from the same team's lineup, for example, the first through fifth hitters. With baseball stats being highly correlated, this approach makes sense if you are trying to put up a high number of points and win a tournament. If a particular team goes off for a bunch of runs, this allows you to get points in an exponential fashion. If the cleanup hitter hits a grand slam with the first, second, and third hitters on base, you'd get points for all of the runs being scored in addition to points for each RBI. Of course, the lineup could go ice cold, but baseball is a long season and you need to enter it knowing that you will lose more nights than you'll win. Think of stacking as the ultimate boom-or-bust strategy.

When you do cash, you want to cash big. Frequently cashing at the bare minimum payout in tournaments is fine, but you'll have a greater return on investment in the long run if you cash less frequently, but end up with more scores in the top 5 percent or top 1 percent. Payouts are skewed so that the top five to ten lineups win exponentially more money. Stacking can lead to many losing nights but reward you every once in a while and give you a chance at coming in first. It's much more difficult to pick and choose eight batters from different teams who all happen to have big nights.

Weather

One thing you should always check when making your lineups is weather. First and foremost, baseball is the one sport in which postponed games can ruin your lineup. If you have players in your lineup who are a part of a game that gets rained out, you're not going to get any points from them

---

and will have a very difficult time winning any money. Rain delays can also play a large factor with starting pitchers. If a few innings are played and then a two-hour rain delay comes along, the starting pitchers likely won't come back to the mound once play resumes.

Plenty of other atmospheric elements come into play too. Temperature, wind speed, wind direction, humidity, air pressure, and stadium elevation all impact how far a batted ball will fly. Coors Field is of course a major outlier due to its extreme elevation. Historically, batters at Coors have scored nearly a full point more on DraftKings than their salary-based expectation would suggest.

Batted Ball Data

In recent years, metrics from Statcast, such as exit velocity, have led to some controversy among baseball die-hards. Some believe it's nonsense, while others think it can help predict future performance. This is an extension of the *Moneyball* idea, popularized by Billy Beane and the Oakland Athletics in the early 2000s. The new way of gauging players is based on sabermetrics and crunching numbers, not the old-school eye test.

Baseball is a lucky game. A 110-mile-per-hour line drive can go straight into the third baseman's glove, while a blooper can fall in between the second baseman and right fielder for a base hit. However, you'd definitely prefer to have a player who is consistently hitting the ball harder—and that's not up for debate. Batted ball data is an excellent predictor of DFS success, with stats like exit velocity, batted ball distance, and hard-hit percentage all having linear relationships with fantasy output.

Players with an exit velocity average of at least ninety-five miles per hour over the past fifteen days have produced more than a half point better on DraftKings than their salary would suggest. Meanwhile, players with an exit velocity of eighty-five miles per hour or below over the past fifteen days have been almost an entire point worse than expected. The first group is about the top 5 percent, while the second is near the bottom 5 percent.

The same can be said for pitchers and the batted balls they allow. Pitchers who have been getting hit hard in recent starts tend to continue to get hit hard and, in turn, produce poor point totals. Pitchers allowing weak contact over their past few starts are good options to include in your lineup, especially if they can strike batters out too.

These advanced metrics are far better predictors of success than a player's past fantasy performances. Having access to this information can give you a huge leg up when selecting your lineup.

FACT

One of the best sites for DFS tips, tools, and analytics is *FantasyLabs*. It was founded in 2015 and is considered the industry leader in terms of helping DFS players build winning lineups. It has player projections, models, trends, batted ball data, bargain ratings, matchup tools, weather information, a lineup optimizer, stacks builder, and much more. In 2018, *FantasyLabs* introduced a groundbreaking player prop tool that allowed bettors to capitalize on mispriced player props in the betting market.

Betting Odds

Betting odds play a large role in daily fantasy sports. Perhaps the most sought-after number by DFS players is a team's implied run total, which can be found by looking at the total and moneyline odds for a game. Oddsmakers know what they are doing, and you're not often going to want to play hitters on a team with an implied total of 3 runs or pitchers facing a team with an implied total of 5.5.

Moneyline odds are also crucial. With wins being an important stat in DFS for pitchers, you're not going to want to play a pitcher on a team that is a +250 underdog. You want to select a pitcher who is a big favorite (think –150 or more). Another thing to pay attention to is whether a big favorite is home or away. Hitters on away favorites have been better than away underdogs and home favorites or underdogs. Favorites of course do better than underdogs, and home favorites—especially large ones—aren't guaranteed to bat in the ninth inning.

Lineup Order

In order to produce points, hitters need to get up to bat. You'll want to capitalize the number of plate appearances your players get by focusing on hitters at the top of their respective orders. The first through fourth hitters often get at least four plate appearances a game, and often get up to bat five times. Meanwhile, the seventh through ninth hitters have a decent chance of having one less plate appearance than the top of the order. One technique of cash game players is to use as many leadoff hitters as possible. In the long run, this will maximize plate appearances and potential fantasy points.

Starting Pitchers

Many of the best players in the DFS industry take a "don't screw up" approach when it comes to pitchers. With more consistent results than hitters, decent performances by pitchers is something you'll need to get consistently to win. This is why players will often choose to "pay up" for high-priced pitchers who are both consistent and have a high ceiling.

Historically on DraftKings, pitchers priced at $12,000 or more have averaged over 2.5 points more than expected. If you're looking to roster several high-priced batters and go cheap on pitchers, be aware that arms priced at $6,000 or less have averaged about –0.4 points less than expected, which isn't that much to begin with given the low salary. Times when it may make sense to play a cheap pitcher are when they have just been called up from the minors and are making their first start, or if they have a chance to rack up a decent amount of strikeouts.

FACT

FanDuel was founded in New York City in 2009 by Nigel Eccles, Lesley Eccles, Tom Griffiths, Rob Jones, and Chris Stafford. As of 2018, FanDuel had six million users. In July of 2018, FanDuel was bought by Paddy Power Betfair, a popular Irish bookmaker. Just like DraftKings, FanDuel decided to enter the sports betting marketplace in addition to providing DFS games. In July of 2018, the FanDuel Sportsbook at the Meadowlands Racetrack in New Jersey opened for the first time.

How to Bet Fantasy NBA

Baseball is not a sport in which you want to pay close attention to point projections. A player could be projected to get 8 points, but there's a decent chance he ends up with 0. Basketball is the complete opposite, as projections play a huge role in models and lineup construction. If a player is projected to score 30 points on DraftKings, oftentimes he'll end up between 20 and 40.

NBA is currently the only major sport in which both sites do not allow late swap, which can certainly be frustrating. This, companied with how important injuries are in the NBA, make it the most important to pay close attention to news on *Twitter*. In recent years, star players are also being rested more frequently than in the past and the news may not be announced until late in the evening. These situations often open up opportunities for inexpensive players to play a much larger role.

Usage Rates

One of the most important stats to know is usage rate, which is a player's percentage of plays finished when he is on the court. This includes shots, free throws, and turnovers. The best players in the league will be upwards of 30 percent. Knowing a player's usage rate when certain players are on or off the court is particularly helpful for when certain players are injured. If player A's usage rate is just 15 percent when his star teammate is on the court with him, but 30 percent when he isn't, you would expect him to have a much larger role if the star didn't play that night.

Betting Odds

Betting odds play a large role in fantasy basketball too. Similar to baseball, a team's implied total is perhaps the most important element. Though players can score points in DFS in low-scoring games by accumulating rebounds, blocks, and steals, it's easier to predict how many points a team and its players will get on a given night using betting totals.

There is also some thinking to do when it comes to the spread, as massively favored teams can blow a team out early on and rest their stars for the fourth quarter. This has happened plenty of times in recent years with the Golden State Warriors.

Minutes

In baseball, players at the top of the order get more plate appearances and are in turn more valuable than players at the bottom. In basketball, those who play a lot of minutes give DFS players an edge. Historically on

DraftKings, players who average more than thirty minutes a night have scored 1.3 points more than expected. Cheap players at $4,000 or less who are expected to play more than thirty minutes on a given night have produced over four more points than expected, which goes to show how valuable the players replacing an injured teammate in the starting lineup can be.

Pace

Each team in the NBA plays a slightly different brand of basketball and not every matchup will be the same. One important statistic to pay attention to is pace, which is the average number of possessions a team averages over forty-eight minutes. In the 2017–18 season, the Pelicans led the league with a pace of nearly 103, while the Kings were last with 97. When selecting your NBA lineup, you want to target players from teams who play at a high pace, especially when they're facing a fellow high-paced team. If two teams with high paces face off, you can expect a higher number of possessions, shots, and points scored. DFS players would want to select players on fast-paced teams, while avoiding players on low-paced teams.

How to Bet Fantasy NFL

The NFL is in between the NBA and MLB in terms of randomness and projections. Players are not as consistent as they are in the NBA, which is largely due to how important touchdowns are. Even the top-skill players aren't going to find the end zone every week, and this can lead to a big swing in points, even if all of their other statistics looked fine. On the other hand, quarterbacks, top running backs, and wide receivers all have at least somewhat of a floor, which is not the case in baseball, where 0 points is a rather possible outcome. Even on a terrible day, you'd expect to see a handful of points out of the top football players. On their best days, several touchdowns and hundreds of yards can be racked up. Here are some important factors that should enter your equation when making an NFL lineup.

Stacking

Just like in MLB, stacking players on the same team is a popular strategy in the NFL. This is frequently done by pairing a quarterback with a wide receiver or tight end. Though it carries some risk, the reward is certainly worth it, as your points can come in bunches. Every time the receiver picks up yards or scores a touchdown, the quarterback will also be receiving points. If a quarterback has a terrific day, it's likely that one of his receivers does, and vice versa.

ESSENTIAL

The NFL is the most matchup-based and game-plan heavy of all the sports. When filling out your lineup, always think about each team's plan of attack. Is a team's red-zone defense more prone to allowing passing or rushing touchdowns? Is one team better against the run, but bad against the pass? Will pressure on the quarterback lead to more short checkdowns to running backs and receivers? There are tons of angles to examine for every game on the slate. When you roster a player, there should be a reason behind it. For example, "X player is going to catch eight passes for over 100 yards because of X,Y, and Z." Decide how you believe a game will play out and then make decisions on which specific players will do better or worse than most people are expecting.

Weather

Along with the MLB, the NFL is one of the few sports in which checking the forecast is an important step when making lineups. Though football players will play through rain or snow and postponed games are essentially never an issue, it's still important to factor in the elements. Games with heavy precipitation are going to cause trouble for offenses. The same goes for games with high winds.

Historically, games with average winds of at least ten miles per hour have led to less value for offensive players. On DraftKings, quarterbacks have averaged about 1.25 points less than expected, with wide receivers and tight ends coming in at about a half point less than expected. Surprisingly enough, running backs have also been hurt at a similar clip as wideouts and tight ends. However, in *really* windy games, when the average has been over fifteen miles per hour, running backs have outperformed expectations by nearly 2 points.

Since the wind hurts offenses, it's understandable that defenses have benefitted. In winds greater than ten miles per hour, defenses have outperformed expectations by over a half point.

Betting Odds

Betting lines and totals play a huge role in NFL DFS, just as they do in every other sport. NFL totals have a wide range, as totals have ranged from 30 to 60 over the past fifteen years. Of course, you'll generally want to target offensive players in the games with high totals and defenses in the games with low totals, but that doesn't always have to be the case. Betting odds can also provide a great gauge of ownership, as players on heavy favorites and teams with high expected point totals will tend to have higher ownership. This is important information to keep in mind, as targeting less popular players in games with a slightly lower total is a strong contrarian strategy.

CHAPTER 17

The Mental Game

Throughout this book, we've discussed all the important aspects of betting. We've learned the basics, set up our bankroll management plan, set realistic expectations, adopted our contrarian and sharp action betting philosophy, learned how to make a pick, place a bet, and target each of the major sports. We are now ready to enter the betting arena. However, our work doesn't end here. In a way, it's only just beginning. It will take lots of time and effort to truly master the art of betting. Before we depart, here are a few final tips to remember as you progress on your betting journey, including the importance of tracking your plays, doing your homework, building a betting community, and adopting the "grinders with blinders" mentality.

Track Your Plays

One of the smartest moves you can make as a bettor is to track every single bet you make. Many casual bettors never think to do this. Maybe they consider it to be too tedious or time consuming. Or maybe they just don't see the benefit of it. Sure, tracking your plays would be fun if you're winning. You can sit back and smile, patting yourself on the back for all your wins. But what's the point of tracking your bets if they ended up losing? Public bettors want to forget about their lost bets and move on. Seeing them staring you in the face makes you feel worse, like someone is rubbing it in.

Most public bettors track their performance based upon their bank account. If it's higher than yesterday, that's a good thing, because it means they won their bets. If it's lower than yesterday, that's a bad thing, because it means they lost their bets. But there is so much more that goes into betting than just wins and losses. If you brush a win or a loss aside without analyzing why it won or why it lost, you are forfeiting a crucial opportunity to get better.

By keeping a running record of all your plays, you can not only keep a closer eye on your performance, but more importantly, learn about who you are as a bettor. If you're computer savvy, file your plays in a spreadsheet. If you're more old school, keep a notebook. The methodology doesn't matter. The only requirement is that you document every bet you make.

Once you bet a game, write down as much information about your pick as possible. Don't just write down "Yankees." Provide depth and context. What kind of bet was it: moneyline, spread, or total? Were they a favorite or an underdog? What price did you bet them at? Were they at home or on the road? Did the line get better or worse after you bet it? Did you beat the closing line? What percentage of bets did they receive? Were they coming off a win or a loss? What was the total?

More importantly, what made you decide to bet the Yankees? Was it because they were contrarian in a heavily bet game? Or because they had sharp reverse line movement, a steam move, or a line freeze? Were they getting much more money compared to bets? Did you like the matchup against the opponent? What about the matchup did you like? Did you decide to bet the game on your own, or did you take advice from someone else? If you did take advice, who did you listen to? What was their reasoning?

Once the game is over, you can award yourself a win, loss, or a push. But the more important thing is analyzing your decision-making process and learning who you are as a bettor.

ESSENTIAL

One of the best tools for documenting and tracking your plays is the free Action Network: Sports Betting and Live Odds Tracker app. Once you make a pick, add it to the bet tracker and it will keep a running record of every play you make. It will provide a report card, showing your win-loss rate, the number of wagers made, your win percentage, units won, and ROI. It also lets you track your bets in real time, with live scoring and a bet win–probability meter.

Know Your Strengths and Weaknesses

By documenting your plays and providing details and context for every pick, you can learn your strengths and weaknesses as a bettor. This is critically important because it will open your eyes to what aspects of betting you're doing well at and other aspects you're struggling with. By knowing your strengths, you can focus on them and lean on them. By knowing your weaknesses, you learn exactly where you need to spend more time working to improve.

Maybe after documenting your plays for a few months you find that you're doing great betting on road underdogs, but you keep losing home underdogs. Or maybe you're much better at picking totals in baseball than you are at picking moneylines. Maybe you're putting too much emphasis in specific stat categories or head-to-head matchups. Maybe you're betting your games too early in the day and losing out on better odds. Or maybe you're waiting too late and betting bad lines after they've moved too far.

Always look for bias seeping into your plays. Even the most hardcore contrarian bettors can struggle with this. Maybe you learn that you're showing elements of favoritism by betting on one team far more often than others. Or maybe you're doing great with your plays on the weekends, but struggle on weeknights. Or maybe you're winning a lot of games on TV that are played in primetime, and losing games that are played during the day and aren't televised.

After a full calendar year, you can then begin to discover what bet types and what specific sports you're best at. Maybe you're much better at college basketball than you are at baseball. Or maybe NFL totals are your strong suit, but spreads give you trouble. Or maybe you thought you were doing terrible in college football, but you're actually doing pretty well.

Stick with what you're good at. Be more cautious with what you're struggling with. Learn your blind spots and where you need to improve. Pay close attention to the amount of bets you're placing each day. Maybe you realize that you are betting too many games. When you bet ten games per night, you rarely turn a profit. But when you stick to two or three bets per night, you have much more success.

No Pain, No Gain

When you first start betting on sports, ask yourself this question: what kind of bettor do I want to be? If you just want to place the occasional wager for fun during March Madness, the World Series, or the Super Bowl, this book will help you make the smartest bet possible. But if you really want to become a serious and successful sports bettor, you need to be prepared to put in the work.

If you want to get in better shape, you need to spend hours in the gym. You need to sweat. You need to make it a daily habit and a routine. The same can be said for betting on sports. The more time you put in, the better you'll become at it.

The best way to get better is by doing your homework. This means immersing yourself in sports betting and watching lots of games. Know your sport inside and out. If you want to get better at betting on the NFL, watch as many NFL games as you can. It's not enough to just watch *Monday Night Football* every other week. You need to watch all the games on Sunday and Thursday as well. Watching games allows you to keep your finger on the pulse of sport. You pick up on its nuances. You will learn the teams, the flow, the rules, what separates winning teams from losing teams, and what advantages or disadvantages specific teams possess.

When you're watching games, be a student. Have a notebook and pen in your hands. Take notes during the game. Look for tendencies. Jot down important information that you can use to your advantage later. Think of yourself as a professional scout. Try to keep notes on every team you watch.

Who are their best players? What are their coaching tendencies? What is their style of play? The goal is to have an encyclopedia of knowledge for each team that you can revert back to when deciding to bet on or against that team in the future.

Maybe you notice that a specific MLB team struggles against left-handed pitching. Or an NBA team fouls a lot down the stretch, leading to high-scoring games. Or an NFL team is great against the run but gets torched in the air. It may not seem that important at the time, but over the long run these nuggets add up. Always look for any edge you can find. It could help you win a bet down the road. Remember, you are your best analyst.

ESSENTIAL

The start of every new season is an especially exciting time. Bettors can't wait to get going and place their first wagers. Oddsmakers release lines on preseason games, which bettors can bet on. However, it's strongly advised not to bet on preseason. The biggest reason is that the teams aren't trying to win. The win-loss records do not count. They are exhibition games and the starters do not play the whole game, if at all. In preseason, it's more about getting your system in place and scouting young players. Also, these games are extremely low-bet, which means there isn't any contrarian value. While it may be tempting, bettors should avoid betting preseason. Wait for the regular season, when it really counts.

Build a Betting Community

In the end, you are the ultimate arbiter of your bankroll. You decide who you want to bet on. However, this doesn't mean you have to be all alone when it comes to betting. When you're starting out, seek out experienced bettors who have been in the game much longer than you have. Watch games with them. Pick their brain. Learn their thought process and how they select games. If you show an open mind and a thirst to learn, these bettors will welcome you in with open arms. After all, everyone started out as a square bettor. You'll be surprised how willing experienced bettors will be to pass down their knowledge and help you win.

Over time, try to foster your own betting community. Surround yourself with people who are smarter than you. Read books written by professional bettors. Always keep learning. Look for like-minded bettors who share the same contrarian philosophy. When it comes time to select a play, bounce ideas off your betting friends. See where you overlap and where you disagree. Talk your way through a game with fellow bettors you value and trust.

ESSENTIAL

One of the best ways to interact with fellow bettors is through *Twitter*. It is the most popular social media platform among bettors. In fact, it has given rise to its own subculture called *Gambling Twitter*. All day, bettors from across the country (and the world) will tweet about games and discuss lines. You can even send direct messages or private messages to fellow bettors if you have a question. *Twitter* is extremely helpful for staying up to date with breaking injuries and up-to-the-second line moves. All sports bettors should create a *Twitter* account.

Always stay plugged into what your non-betting, sports-loving friends are doing and saying. Chances are some of your best friends will be perfect examples of "public" bettors. Ask them who they like. See which teams they're talking about. Use your average Joe friends as a barometer for the "public." If your uninformed friends are all over one team, chances are the entire public is too. This is the easiest way to know you're on the contrarian side. Always try to be on the opposite side of your public friends.

Learn from Losing

The goal of every sports bettor is to turn a profit. When you're doing well, you're invincible. There's nothing better. You feel like you're on top of the world and are bound to win every single bet you make. It's easy when you're winning. When you're losing, that's when it gets hard.

Every single bettor suffers through agonizing losing streaks. It's part of the game. How you deal with losing streaks will define your future as a bettor.

When you're winning, you get spoiled and you get lazy. You lose your discipline and start taking chances you wouldn't normally take because you're riding high. The truth is, you don't learn anything from winning. You take your win and move on. There is no self-reflection, looking inward, or studying your process.

It might sound crazy, but you won't truly see the light until you lose big. When you hit rock bottom, you reach a crossroads. You can either quit betting altogether, or you can continue. If you continue, you become a much better bettor. Nothing sharpens you up quicker than losing money. You learn to be incredibly selective and study your games much harder. It forces you to be disciplined because your real, hard-earned money is on the line. It might feel like hell at the time, but in the long run it's better to experience a bad losing streak early, to get it out of the way and learn from it. As Winston Churchill once said, "If you're going through hell, keep going."

QUESTION

If you're losing, should you change your betting approach?
The simple answer is "no." Bettors should never allow the fear of losing to influence their decision-making. If you're in a tough stretch, don't lay off because you're scared. If you went 0–5 last night, the obvious reaction is to take the next day off. However, this reactionary thinking will cause you to miss profitable opportunities, simply out of fear. Your approach should never change, no matter how well or how poorly you're doing. If a game has value and fits the contrarian blueprint, take it. Always remember: scared money don't make no money.

Grinders with Blinders

In order to succeed at sports betting long term, you need to get your mind right and adopt a "grinders with blinders" mentality. This means ignoring the noise and trusting the process. Betting will take you on an unbelievable roller coaster of emotions. You will experience the highest of highs and lowest of lows. It's easier said than done, but you should always try to stay even-keeled. Never get too high or too low. Ride the wave, but never let it change your mindset. You're never as good or as bad as your current record dictates. You're always somewhere in the middle. Always stay the course and think long term.

Sports betting isn't easy. If it were, everyone would do it and become mil-lionaires. But this doesn't mean it's impossible. Remember to always believe in yourself. It takes a long time to really get the hang of it, but you can do it. Just take it one day at a time. The goal is to get 0.01 percent sharper every single day. Learn to recognize situations. Losses will happen, but always try to learn from them. The next time a similar situation comes around, capital-ize on it. Never be content. There is something new to learn every single day.

Never forget: it takes guts to be a sports bettor. We're a special breed, and not everyone has what it takes to enter the arena and take risks. You have to be equal parts fearless, smart, and incredibly disciplined. Take pride in this. Embrace the sweat. Always keep grinding. In the end, that's how you'll turn sports betting from a hobby into an investment.

"It is not the critic who counts; not the man who points out how the strong man stumbles, or where the doer of deeds could have done them better. The credit belongs to the man who is actually in the arena, whose face is marred by dust and sweat and blood; who strives valiantly; who errs, who comes up short again and again, because there is no effort without error and shortcoming; but who does actually strive to do the deeds; who knows great enthusiasms, the great devotions; who spends himself in a worthy cause; who at the best knows in the end the triumph of high achievement; and who at the worst, if he fails, at least fails while daring greatly, so that his place shall never be with those cold and timid souls who neither know victory nor defeat."

—*Theodore Roosevelt, "The Man in the Arena" speech, 1910*

APPENDIX A

Glossary

action

A bet of any kind.

added game

A game that was a late addition to the list of games bettors can bet on, typically a rescheduled game or the second game of a doubleheader in baseball.

arbitrage

When you bet all possible outcomes of an event at different odds to guarantee a profit.

ATS

Short for "against the spread." A win-loss record given to a team based on how often they cover the point spread. If a team has played five games and covered three of them, they would be 3–2 ATS.

backdoor cover

When your spread bet is losing for much of the game but comes back unexpectedly to cover and win at the very end.

bad beat

When your bet is winning and looks like it's bound to cash but loses at the very end in heart-breaking fashion.

bankroll

The amount of money a bettor has at their disposal to bet on.

bet signals

Automated alerts coming from the sportsbooks. These are triggered when professional bettors place a lot of money on a specific game, team, and number. See also: "line freeze," "reverse line movement," and "steam move."

bet to risk

Betting a specific amount, regardless of the odds. Your bet size will always be the same but the payout will vary, depending on the odds.

bet to win
Betting a variable amount based on the odds. Your bet size will change each time but the payout will stay the same.

bets versus dollars discrepancy
Comparing the percentage of bets to the percentage of dollars a particular team or side is receiving to better understand which side the professional bettors are on.

betting sheets
The papers a sportsbook prints off outlining all their offerings (games available to bet on and their lines) before the day starts. Each sport has their own betting sheet.

betting syndicates
Professional bettors who team up and combine their knowledge and resources.

betting system
A model that hones in on a profitable situation in the past and then looks for present-day games that fit the same criteria.

board
Also referred to as the sports betting schedule. This shows every game a bettor can bet on.

book
The nickname for a bookmaker or sportsbook who takes bets on games.

bookie
A person who illegally takes bets on games.

buying back
Occurs when professional bettors intentionally bet one side in order to move the number in their favor. Once the odds move to their desired number, they bet the other side for an even larger amount than the original steam move.

buying points
When a bettor pays the house an additional fee to get a better number on a spread or total.

chalk
The team that is favored.

closing line
This is the final number that the line closes at when the books stop accepting wagers. It happens right before the game begins.

closing line value (CLV)
The value of a bet relative to where the line closes. Consistently beating the closing line is the mark of a sharp bettor.

confirmation bias
Seeking out data or trends that fit your preconceived opinion.

contrarian betting
The philosophy of betting against the public. Contrarian bettors look to take advantage of public bias and bet on games being overvalued by average Joe bettors.

cover
Whether or not a team wins a spread bet. If you bet a 3-point favorite and they win by 4 points, you covered the spread and won your bet.

daily fantasy sports (DFS)
Betting on players across all sports. Bettors pick players on any team, build a lineup, and compete against other bettors.

dime
A $1,000 bet.

double-siding
When a handicapper tells half of his clients to bet one side of a game and the second half to bet the other. No matter what happens, he can say he chose the correct side.

edge
When a bettor has an advantage against the sportsbook or casino. This means that they have a positive expected value.

even money
A bet without any juice (+100).

exotic
Any kind of bet that isn't a straight moneyline, spread, or total bet. The most common exotics are prop bets and parlays.

expected value (EV)
The expected value you would receive on a bet based on the probability that it will occur. Bettors always strive for bets that have positive expected value (EV+).

fade
To go against or bet the opposite side.

fading the trendy dog
The rare occurrence where contrarian bettors can bet on an undervalued favorite.

favorite
The team that is expected to win the game.

field
In a prop bet, bettors can oftentimes bet the field. This means betting on all other teams or players not listed in the bet. For example, a prop bet may say: What color Gatorade will the Super Bowl winner dump on the head coach? Red -150, blue +200, field +300. If you think it's any color other than red or blue, you would be "field."

flat betting
Risking the same amount on every game, always risking 1 unit (not to win 1 unit), only risking 1 percent to 5 percent of your bankroll per play.

future
A bet on something that will happen down the road. For example, you might place a futures bet on Patriots +500 to win the Super Bowl before the season starts.

gambler's fallacy
The false idea that if something has happened more often in a normal period of time, it is bound to happen less often in the future.

getting down

The act of placing a bet.

grand salami

The over/under total for how many runs, goals, or points will be scored in all games in one day.

handicapper

Someone who breaks down the information on a particular game or event and makes an educated guess on the outcome.

handle

The total amount of money that a sportsbook takes in on a game or event.

heavy juice

A higher price on the standard –110 juice, typically up to –125.

hedging

This is a popular strategy commonly used with futures bets. Say you bet the Vegas Golden Knights at 75/1 to win the Stanley Cup before the season started and then they make the Stanley Cup Finals against the Washington Capitals. You could either "ride out" your Knights futures bet, or place a bet on the Capitals to win the series. By betting the Caps and "hedging" your Knights future bet, you guarantee yourself a payout no matter what happens.

hold

The amount of money the house holds onto after all bets have been settled, also known as the profit.

hook

The extra half point on a bet. In football, bettors might get the hook so they can get +3.5 instead of +3.

house

The sportsbook or the casino that accepts all the wagers.

implied probability

This converts the betting odds into a likelihood percentage (chances of winning from 1 percent to 99 percent). For example, say the Astros are playing the Rangers and Houston is a –175 favorite and Texas is a +150 dog. Houston's –175 odds would translate to a 64 percent implied probability to win the game. Meanwhile, Texas's +150 odds would translate to a 40 percent chance of winning the game.

juice

The tax or commission bettors must pay the sportsbooks in order for them to accept your wager.

Kelly criterion system

Developed by J.L. Kelly Jr. in 1956, this system weights your bets based on confidence level. The more confident you are, the more you bet. This system is used by experts and can be highly profitable, but it can also be highly dangerous.

key numbers

The most common margin of victory or defeat. In football, the most common key numbers are 3 or 7.

lay

When you bet a favorite on the spread, you lay points.

lean

When you "like" a bet but haven't actually bet it, or place less money on it than you would otherwise.

liability

When a sportsbook has heavy action on one side and stands to lose big money if that side wins or covers.

limits

Also known as betting limits. The maximum amount of money sportsbooks will allow their players to bet. Limits differ based on the sportsbook, sport, and wager type.

line freeze

Line freezes take place when there is heavily lopsided betting on one side but the line refuses to budge toward the team getting the vast majority of bets.

line shopping

Going to multiple sportsbooks to find the best and most profitable line for each game.

lines

Another name for odds.

listed pitcher bets

A type of bet in baseball in which if either listed starting pitcher does not start the game, the bet is void.

live line

Also referred to as live betting, in-play wagering, or in-game wagering. This is the line on the game at any given moment while the game is in progress.

long odds

Large betting odds, which occurs if there is a large gap between two teams' power ratings.

Martingale betting system

A betting system in which you double your bet after each loss so you can recoup what you just lost and turn a profit. By doubling down, you are increasing your risk and are more likely to go broke.

middling

When bettors bet both sides of a game after a major line move so they can "play the middle" and win both bets. For example, say you bet the Patriots −6 against the Steelers and Ben Roethlisberger gets injured in practice and is ruled out for the game. The books would take the game off the board and might reopen the line at Patriots −13.5. If you bet Steelers +13.5 (and already bet the Patriots −6), you could "play the middle." This means that if the Patriots won by exactly 7 to 13 points, you would win both bets.

mobile betting

When you place a wager on your phone through an app or website.

moneyline
Betting on which team will win the game.

moving on air
When a sportsbook adjusts its lines to mirror what other sharper sportsbooks are offering. For example, if a square or public sportsbook of posting Giants –7 against the Cowboys and a sharp book is posting Giants –8, the square book may "move on air" and adjust their line from –7 to –8 to align themselves with the sharper market, regardless of whether or not they took in any action on the Cowboys.

moving the line
When oddsmakers adjust their lines because sharps are betting one side heavily.

mush
Someone who brings bad luck to bettors.

nickel
A $500 bet.

no action (NA)
When a bet is voided and the sportsbook gives you back your money. The most common no action scenario is in baseball when a game is rained out.

odds
The price given to every team that bettors can bet on.

oddsmaker
The person who sets the odds or betting lines.

off the board (OTB)
When a sportsbook or casino takes down the betting lines on a game and no longer accepts bets. Oftentimes it will occur when a major injury takes places, such as a quarterback in the NFL. Afterward, the books will typically reopen the line at an adjusted number.

opening line (opener)
This is the first line that the sportsbooks release on the game. It will then move (or not move) based on the action the sportsbook is taking in.

over/under (O/U)

See "total."

parlay

When you tie multiple bets into the same bet. If one bet loses, the entire bet loses. If all bets win, the winner enjoys a large payout.

partial game lines

Spreads that are only for the first half, the second half, or one of the four quarters of a game.

percentage play

How large your unit size is compared to your starting bankroll. If your bankroll is $1,000 and your unit size is $20, your percentage play is 2 percent.

pick (PK) or pick'em

A 50/50 toss-up between two evenly matched teams. There is no clear favorite or underdog. Bettors can "pick" which side they prefer. This appears as a line of zero (0).

pleaser

The opposite of a teaser bet. Instead of getting better odds and additional points, you are getting worse odds but at a much better price.

plus money

An incentive to bet on an underdog, affording bigger payouts when an underdog wins.

power ratings

A statistical representation of how strong every team is compared to each other.

prop bet (proposition)

A bet on anything other than the outcome of a game, such as the over/under rushing yards by an individual player or how long the Super Bowl National Anthem will be.

public money

Money coming from novice, recreational, or casual bettors who bet for fun and do not have a clear edge.

puck-line

The spread in hockey. The favorite is −1.5 (must win by 2 or more) and the underdog is +1.5 (can win or lose by only 1 goal).

push

When your spread or total bet lands on the exact number of the odds. Also known as a draw or tie. When this happens, bettors get their money back.

Pythagorean differential

Also referred to as the Pythagorean expectation. This converts each team's point differential into an expected winning percentage.

real-time odds

Live sports betting lines that update automatically as soon as a sportsbook adjusts their numbers.

recency bias

The psychological bias where the public overvalues recent games and results for a team and undervalues the long-term outlook.

reduced juice

A lower price on the standard −110 juice, typically −107 or −105.

reduced juice sportsbook

Rare and relatively unknown to public bettors, a sportsbook that offers lines well below the standard juice and is the best-kept secret and favorite type of sportsbook for serious, experienced, and professional bettors.

return on investment (ROI)

The net profit a bettor makes based on how much money they started wagering with.

reverse line movement (RLM)

When the betting line moves in the opposite direction of the betting percentages, one of the clearest indicators of smart money.

rotation number
Also referred to as the NSS number, ID number, game number, or Vegas rotation number. This number is located to the left of a team and unique to the team, sport, and event. It is universal across all sportsbooks.

run-line
The spread in baseball. The favorite is –1.5 (must win by 2 or more runs) and the underdog is +1.5 (can win or lose by only 1 run).

runner
Someone who places a bet on behalf of another bettor, also known as a number runner.

scalping
When a bettor bets both sides of the same game to guarantee a profit. For example, say the Mariners are playing the Angels and one book is posting Mariners +105 and the other book is posting Angels +103. The bettor could bet both teams and guarantee a profit.

shaded line
A line that occurs when sportsbooks move the odds further in the direction of the popular public side, forcing recreational bettors to take bad numbers.

sharp
A professional sports bettor who has a long track record of success, tends to bet big amounts on games, and bets based on value, numbers, and data.

sharp action
Line movement caused by professional bettors betting predominately on one side or the other.

sharp sportsbook
A sportsbook that sets its own lines, has high limits, and accepts big wagers from experienced, professional players.

short odds
Small betting odds, which occurs if there is a small gap between two teams' power ratings.

side

When bettors pick a side in a matchup, either the favorite or the underdog. It would be on the spread or the moneyline.

smart money

Money coming from professional bettors who have an edge, a long track record of success, and win at a high rate. Books will move lines based on which side is getting sharp money.

sportsbook

The place that offers odds on games and accepts bets on sports. It can either be an in-person facility or an online account.

spread (SPD)

Also known as the point spread. The number set by the oddsmakers to distinguish favorites from underdogs. A favorite gives points and an underdog gets points.

square

A novice sports bettor who bets for fun and tends to bet on favorites, home teams, and overs.

square sportsbook

A sportsbook with low limits that caters to recreational bettors, doesn't set their own lines, and instead follows other books. Lines are often shaded toward favorites and overs.

steam move

An overload of sharp action from professional bettors that causes sudden, drastic line movement across the betting market. Popularly referred to as a "team getting steamed."

straight up

The team who wins the game based on a moneyline bet, not based on the point spread.

survivor pool

Also referred to as a survivor tournament, eliminator challenge, or suicide pool. This is a type of bet where a group of people enters the same contest and all pick one team to win straight up each week. Each person can only pick each team once. Whoever lasts the longest through the season wins the money.

sweat

When you have action on a game and root for your bet to win.

syndicates

Groups of professional sports bettors who team up and combine their bankrolls, skills, and expertise to bet as much money as possible with the biggest edge possible.

tail

To follow someone else's pick.

taking the points

When you bet an underdog in the spread, the opposite of laying the points.

teaser

A modified bet in which you can change the point spread or total on a game. The more you change the spread (tease up or tease down), the lower the payout.

ticket

The betting slip or receipt you receive once you place a bet.

total

The total number of points scored in a game by both teams combined. A bettor can bet on whether it will go over the total or under the total.

tout

Someone who sells picks, typically using over-the-top sales marketing.

underdog

The team that is expected to lose the game.

unit

The most common way sports bettors measure their performance. You either have units won or units lost. In flat betting, the standard unit size is 3 percent of your bankroll. If your bankroll is $100, each unit would be $3. If you are up 10 units, that means you are up $30 overall.

upset

When the underdog wins a game straight up.

variance

Massive ups and downs in betting in a short period.

vig or vigorish

See "juice."

wager

Any kind of bet.

window

The cashier at a sportsbook where you walk up and place a bet or cash a ticket.

wiseguy

A sharp, professional bettor.

z-score

This measures how far one data point is from the average.

APPENDIX B

Online Resources

The Action Network
www.actionnetwork.com
Live odds, insider analysis from industry experts, game previews, betting breakdowns, articles, daily newsletters, bet tracker, podcasts, mobile app, bet calculator, odds converter, betting education academy, live scoring, and play-by-play; *Twitter* @ActionNetworkHQ.

Bet Labs
www.betlabssports.com
Historical betting database since 2005. Create your own betting systems using more than four hundred filters. PRO systems for NFL, NCAAF, NBA, NCAAB, MLB, NHL, WNBA, CFL, and EPL. Live betting hangouts; *Twitter* @Bet_Labs.

Covers
www.covers.com
A leader in sports gaming industry news, featuring regular coverage of industry news and events, as well as detailed reviews and rankings of the best online sportsbooks, including user-rankings.

ESPN
www.espn.com
The industry leader in sports information, such as box scores, standings, statistics, articles, and more.

FantasyLabs
www.fantasylabs.com
Cutting-edge daily fantasy (DFS) tools and real-time analytics, build and backtest models, analyze trends, slate breakdowns, podcasts, tutorials, player props tool; *Twitter* @FantasyLabs.

Legal Sports Report
www.legalsportsreport.com
News and updates on legal sports betting and daily fantasy in the United States.

OddsShark
www.oddsshark.com
Offers odds, percentages, game analysis, and sportsbook reviews.

PredictIt

www.predictit.org

Begun as a research project from Victoria University of Wellington in New Zealand, this prediction market allows you to bet on politics and events. It also allows researchers access to their data to get a feel for how the public views different contents.

Smarkets

https://smarkets.com

London-based betting exchange offering data driven analytics for sports and politics.

Sports Gambling Podcast

www.sportsgamblingpodcast.com

An informative and entertaining podcast dedicated to sports betting odds, news, articles, and contests.

Sports Insights

www.sportsinsights.com

Live odds, betting and dollar percentages, steam and reverse line moves, bet signals, best bet picks, contrarian plays, sharp report, injuries, weather, officials, line predictor, line watcher, live betting hangouts; *Twitter* @SportsInsights.

Sportsbook Review

www.sportsbookreview.com

The premier site for getting reviews and ratings for online sportsbooks.

Vegas Insider

www.vegasinsider.com

A great starting point for anyone looking to get a wide variety of lines from a number of Las Vegas books.

VSIN: Vegas Stats and Information Network

www.vsin.com

A good source for Las Vegas betting information, odds, analysis, and gambling content. VSIN is broadcast on Sirius XM Radio and is the first national radio show dedicated exclusively to sports betting.

Index